DEAD
MAN
WALKING

DEAD MAN WALKING

Teaching in a maximum-security prison

by W. Reason Campbell

Richard Marek Publishers, New York

Copyright © 1978 by W. Reason Campbell

Printed in the United States of America

Library of Congress Cataloging in Publication Data

Campbell, W   Reason.
   Dead man walking.

   1. Campbell, W. Reason. 2. Teachers—
Biography. 3. Education of prisoners—California.
4. English language—Study and teaching.
I. Title.
HV8875.C28   365'.66   78-4868
SBN: 399-90008-X

GLOSSARY OF PRISON TERMS

1. *Big daddy dump truck.* The same as dump truck (# 21), only with emphasis. Once a student referred to me as "big daddy dump truck." The term amused me and I started referring to myself by this name. Some of my students were upset by this and thought I was demeaning myself. They asked me to refrain from using the term. I deferred to their request.
2. *Boned.* The prison term for sexual intercourse. It is synonymous with the more commonly used term, balled.
3. *Bonna ru.* Something especially fine or good. Prisoners refer to their best clothes as bonna rus.
4. *Bricks.* Life outside the joint. A person "hits the bricks" when he is released from jail.
5. *Bull.* A prison guard or police officer.
6. *Carry a lunch pail.* Accepting a routine job on the outside. Many inmates still have the vision of big cars, beautiful women, sharp clothes, and they would rather go to jail or die than become lunch-pail-carrying members of society.
7. *Cat.* The same as dude; only it is a slightly more affectionate term.
8. *Cellie.* Your cell mate. Customarily there were two people in each cell. After a few months of clean time you could usually, upon request, be assigned to a single cell or an honor cell.
9. *Chicano.* A Mexican-American. It is frequently used in racially mixed groups. Once one of my students brought in an article

claiming that the word Chicano was offensive to Mexican-Americans. I discussed the article in class and the majority of Mexican-American students disagreed with it.

10. *Christmas tree.* Bringing a woman to orgasm. The term conjures up the image of the long, pointed, green fir tree with the star on top, the bright candles burning and swaying, the tinsel and the ornaments, the merriment and the spirit of giving.

   I remember once a student in describing a lost love said, "She didn't love me, but she loved the Christmas tree." Poetry.

11. *Clean time.* Time in jail free of write-ups or reprimands or brushes with authority. The question of clean time is the first one asked when going before the parole board.

12. *Cold dude.* Someone who can perform an act without regard to human emotions or human decency. The term can be used to describe anyone from a sadistic guard to a calculating holdup man. Many inmates have respect for this kind of person.

13. *Cop out.* To confess or plead guilty to a crime. Inmates will tell you that it is wise never to cop out to anything.

14. *Crime partner.* Your accomplice in whatever crime you committed.

15. *Dead man.* Someone on Death Row at San Quentin.

16. *Devil.* The black man's word for the white man. It is used particularly by the Black Muslims.

17. *Do your own time.* Don't get involved in what someone else is doing. Take care of yourself.

18. *Duck.* To make a duck of someone is to make him look foolish. It derives, I suppose, from the ungainly walk of such a fowl. It gives inmates pleasure to see someone make a duck of a free person.

19. *Dude.* Any male. Not a derogatory term.

20. *Duke.* A prison leader. If you have the dukes with you, they will assign men to clean up the classroom for you and crack down on any student who steps out of line. I never subscribed to this system and never had any trouble with it. Half the time I didn't know who the dukes were. Sometimes a student would

approach me after class and offer a crew to clean up my room. I would politely turn down the offer and that would be the end of it. I think the dukes were natural leaders and I had respect for them. Prison authorities are always trying to identify dukes and work through them. However, once a man becomes identified with the power structure, he loses the respect of his peers and destroys his dukedom.

21. *Dump truck.* A loud, crude, insensitive person. A lout.

22. *Fat-butt boy.* A young prison homosexual. When you are intolerably horny you go to a fat-butt boy.

23. *Fight, fuck or hit the fence.* This phrase describes a situation that some inmates stumble into. For instance, if you borrow money or cigarettes and cannot repay the debt you have only three ways out of your dilemma; you can fight the man you owe, you can sell your body (this is called giving head or tail) or you can try to escape by trying to scale the fence. If you ignore the debt you will be killed. Sometimes in San Quentin or Folsom a man is killed for a debt as small as a few cartons of cigarettes.

24. *Fox.* A girl.

25. *Freaked out.* Bombed out of your mind, spaced out, temporarily insane, not with it.

26. *Free person.* Anyone who works inside a prison other than an inmate.

27. *Front.* To put on a big show, to pretend to be something you aren't. For instance, inmates who talk very tough are usually in jail for less serious crimes. The ones in for very serious crimes don't front about their deeds at all. Many inmates believe that success is achieved by fronting and that education is only a license to steal. Long-term inmates are amazingly glib and they create fictionalized accounts of their pasts that are works of art. After you work in a prison for a while you become adept at spotting these con artists.

28. *Fruit of the poisoned tree.* A phrase coined by J. Edgar Hoover, I believe, for evidence obtained illegally. Any such evidence is not permissible in court and any other testimony or evidence

based upon the illegally obtained evidence is also thrown out of court, for it is the fruit of the poisoned tree.

29. *Get off my case.* Don't pry into my private affairs.

30. *Get your rocks off.* To achieve a sexual or emotional climax.

31. *Get your shit together.* To pull yourself together, to get your head together and to be able to function properly.

32. *Give head.* To submit sexually to another. The name itself implies oral activity.

33. *Gunsill.* A loud-talking, aggressive inmate. They come, usually, from one of the Youth Authority facilities, and after a while the older inmates sober them.

34. *Hank literature.* Literature written by inmates for masturbatory purposes. It circulates privately, is illegal, and is utterly without redeeming social value.

35. *Hard stuff.* Heroin and opium, in contradistinction to marijuana, speed, goof balls, and less potent drugs.

36. *Hold your mud.* Standing your ground or holding your own in the prison setting. If you panic and can't hold your mud in a prison, you will be gang raped and torn apart. It is the soft, middle-class youngster, usually in on a marijuana bust, who has the most difficult time holding his mud. Prison often destroys these youngsters.

37. *Joint.* Any jail.

38. *Joint-converted Muslim.* A man who has joined the Black Muslims in prison. He is extremely zealous in his new religion, excessively polite and formal with white people, and usually boiling inside with anger.

39. *Juice.* Power. Any man who can make things happen or get things done for you has juice. Inmates who get special favors have "juice." Theoretically all inmates are equal. In reality, there is an enormous struggle for juice. There is also a great struggle for juice among the free people in a prison.

40. *Keester stashed.* Keester is the ass. Stashed means stored. Inmates are frequently stripped and searched and many of them are experts at converting their rectums into storage areas.

41. *Kick back.* To relax, take it easy, control your anger, go with the flow, bro. Foggy dismal days are referred to as kick-back days.

You long to return to your sack, pull the covers over your head and sleep. Time passes quickly and you are closer to freedom.

42. *Low rider.* A person cruising around looking for trouble. The term gets its derivation from someone riding in a car with one foot out the window and slouched down so that only his eyes appear above the dashboard. A low rider has no respect for anyone or anything. He takes no shit. He has no pity or remorse.

The image of the low rider has enormous appeal for the young man who has been kicked around all his life. Low riding is considered a sport. The more people who are shocked by it, the more exciting it becomes. However, there is no low riding in prison. When inmates start aggressive activity, they are either taken care of by other inmates or put in solitary confinement.

43. *Lucky 13.* The code name for marijuana. This was the most popular bit of graffiti that was scribbled on the walls of the prison. "M" is the thirteenth letter of the alphabet and stands for mary jane.

44. *Mary Jane.* One of the many names for marijuana.

45. *Mess.* A gun. When committing a robbery it is important to decide who is going to carry the mess.

46. *Miranded.* After the Supreme Court decision in the Miranda case, it became mandatory for the arresting officer to inform the person of his legal rights before making an arrest. This includes the right to remain silent and the right to secure legal counsel. If the arrested person is not miranded, informed of his constitutional rights, the case can be thrown out of court.

47. *Mule.* A free person who has been intimidated by inmates. If a free person has broken a prison rule and the inmate can prove this, he can get the free person fired. Much of the contraband in a prison is brought in through mules. During the time I worked in a prison, I was never searched, nor to my knowledge was any other free person searched. However, my classroom and room on the prison grounds were searched frequently.

48. *Naline test.* A test to determine if there is any heroin or opium in

9

your system. It is done by urinalysis. Sometimes you can beat this test by having someone else piss in the bottle for you.

49. *Narc.* A narcotics agent.

50. *Never get your nose open behind a woman.* Never try too hard to please a woman. If you get your nose open, she will put a ring in it and lead you to destruction. Many a man stole to supply his woman with material things. Then, when the pressure was on, she copped out on him and sent him to jail.

51. *Old lady.* A girl friend or wife. I was raised in an era when it meant mother, and it took me some time to get used to it in the prisoners' context. Thus, when someone said that he was balling his old lady, I initially inferred that he was describing an incestuous relationship.

52. *P.C.* Protective custody. This is where the conspicuous homosexuals are segregated. Any inmate can request to be placed in protective custody, regardless of his sexual tendencies. If you feel that your life is threatened by another inmate, you can get placed in protective custody. However, there is a social stigma attached to this and not many inmates want to do it. Sometimes an inmate is placed in protective custody against his wishes when prison guards think there is a good chance that he will be killed if he remains on the main line.

53. *Paper hanger.* The old-time term for the bad-check writer.

54. *Pitch and catch.* The term pitch means to be the aggressor in a homosexual act. Many men in prison claim that even though they engage in homosexual activity in prison, they are heterosexual and it is the deprivation of women that causes them to find a different pillow for their lust. These men claim they only pitch. To catch is to submit to the act. The old-timers claim that if you pitch you also catch.

55. *Pruno.* Prison-made home brew. It's concocted from yeast, fruit juices, bread, potatoes and many other ingredients. There are many recipes for it. It doesn't taste very good; but it can give you a buzz. It is, of course, illegal and inmates are punished when caught with it.

56. *Punk.* Someone who submits sexually to a stronger inmate in exchange for protection and small favors.

10

57. *Pushing iron.* Lifting weights in the gym. Many inmates have extraordinary muscular development in their upper chests and arms from lifting weights every day. It's the only acceptable outlet for a physically healthy young man.
58. *Queen.* An unmistakable homosexual. A woman trapped in a man's body.
59. *Ruby do.* What every inmate dreams about every day in prison! A parole.
60. *Rue out.* The same as ruby do. When you get your rue out, you think you have it made; yet 70% of the persons released return again.
61. *Rug head.* A black man. It's never used in the presence of a black man.
62. *Sanchez.* The other guy. The man who marries or makes love to your wife or girl friend while you are in the joint. Whenever an inmate would express concern about a woman, someone would invariably say, "Don't worry about that woman. Sanchez will take care of her."
63. *Screw.* A prison guard. It is a common term in eastern prisons but rarely used in a California prison.
64. *Shank.* A knife. It can be made from a piece of metal taken from the machine shop. It can be a knife smuggled in from the outside. It can be a toothbrush handle filed to a deadly point. It can be a bed spring. It's amazing how many things can be converted into a deadly weapon.
65. *Shanked.* Is stabbed.
66. *Shine on.* To completely ignore another person. It's a necessary process where men live in a climate of enforced proximity.

    Inmates work out their own petty differences by this process. It avoids physical confrontations and has a devastating effect on people who have been conditioned to noisy abusive responses. It was the most powerful disciplinary tool at my disposal.
67. *Short.* Wheels, or an automobile.
68. *Silent beef.* Crimes you were suspected of committing for which you were neither tried nor sentenced. Frequently if there is evidence that a man has committed several crimes, the D.A.

and the judge will make a deal that if the defendant pleads guilty to one of the charges, all other charges will be dropped. However, a complete record of his case is on file, and when the parole board has a hearing they go into these other alleged crimes with the defendant. Since California law has indeterminate sentences, the parole board can keep the prisoner in jail as long as they see fit. Thus it is meaningless to be convicted on one count, because the parole board judges the man on his complete past record and is, in effect, judge and jury for these alleged other crimes. Many inmates feel that a silent beef is more important than the crimes for which they were convicted. And, of course, an inmate is not officially being tried for these other alleged crimes. Inmates feel outraged and tricked by this process.

69. *Skin search.* To strip completely naked and be searched for weapons or contraband. A guard has the right to skin search an inmate at any time for any reason. Inmates are sometimes skin searched several times a day. It is mandatory after having received visitors to be skin searched.

70. *Snitch.* A squealer or informant. Inmates despise these people and will kill them. The majority of people in prison are there because someone snitched on them and this explains the hatred. However, there are many snitches in a prison.

71. *Soul brother.* The term for a black man used by a black man to refer to another black man. It isn't a demeaning term and is frequently used.

72. *Stone fox.* A beautiful girl.

73. *Stuff.* A gun. Sometimes it is used to refer to dope or marijuana or stolen material.

74. *Tailor mades.* Brand-name cigarettes. They are in contradistinction to the roll-your-own cigarettes which are cheaper and more common in a prison. If a dude always smokes tailor mades, that means he has money and is a little higher on the social scale than his associates.

75. *Take his head.* The same thing as "to off someone." Frequently it is used as a threat rather than as a description of the deed.

76. *The Man.* Legal authority. It could be policeman, judge, parole board. Always, you must be wary of the Man.
77. *To off someone.* To kill someone. You almost never hear someone say, "I killed someone." You will hear instead, "I offed the dude."
78. *Turned out.* This means that an inmate has been used as a sexual object. Frequently it refers to his initiation into this mystery.
79. *Wife.* A male girl friend in a prison.
80. *Zoo-Zoos and Wham-Whams.* Goodies and candy bars bought at the canteen.

DEAD
MAN
WALKING

CHAPTER 1

Prison is a place where you write letters and can't
think of anything to say.

From a Student Theme

"These men are not in here for pushing ducks into the water or for refusing to leave the library," principal Hugo Belson said. "But they are human beings, and some are better and some worse than the rest of us. Their ages are from eighteen to twenty-five. Don't forget, the best student you'll have was undoubtedly expelled from a public school because he was the worst one they had.

"Never trust an inmate or grant him special favors, because if you do he'll use you and have you in trouble fast. Suppose an inmate comes to you and tells you he's heard his girl friend is sick and he's not allowed to write to her. He says he has written a letter to her and wants you to mail it for him on the outside. His story is so pitiful you decide to mail the letter, even though you know it's against prison rules. After the letter has been mailed, the inmate comes to you and says that the letter is proof you've broken a strict prison rule and he now has evidence that could cost you your job. At first he will ask for a few packs of cigarettes to keep quiet; in giving them to him, you've broken another prison rule. Before you know it, you'll be trotting in and out with

17

dope, and in danger of serving a prison term yourself. It has happened around here, believe me. We suspected the last English teacher, but we never caught him at it."

Hugo Belson then showed me through the educational area of the prison. The inmates dressed in blue denim were working busily at their desks.

I told principal Belson my experience was in teaching through discussion rather than using standard textbooks and asked him about the inmates' attitude toward this approach.

"It won't work," he said. "These inmates are hostile and will twist any subject to their own advantage. It's impossible to involve them in a discussion of anything but dope and sex. Also, they're not kept busy in a discussion group; and when these men aren't busy they get into trouble."

We returned to the principal's office. "Teaching in a prison leaves a taint on a man. You'll have a difficult time getting back into public schools if you should ever want to. But you can have the job if you want it; you look strong enough to handle it."

I took the job. I had just had a textbook publisher's contract cancelled, and instead of collecting the $2,500 check I had expected, I found myself flat broke and scrambling to survive.

My wife and two small children were to remain in San Francisco, and I was to live in barracks 3,000 yards from the prison for the first year, visiting my family only on weekends. Vacations consisted solely of Thanksgiving and Christmas, for we taught straight through the summer. After one year I would accrue five days vacation and would use this time to move my family nearby.

"The majority of your students are capable of killing you, so don't take chances," continued Belson. "Don't allow a student to get behind you. Watch your wastebasket; a favorite trick played on new teachers is to jam the wastebasket with paper and set it on fire. These men can flick a lighted match into a full wastebasket from almost any corner of the room. They've had plenty of time to practice, and are expert at it. If you have a fire, set the basket out in the corridor and dial 222 for the fire department.

18

They'll put it out for you. Don't get flustered if this happens to you; they're testing your reactions. These men will watch every move you make and will probe every aspect of your personality. If you have a weakness they'll find it and exploit it mercilessly.

"You have more control here than in any public school. We don't have a PTA," Belson said with a smile. "If a student causes you difficulty, you can get him sentenced to ten days in isolation on your say-so alone. He won't get much more to eat there than a bologna sandwich a day. Your complaint against him will be placed in his jacket and, as we have indeterminate sentences, a bad report from you could easily cost a man an additional year in jail.

"No inmate's word is valid against the word of a free person. These men have lost their civil rights. You are an absolute authority in your classroom. They know this, and won't stretch your tolerance. They respect authority, but if they think you're weak they'll drive right over you. So don't be afraid to write someone up. If something happens and you're not certain who did it, pick someone who might have done it and beef him. It doesn't matter if it's the wrong person; you'll have established yourself as a cold dude and they won't give you any more trouble.

"Oh, by the way," he added, "there's a phone in each classroom, usually just behind the desk. If trouble starts, dial 333 and the goon squad will be there to rescue you. If you don't have time to dial, just kick the phone off the hook and help will be on the way in eleven seconds."

I was to report the next day for a prison briefing, and would start teaching the day following. The prison itself consisted of a long corridor with cell blocks jutting out from it at either end and an administration building in front of the prison complex. The cell blocks were several stories high, and their barred windows overlooked the entranceway and the yard. The buildings were surrounded by high double fences; a guard tower stood at each corner.

If a prisoner tried to escape, he had to climb the first fence,

19

getting over a tangle of flaring barbed wire at the top. Then he had to drop to the ground and run a few yards to a second fence identical to the first. During this time, he would be an easy target for the tower guards. If he did manage to get over both fences, there was considerable open space where he could be picked off.

During the time I was at the prison, two attempts were made to "hit the fence." Both occurred at noon. In the first instance, two inmates, in full sight of the several hundred others in the yard, bolted and tried to climb the fence. One youth, who was in prison for a minor offense, was killed. He got over the first fence but was knocked off the second when a bullet caught him in the head. The second man, who was serving a long term, escaped.

The inmate who escaped was accused of murdering the one who had been shot. According to California law, if you incite someone to escape and he is killed, you are guilty of murder.

The inmate who had been killed had a YA or Youth Authority status, meaning that the crime for which he had been convicted would be reduced to a misdemeanor if his parole record was good. A misdemeanor is not reflected on a criminal record. Unfortunately, these YA men were allowed to mingle with the "B" numbers who had been convicted of more serious crimes.

The second escape attempt was made by a teenage Mexican student who had only a few weeks time to serve before parole. He had received a Dear John letter and went berserk. He wasn't killed, but the thumb and forefinger of his right hand were blown off, and a hole was carved in his left forearm as he tried to climb the first fence.

His teacher resigned shortly after this incident. The student had been one of his sixth-grade pupils and he had considered him to be "gentle as a lamb."

I had a class the afternoon just after the shooting had taken place. The students were shaken. Many of them had been witnesses to it and had been horrified at the sight. Feeling was high that the shooting was unnecessary because the young man was crazy out of his mind and could have been captured before he got very far.

A student pointed out that if a man runs onto a crowded

superhighway, you cannot blame the driver of the car that strikes him. Thus, if the inmate knew he would be shot while attempting to climb the fence, he should be responsible for the consequence of his actions. Others violently disagreed, pointing out that while the guard in the tower can make a choice, the driver cannot. An interesting discussion of values followed.

My second day on the job I was taken on a tour of the prison. The cell blocks were of gleaming steel, and everything was extremely clean. I was shown a shower room in one of the cell blocks, where a guard was supervising the inmates to see that no horseplay or homosexual activity occurred.

"They're a bunch of fucking animals," the guard said. "A bunch of fucking animals."

Most of the men were handsome, healthy and well built. Most of them practiced weight lifting, and their muscular development was extraordinary.

"What do you mean by animals?" I asked.

"A bunch of animals," he repeated. "Do you see that bastard over there?" He pointed to one of the men. "Do you know what he done? He raped a girl. But that ain't the full story, because they don't put things like that in the paper. Do you know what he done after he raped her? He shit on the floor and smeared it on his prick—then he made the girl lick it off, and then he cut her throat. Do you think you're going to teach these fucking animals anything? It's just a waste of the taxpayer's money.

"OK, you animals," he said, turning off the showers, "get on out now and let the next batch in."

The inmates were subdued and did not look at the guard. They did as he asked.

That evening I spent my first night in the bachelors' quarters on the prison grounds. This consisted of a long one-story building broken up into individual cubicles. In each cubicle was a desk, chair, bed and washstand. The cubicles were only slightly more habitable than the cells.

During the evening and throughout the night I heard strange howls coming from the prison. They were nonhuman, as if some

21

animal were in great pain. I was taken back mentally to some primitive landscape, and thought that early man, when he first tried to comprehend this troubled earth, must have stood by his cave at night and uttered sounds like these.

The next day I inquired about it and one of the guards said, "Oh, that: you'll get used to it. It's just the animals in isolation. They get lonely and make noise. Sometimes we have to turn the hose on them, and that quiets them down."

Strangely enough, after a while I did get used to it.

I started teaching. My first class consisted of fifteen students picked at random from the main line. New classes were not to start for another two weeks; this class was set up to accustom the students to a school situation, and to give me a chance to get adjusted to my new job before the term began.

As there were plenty of geography books available, it became a geography class. No credit was to be given for the work, but I was instructed not to let the students know this.

I handed out the geography books and assigned the students to read the chapter and answer the questions at the end; the kind of unimaginative teaching I deplore. Furthermore, the geography text had been published by the same company that had cancelled my contract and left me stranded. I felt that fate was rubbing my nose in the mud for trying to improve educational methods.

The students went quietly and politely about their "donkey" work, with the exception of one black student who sat in the front row, staring into space without opening his book. I watched him for a while and then noticed a twitch and an expression of great pain cross his face. I walked over to him and inquired quietly if something was wrong.

"Mr. Campbell, a worm is eating at my insides. I am being eaten alive inside."

"Can I send you to the hospital?" I asked.

"It won't do no good. I been there. They say nothin's wrong with me."

"Well, what can be done?" I asked.

"Ain't nothin' can be done," he said. "Only if I be still, sometimes that worm don't eat so fast."

22

I didn't question him further, but when he shuddered I could almost see that worm taking a bite out of his intestines.

His name was Richardson and he didn't come back to class the next day. I heard he had been transferred to the mental ward at Vacaville. He later died of cancer of the bowels.

CHAPTER 2

I feel silly writing this so I am going to stop. I don't want you to know too much about me. I don't know you.

From a Student Theme

During the next few days I began to learn about prison. One of the first things I had to master was the prison language. Terms such as "low rider," "kick back," "shine on," "bull," "shank," "the Man," "dude" and "front" were completely unfamiliar to me. I discovered in prison, "mother" is only half a word.

To "shine someone on" means to completely ignore him. This is an important and subtle psychological tool in a prison, for one is constantly in close physical contact with others. Sometimes, in walking the corridor, I would fail to nod to one of my students or would not notice his greeting. The student would brood about this for days and then suddenly burst out in class with the accusation that I hated him. As these men are removed from normal social relationships, the slightest discouragement on the teacher's part can be devastating. On the other hand, shouting or getting angry with them merely increases their hostility.

As I became accustomed to prison language, I started to use it in my own speech. An inmate who I had thought was somewhat hostile to me approached me after class one afternoon and said,

24

"Mr. Campbell, I wish you wouldn't use prison slang. It don't sound right coming from you. Most of us like to think of the teacher as someone better than us, and when you talk like that it's like saying education don't improve you any."

After that, I always tried to speak correctly in the prison. However, the language is very expressive and I found myself using prison argot in private conversations.

In one instance my own midwestern vernacular collided with prison terminology. Before the final bell I would say, "All right, in a few minutes I'm going to turn you out to pasture. This was always greeted with shocked expressions. Later, I found out that "turned out" is the prison term for male rape.

I discovered that teaching in a prison was very different from teaching in a public school. Classes were smaller. There were rarely more than twenty-two students in a class, and my total pupil load was approximately eighty students. In my public-school teaching experience there had often been thirty-five students per class and as many as one hundred fifty students, total pupil load.

In the prison high school, unlike in the public schools, I did not have a student whose reading score was below seventh-grade level. If I found a student who was unable to read simple stories, he would be recommended for elementary school, where he would remain until he was equipped to do high school work.

A number of students were functionally illiterate when they came to the prison, although they were high school graduates. These men started in the prison's first grade, learned the alphabet, and worked their way up through the higher grades. One black student advanced from first-grade to acceptable high school work in little more than a year. I asked him how it had been possible to become a high school graduate without learning to read, and how, with his quick mind, he had been able to sit through twelve years of public schooling without mastering the alphabet.

"I was absent a lot in elementary school," he replied. "In high school, I found out the best way to get promoted was to cause so much disturbance the teacher didn't want me back. I really wanted to learn to read, but I didn't know how to tell anyone. The high school teachers didn't have the time to help me, anyway."

There are many books and statistics that clearly demonstrate the failure of our educational system to teach the simplest skills to many of our young people. In a prison, however, one deals with damaged lives rather than statistics.

In prison classes the level of maturity is higher than in public school and fewer distractions exist. Clowning is not permitted, and disciplnary problems are relatively rare. However, there is always a strong feeling of depression among student inmates, and laughter is not shared with loved ones. It is not possible to be truly happy in a prison setting; when you tune in on your students you tune in on despair.

Custody rules, and many guards, are hostile to the educational department. This is due, in part, to the teachers' higher pay, the low educational level of the guards, and the fact that it is easier for a teacher to establish a friendly relationship with an inmate than it is for the guard who must order him around.

Students in a prison are generally more eager to learn than are public school students. Wife killers, others who have committed "crimes of passion," dope addicts and marijuana users are model pupils. One older con confessed to me he liked the California drug laws, since the prisons were improved by the bringing in of a "higher class element."

Young men who have been continually in and out of prison, many of them since they were eight years old, present a great problem. They have been institutionalized so long that whatever families they had are no longer interested in them. All their friendships have been formed in prison. Most of their memories of Christmas and other holidays are of those spent in the joint. Their sex lives begin with a moist, warm and yielding watermelon cut in half and buried in a field on a prison farm, and end in homosexuality by the time they are twelve. They are seldom out of jail for more than six months at a time, and on getting out, they are incapable of dealing with a free society. They run away from foster homes and perplex the counsellors who try to help

26

them. Some are intelligent, likable human beings; however, they are unequipped to cope with the ways of the outside world.

Some young men take great pleasure in breaking the law. Psychiatry, perhaps, has been able to identify them but has, so far, been unable to change them. These men are not a problem in a classroom, for there is relatively little they can steal.

I once asked the question of my students, "Would you prefer to serve a six month's sentence or take a whipping?" Almost to a man, they preferred the sentence. I considered this strange, as I would much rather take a beating and earn my freedom. They considered my point of view masochistic.

When I started to teach, one class immediately caused me trouble. It was the last period in the day, from 2:30 to 4:00. Every Friday I would become restless, since I was anxious to wipe away the prison grime and return to my family in San Francisco. I longed to hear children laugh, to see women, and to be with people who had hope for the future. The students sensed my restlessness, realizing, at the same time, nothing was waiting for them over the weekend other than more misery and frustration. My temper was short and got the best of me.

A young, red-haired student, O'Leary, had been notified he was to be paroled in two weeks. He had presented no problem until this time, but after hearing he was going home, he thought he could do as he pleased. He came into the classroom looking for trouble. I tried ignoring him, but this had no effect. He took a sheet of paper, crumpled it into a ball and threw it onto the floor.

"Mr. O'Leary, pick up that paper and throw it in the wastebasket," I barked.

He did not respond.

"Pick it up."

"I ain't gonna do it. I'm getting out of here in two weeks."

"Pick it up." Again, he did not respond.

"I'm giving you a direct order. Pick it up."

I now found myself in direct confrontation with him. I felt my authority in the classroom would be destroyed if I backed down, yet I didn't want to get him into trouble just before his parole.

I later learned how to handle a situation like this with ease.

The first rule was to avoid direct confrontation. When I first became aware of his attitude I should have called him outside and privately told him, "O'Leary, don't mess with me. I'm pleased you're going home. Go on back to your unit and stay there. I'll carry you on the class roll. But if you give me trouble, I'll give you trouble. Now get out of here."

I didn't handle the situation properly. I ordered him out of the classroom and told him I would have to write him up. He then left the classroom, but sat on a bench in the corridor instead of returning to his unit. I finally went to the phone, called the guard and had him removed. Later I filed a report on the incident.

The next day O'Leary returned to class looking very contrite. Hugo Belson had read my report and had threatened O'Leary with an additional six months in prison when he went on trial for refusing to obey a direct order. I withdrew my complaint.

O'Leary then took another tack. He was pleasant in class and when I asked him for a theme, he handed in a sixteen-page document. It turned out to be a pornographic story, or what the inmates call "hank" literature. These stories contain elaborate descriptions of every perversion known to mankind and are written by older, more literate cons who rent them out for cigarettes and other favors. There is a library of these stories that circulates in prisons throughout the country, and the most prurient are kept alive by convict "troubadours," just as folk tales were passed on by wandering minstrels in the Middle Ages.

The particular story handed in by O'Leary was about a beautiful young girl who was abducted and sold into white slavery. Her first captors were truck mechanics, and a graphic description followed of how they penetrated her fore and aft simultaneously, using axle grease as a lubricant. There was vivid description of dark stains trickling down her attractive legs.

I returned the story to O'Leary and told him it was not acceptable. I said when men live in degradation they are attracted to degradation and tried to explain there is beauty, warmth and tenderness about a woman. When he discovered this, a story such as the one he had handed in would sicken him.

He didn't buy it. "Naw," he said, "Businessmen and dudes

28

that have families and carry lunch pails go for that stuff just as much as the dudes in prison."

Two days later a guard caught him with the story. O'Leary claimed I had assigned it as a theme and had encouraged him to read it to the class.

Hugo Belson called me in, and I explained what had happened. He accepted my story but claimed O'Leary was trying to make a "duck" out of me, and I should be careful. He said O'Leary had purposely let the guard discover the story in an attempt to get me into trouble. He added that, even though it was a setup, gossip would spread among the guards that I was encouraging my students to write dirty stories.

I talked to O'Leary about this, and he freely admitted he had fabricated the story in an attempt to get himself off the hook. When I asked why he would want to implicate me, he said, "You're a free person; you can take care of yourself."

The following day an inmate told the class that when he was a burglar he always carried a blow torch and a blank key. He would heat the key until it was malleable, insert the key into the lock, and open it. O'Leary perked up when he heard this, convinced his stay in my class finally had produced something of practical value.

However, he returned to me the following day in a huff of righteous indignation.

"Mr. Campbell, you're makin' a duck out of me," he cried.

"What do you mean?" I asked.

"I was talkin' to my cellie about that hot-key trick. It won't work. All it will do is plug up a lock so no one can open it. It's a bum trip and it ain't funny. I coulda tried that on the outside and been caught. You should be teachin' us English, not takin' us on trips that could get us in trouble."

During O'Leary's last day in class I turned my back to write something on the blackboard—and it happened. My wastebasket, jammed to the top with paper, was on fire.

I looked at the shooting flames and realized all eyes were focused upon me to take in my reaction.

"Where are you from?" I asked O'Leary.

29

"L.A.," O'Leary replied.

"Well, here's a little present for you men from the L.A. area."

With my foot, I spun the wastebasket into the middle of the room.

"I know how homesick you all are for a little smog. Breathe it in and be happy."

"I didn't do it," O'Leary sniveled.

"Of course you didn't," I said gleefully, realizing this time the deck was stacked in my favor. "A fine, upstanding lad like you, Mr. O'Leary, ready to go back into society as a clean-living example of how prison can rehabilitate a man. Why, I bet if I called you outside you'd tell me who did it, and I could have the guy put in the hole for thirty days."

The other inmates were coughing and laughing, but they were laughing at O'Leary, not at me. I let them suffer a little, and then someone got a butt can from the corridor, jammed it into the wastebasket and smothered the fire. The students took off their jackets and helped fan the smoke out the windows. They found soap somewhere and cleaned up the charred mess on the linoleum floor. I never reported the fire and never had any more trouble in that classroom.

O'Leary was released the next day, and entered Soledad prison three weeks later on a new charge.

CHAPTER 3

Prison is a place where you learn that nobody needs
you, that the world goes on without you.
From a Student Theme

Many people who worked in the prison told me they experienced a sinking feeling when the gate first closed behind them. Entering the prison never depressed me. When the first gate was closed, I would wave to the guard in the tower and he would throw a lever, opening the massive wire-mesh door for me. Once I was inside, the door would magically close behind me. If I had forgotten something and wanted to go out, a wave of the hand would open the door again.

I would walk up the path, bordered with flowers and expansive lawns, to the main administration building. It was a busy place, with many women secretaries. There was also a sprinkling of denim-clad trusties who performed custodial and gardening tasks.

I would walk through the administration building, across a stone courtyard, to the central-control area. A guard would buzz another door open for me. Then I would walk a corridor to an iron gate that entered into the prison proper. There, a corridor guard would unlock the gate with a big iron key, and I would be inside. If no guard was visible, I would tap on the bars lightly with my key until someone arrived to let me into the prison.

31

Then I would walk down a long corridor with white chalk lines on either side. Inmates, going to and from assignments, were required to walk between these lines. Every so many feet there was an iron grating that could be brought down, blocking the corridor. This prison was built like a water-tight ship with compartments that, at the first sign of trouble, could be sealed off by the throwing of a switch. Then the guards could systematically work through and secure each area. It was not possible for a riot to engulf the entire prison.

Everyone was made acutely aware that doors would not be opened to prisoners who took hostages. If an inmate marched a free person to the main gate and threatened to cut his throat, the response from the tower guard would be firm and clear: "Cut his throat and when his body drops, I will kill you."

This was a rough rule, but I subscribed to it. I would rather take the chance of having my throat cut than live in constant fear that some yo-yo was going to use me as a shield to escape from prison.

Although I did not have much personal contact with the guards and cannot give a detailed observation or evaluation of what they were like, I will describe what I saw.

Guards did let us into the prison every day and for the most part they were courteous and friendly. Although once in a while there would be a grumpy one on duty. There was a guard assigned to the education area, but I rarely saw him. He patrolled the first floor; my classroom was on the second floor and distant from the stairway. Later, during my last six months in the prison, when educational funds were received from the government, another guard was assigned to the second floor. His name was Johnny and his primary function was to make certain no prisoner wore a cap in the education area. He checked out each classroom and, if any student were wearing a cap, he immediately accosted him and made him take if off. He started marching into my classrooms when he spotted a cap on a head. I politely asked him to tap on the glass and get my attention if he saw an infraction of this rule, and I would handle it. So, whenever I heard a tap and saw Johnny's face, I would nod to the guy wearing the cap and nod to Johnny and the cap would disappear.

Johnny was a gentle soul, not greatly disliked by the students. He had been in prison work for more than thirty years and the students told me when he was a young man, he had been gang raped during a prison riot and it had affected his mind. They claimed he had been castrated. I doubt it.

I did get to know a few more of the guards who lived in the bachelors' quarters with me. One was named Leonard and had been transferred from Susanville to stay in the bachelors' quarters until he could move his family down from the mountains.

I complained once about my wife spending all my money on clothes and Leonard said, "I wish I had your problem. My wife is a full-blooded Chocktaw Indian and she slops around the house in a kimono all day. I can't hardly git her into a dress."

Leonard was conscientious. It was his duty to make the rounds in the middle of the night and see everyone was in bed. One of the rules was that every guard, when he made the bed check, must see flesh. There were pictures in the guard room of a bunk with a dummy in it that inmates had constructed so that it looked like a human form was beneath the covers. The escapees had cut through the window bars with a hacksaw, dropped to the ground and gotten over the fence undetected. The guard who had reported them present when he made the bed check was fired.

This was not going to happen to Leonard. If an inmate burrowed beneath his blankets, Leonard whistled and banged on the bars until the man stirred. If he got no response, he unlocked the cell door and peeked beneath the blankets until he saw flesh.

Inmates were furious with guards who rattled on the bars and woke them in the middle of the night by pulling their covers. It was an invasion of privacy. It was inhuman. Yet it was Leonard's job and he followed the rule to the letter.

Another guard, whom I didn't know but who also lived in our quarters, was fired for bringing liquor on the grounds. The first thing visible as you entered the prison was an enormous sign stating it was a felony to bring liquor, drugs, cameras or firearms onto prison grounds. This man had been on an airline flight and when the stewardess had offered him a drink in a small bottle he had slipped the bottle in his pocket and had forgotten about. The bottle was discovered in a jacket pocket in his closet on a routine search of prison grounds. He protested it was not his intention to bring liquor on the grounds, and he had forgotten about the small bottle. Nevertheless, it was a clear violation of the law and he was dismissed. However, no criminal charges were brought against him.

Another guard got into trouble because he gave a mother and child a ride from the main road to the prison front gate. The prison complex was about a mile back from the highway. There was no bus that ran from the prison to town and visitors who did not come by car would have to get a taxi ride from town to the prison.

The young mother, who did not have the money for a taxi, prevailed on the bus driver to let her off at the side road and was walking the prison approach road in a rainstorm when a guard driving to work spotted her and gave her a lift to the main gate. This broke a basic rule about fraternizing with inmate's families and the guard was reprimanded for it.

I broke a prison law during my stay in the bachelor's quarters. My family went East for a two-month visit and we gave up the apartment in San Francisco. I was to find a place in the area to house them when they returned. I did find a house but it was not available until fall. They could not take our family dog, Blue, with them and I arranged to board him with someone in Palo Alto.

I did not visit Blue during his first few weeks of boarding out because I was told it was better to let a dog adjust to his new surroundings. However, after the first month, I got an emergency call that Blue was dying. When I arrived there, he was wobbly, but still on his feet. He had eaten all right for a few days, but tailed off and had refused all food for the last two weeks. He was a hairy skeleton with a pink tongue.

"Blue, something has to be done about you," I told him, and I put him in the car and drove back to the prison with him.

I bought some dog food along the way and two bowls for food

and water. I carried him into my tiny room unnoticed and offered him some food. He didn't eat. I put him on the bed and went to sleep petting him and whispering crazy stories into his stupid ear. In the morning he was hungry as a wolf. I fed him and left him in my car that was parked in an open shed near the dormitory. He was weak enough so that he slept in the car all day long, and I exercised him when I came out at five o'clock. In a few days he was chasing jackrabbits, which were in abundance in the fields surrounding the prison.

I knew I could be fired for keeping a pet on prison grounds. I was willing to take my chances for this infraction, and that wasn't what bothered me. What did disturb me was if I did get busted, I would have a hard time explaining my problem to my next prospective employer. What happens when you fill in the blank space marked REASON FOR LEAVING LAST EMPLOYMENT with "Dismissed for sleeping with a dog."

No trouble arose and when my family returned, Blue joined them in perfect health. Probably no one bothered to go after me because it was the riot season and trucks arrived every day with additional tear gas cannisters and gas masks.

I did have one run-in with a guard. One evening I was late leaving the prison and the main gate was closed. When this happens the tower guard can let you out through a side entrance which he controls electronically. I had my car repaired that day at the inmate-run gas station and expected to pick up my keys in the main building, as was my custom. There were some guards milling around the side gate and I asked one of them what I could do about the keys to my car. He was a short man in his fifties with a very red face. He motioned toward the guard tower and called out, "Give this woman her keys."

"What did you say?" I asked incredulously.

"Give this woman her keys," he repeated.

"I'm a man not a woman," I said, "and I'm also not an inmate and am not going to put up with that kind of bullshit." I moved toward him.

"Give this person its keys," he said snidely.

The tower guard passed the keys down in a bucket that slid along a wire. I picked the keys out of the bucket, glowered at the guard and started to walk away. Then I turned, went back to the guard, and asked, "What's your name?"

"Never mind what my name is," he said.

"Tell me your name," I demanded. "I can find out what it is if you won't tell me."

"It's Sergeant Jones," he said.

I walked back to the barracks. I was furious. I had heard many stories from inmates about how the guards would taunt them by saying obscene things about their mothers, sisters, or wives, or would refer to them as homosexuals, or would call them out of line, order them to strip naked by saying, "Hurry up, I want to see your pussy," then would laugh at them and have them put on their clothes again.

Whenever an inmate came to me with a story of this kind, I told him to just shine it on and the guard could do nothing. If the inmate got angry or became violent he was just playing into the hands of the guards, who could slap him in the hole and give him a write-up that would shoot him down when he went before the parole board.

No one would take the word of an inmate over a guard, so it was useless to protest the provocation. Also, it was the view of many in authority that these men had to learn self-discipline and how to control their anger. So this kind of treatment was considered therapy rather than harassment.

However, I was not an inmate and did not need the therapy. The next day I described the incident in one of my classes. I was careful not to give the name of the guard who had badgered me. The students were curious as to the name of the guard. They made many guesses but no one mentioned the real name.

I asked them what they thought I should do about this incident. Their first response was that I should meet him off the prison grounds and beat him up. I pointed out he weighed 140 pounds and I was nearly 70 pounds heavier and fifteen years younger and it was no contest. I said it was a sickness and should be treated like one.

I then asked their opinion about whether or not I should write a letter describing the incident to the assistant warden. I pointed out if I did this it would be for their sake rather than mine, because I thought guards like him should be weeded out so they did not demean inmates.

There was disagreement about this but the majority thought it would not do any good and would only cause more hostility against me. When I made the statement that every citizen had an obligation to correct injustices done to others, they laughed. "You save yourself first, baby. That is the way the world operates."

"If I report this incident, can't you see I'm trying to help you?"

"How does that help us?"

"I'm trying to get rid of guards who have no business working with inmates."

"You're naive. You won't get rid of the guard and you'll get yourself in a world of hurt.

"Don't be a snitch. Take care of your own business." This was the code of the inmates.

I sat down to write the letter but never finished it. After a few weeks the incident was too far in the past to complain about.

Several months later I met the guard who had taunted me when I was walking back from a chess match in the prison at about ten o'clock at night. He was stretched out on the ground near the prison truck.

"Will you help me?" he asked.

"What is the trouble?" I asked, walking toward him suspiciously.

"It's my back. I got a hitch in it. I can't walk right. I can't even get in the truck. Can you help me?"

"What do you want me to do?"

"Pick me up and put me in the truck. It'll go away in a little while and I'll be all right."

I picked him up and put him in the truck. He was like a basket of feathers.

"I hate this job. I gotta wife and family and it's the only job I could get and I gotta stick it out. I could have called on my radio for help, but I don't want them to know about my back or they would fire me. You won't snitch on me, will you?"

"No, I won't tell," I said.

37

We talked for a while, then he drove away toward the firehouse. I saw him around after that, but I never spoke to him again.

The ratio of guards to inmates was high in this prison because of the large number of volatile young men who were housed there. Guards watched them as they went to work or school or lined up for chow or queued up in their units. Guards pulled them out of line regularly for shaves or haircuts or for unbuttoned pockets.

In a prison such as Folsom or San Quentin prisoners could go all day without seeing a guard. Here they could not. However, in this prison there were few murders, while at Quentin they averaged a murder a month and sometimes more. Some of the inmates who protested the most about close supervision would, nevertheless, not want to be transferred to a prison where there were not many guards.

My students hated prison guards and a few of them would write profiles of them to hand in as themes. This presented a problem because I did not want my classes to turn into anti-establishment dialogues. Also, I did not allow anyone to be under personal attack. However, we did have freedom of discussion and the generic title, guard, was worthy of exploration; as was teacher, inmate, policeman, dope addict, etc.

One student wrote a composite of the background of a security guard named Albert. In high school Albert was the fat kid who never got the girl. He never participated in sports and was a loser in everything he did.

Albert wanted to be a California Highway Patrolman, but he couldn't pass the tests for this job, so the only thing open for him was that of security guard in a prison. He hated the inmates because they were stronger and better looking than he was. He liked the sense of power it gave him to control the lives of others.

In my classroom Albert became the name of all young prison guards and I received poems and stories about Albert. This was an acceptable way for them to work off their aggression. I remember one story described how a student coming from an English class, where he had been studying a dialogue of Plato, is accosted by a guard named Albert who says, "Go to school, you stupid jerk, and get your mind right. Maybe that will teach you not to rob and kill and rape women."

At first the student gets angry at this "ignorant piece of lard and gristle" who is telling him to get his mind right. Then he realizes that Albert is in prison, too. And if Albert isn't careful, he is going to find himself with a life sentence, day in and day out, hassling a bunch of cons. Albert is trapped, and without education he can't escape; and it serves him right. So he looks at Albert and says, "Right on, Albert. Right on."

We had a lot of fun with the ideas in that theme. The idea of captors as captive, the idea of education releasing your mind even though it doesn't make money for you; the idea of conning through writing. For this theme was written to make the reader believe education was a good thing.

The teachers who worked with me had high academic qualifications. Three of them had been high school principals or superintendents; two were Ph.D's; two were retired military officers; one was a retired millionaire. Most of them were in their fifties or sixties. Later some younger teachers were hired. We did not get together socially after work and our only contact with each other was in the teacher's room or at lunch.

We got along well with each other and there was no petty squabbling or backbiting that sometimes does occur in public school teaching. We did not talk much about school or students in the teachers' room and, in fact, I did not spend much time there, nor did many of the teachers. We were a highly individualistic group.

CHAPTER 4

I have tried by putting on paper, which cannot be put on paper in the proper focus or dimension, the every-day life I live in a fenced-off section of nowhere.

From a Student Theme

My early days in the prison were spent adjusting to the ways of a ponderous and inflexible structure. Across the hall from my permanent teaching room was the newspaper office where the bimonthly paper was put together. When I was hired, I was asked to take over this paper. Hugo Belson explained it was a difficult assignment and not one that should be given to a teacher new to prison, but he had no other choice.

I accepted the job, confident I could handle it. My brain bubbled with all kinds of ideas. I was going to get on the mailing list of every prison newspaper in the country, familiarize myself with what was being done, then come out with a format that would incorporate the best of everything in prison journalism.

I thought we would get local editors to come in and talk to the prison editors, giving advice on how to run a newspaper. From this, careers in journalism might open up for my editors.

The first meeting I had with the prison newspaper staff, I mentioned they were under suspicion of trafficking in marijuana and I could not issue passes to them allowing them to roam the prison.

They claimed these marijuana charges were false and they needed passes to attend various activities such as Chess Club, Toastmasters Club, Narcotics Anonymous, etc.

I said I would do what I could for them and talked to Captain Vasquez, the captain of the guards; he presented me with six passes signed by him and to be countersigned by me, giving freedom of movement to my reporters. The next day I passed these out and they were delighted, also incredulous I could get results so quickly.

However, the following day Hugo Belson approached me after class, dropped the six passes on my desk and said, "I just saved you a lot of trouble. You let the inmates make a duck out of you."

"I got it cleared by the supervisor of education and signed by the captain," I said.

"I know, but you've made many of the guards angry. They're asking me, 'Who is this guy Campbell who is issuing his own passes and screwing up our security?' I asked them to pick up the passes and I'm returning them to you. You can hand them out again, but, believe me, you'll get into trouble if you do."

"I'm not trying to cause any trouble. I'm trying to get a paper out. How can I do that when I can't get reporters released to cover the events?"

"You could keep a list of when the events are scheduled and get reporters ducated [ticketed] in for that day," he said.

"All right, I'll do that. But first, I need an editor-in-chief to supervise things. How do I go about finding one?" I asked.

"I don't think you should select the editor yourself," Belson said.

"Why not," I asked.

"Because, you're too new around the prison. You're liable to come up with someone who will use it as a front for running [playing] games."

"What do you suggest I do?"

"Get a security guard in charge of custody to pick someone for you."

41

Belson was not in command of the education department at this time. The supervisor of education was John Draper. Draper's wife, a genteel lady who never raised her voice, also taught in the school. Between them, they earned between forty and fifty thousand dollars a year and lived on the grounds in a rent-free house. They had no children and over the years had invested their money wisely. It was rumored they were worth more than a million dollars.

Mr. Draper was in his early sixties and had been kind to me, advancing me money when my early paychecks were late in coming. I explained to him that I needed an editor to run the paper for me and that Belson had suggested I get custody to supply me with an editor.

"You can have anyone you want, young man," Mr. Draper said expansively. "I don't care if he's in San Quentin, Soledad or anywhere else in the California prison system. I'll get him for you."

"Thank you, Mr. Draper," I said. Since I didn't know anyone under lock and key in California other than my students, this kind of help was useless.

"If I were you, I wouldn't pay any attention to Belson. He doesn't have any power. But what I say goes," Draper said.

I returned to my classroom with another lesson in penology under my belt. There are always people in power and others out of power. Although policies in a prison change very little, the administrations change frequently.

Draper lasted three months, then resigned after nearly thirty years service. He was caught in a power squeeze and forced to resign. I never did know what upended him.

Since I had no one for the job, I decided to put in my request for an editor from custody as Belson suggested.

In a few days Carter appeared. He was a short dude in his early forties with a calm professorial air. He had been in jail for nearly twenty years and had no newspaper experience. He had, however, been on trial for his life for stabbing his English teacher in San Quentin.

"How in hell did custody decide you should be the new editor?" I asked in disbelief.

42

Carter began to rap. He was a fantastic storyteller. He took the warp and woof of his existence, the poverty, the violence, the ugliness, put it on a new loom and rewove it so that it came out a tapestry of dignity and courage.

Carter had nothing but praise for his San Quentin English teacher. The stabbing occurred when he was younger and hostile and given to violent outbursts. The teacher had not been seriously hurt. Yet, since Carter was serving a life sentence, he came under the 4500 code of California law which states that "every person serving a life sentence who assaults another with a deadly weapon or by means likely to produce great bodily injury is punishable by death."

There is a logic behind a rule like this. Adding time to the sentence of a person who is convinced he is never going to get out of prison is no deterrent. Those under life sentence could declare open season on all free people if they knew they would only get more time for it. It would be like hunting toads in their garden.

Strange things sometimes go through the minds of people who have a long time to serve. I remember I had one student, Jackson, who was quiet and well behaved. He had started out in the elementary school and, over a period of years, worked his way up to high school. He had been involved in some brutal murders when he was young and would be in jail for a long time.

Jackson came up to my desk after class one day when I was mildly depressed. My car had broken down again and I was wondering how I was going to get the money to get it repaired. Apparently, I had communicated this gloom to my class.

"Mr. Campbell, is it true if a free person gets killed inside prison his family gets $17,000?" Jackson asked.

"No, it's not true. Why do you ask?"

"Well, I was just thinkin'," he said matter-of-factly but in all seriousness, "You don't look too happy to me and I know that you love your family and that's why you work in a funky place like this. So, if I was to kill you, you'd be out of your misery, your family would get money and I would go to the gas chamber and be out of my misery, too."

"Is it really that bad, serving long time?" I asked.

"It isn't so bad. It's just that I want to be useful. And I just don't think I'll get out of here, ever. And I'll never be useful to anyone."

"Don't you think I'm more useful as a teacher than a corpse?" I asked, getting caught up in this absurd discussion.

"Naw it don't make no difference. Nobody's going to do nothin' with anything we learn now. What good is it for me to learn anything if I'm gonna walk around here for the rest of my life?"

"Maybe you'll get out," I said. "Maybe there will be an earthquake and the prison will split wide open, and you will not run away but will stay and help rescue injured people and then, at the last moment, a rock will fall on you and crush you and you will be a hero in every penitentiary in the world. The future is hard to predict, Jackson."

"Yeah," Jackson said, ignoring my hyperbole. "No offense, Mr. Campbell. I like you. I was just sitting there tripping out in your class and the idea came to me. It seemed like a good idea for both of us. And if you really are a reincarnationist like you say you are, it shouldn't make any difference to you, either."

I started to say, "But I'm worth more than $17,000." But that was insane, because that was Jackson's price tag. The prison didn't pay anything. I started to thank him, but that was even crazier, because no man in his right mind thanks a man who has just offered to kill him.

Carter started telling about his early days in prison; I became intrigued. He was a charming man, radiating power and reassurance. He glossed over the stabbing incident and went directly to when he was on trial for his life. One of the jurors was a woman and she fell in love with him during the trial. Apparently, the vibrations were very heavy between them and she held out for his acquittal. After the trial, she managed to contact him and they started writing to each other. This correspondence blossomed into love, and she left her husband and was waiting for Carter to get out of prison. She also had a son, and son and mother would make monthly visits to the prison to visit Carter.

Carter brought along some of the letters from himself to his

44

bride-to-be, to demonstrate his literary prowess. He also had a few chapters of a book he was writing with another inmate in Folsom prison which, according to him, had already been sold to a publisher. I looked at a few pages of the manuscript and they were good. I didn't pry into his personal life by reading the letters, but I did glance at them enough to convince myself his romantic story could be true.

I offered him the job and he agreed to give it a try. We scheduled a meeting with the rest of the staff for the following day.

Again, Carter put on a superb performance. We had a few tables and typewriters. Carter stood with one foot on a straight-backed chair and, in a low-key delivery, told about his prison experience. "I have been in the joint for twenty years," he said. "You are young, you're just passing through. But this is my home. The joint is my town. I know every trick, every game, every bit of brutality, and I love it. It has the cold, clammy, twisted warmth of the belly of a snake, but I love it. It is funky and perverted, but I love it.

"Forget about the outside. Forget about women and liquor and dope and cars and piles of money. Let's all work together to tell the story of my city."

The reporters, all of whom were in their early twenties, responded warmly to this speech and we did not stress there was no way we could possibly be allowed to put out a newspaper that could tell the truth about a prison or describe the city that Carter wanted to portray.

I did ask the men to bring to me what they had written, regardless of whether it was publishable in a newspaper. I received a few poems and an article on education cribbed from a back issue of *The Saturday Review*. I didn't spot the source, but I showed it to another student who brought me the issue where the material had appeared.

One of my reporters wrote an article on how to make your home burglarproof. He was in jail for committing hundreds of burglaries. This article had already been published and was interesting and authoritative. I talked to him about it and he

45

showed me another series of articles he was writing about museum forgeries, which he knew something about. He had an additional article about coin collecting and stamp collecting that described how he operated in this market. Unscrupulous dealers tipped him off as to where the best collections could be found and then bought from him the things he stole.

The guy was obviously highly intelligent and had gotten into thievery because he could fathom the most expensive things to take. He claimed most burglars get outrageously gypped when they sell coin or stamp collections. They are pleased with anything and it is the dealer who makes the profit.

He claimed he got out of this racket because the dealers were too corrupt and he wanted to expose them. His problem was he never had been busted for these robberies and didn't want to serve more time for revealing them.

There were a few other stories and essays. There was one fanciful tale about a mythical inmate named Huck who managed to figure out a way to unlock doors. At night he got out of his cell, opened the cell block door and managed to work his way to the roof of the prison complex, where he ran and played. By morning, he would be back in his cell again. What made the story appealing was Huck didn't follow the conventional pattern of escaping or tormenting guards or getting even with anyone with his strange power. Huck was weird. But when you were lying on your steel cot, late at night, you could hear him walking on the roof or prowling in the corridors. And he was you; and he was free. Legends are made from stuff like this.

Of course, none of this material was suitable for a prison newspaper. Carter agreed to take on the first major news story himself. This concerned the harvesting of the plums in the San Joaquin Valley. Governor Reagan had assigned convict labor to help pick the fruit. More than two hundred low-security prisoners were temporarily billeted in the gymnasium of our prison while they assisted in picking the plums in the surrounding countryside, with guards riding shotgun on them.

Carter worked in the evening supplying towels and bedding for these new arrrivals; so he was the logical one to write the story.

In the meantime, I asked Carter to come in and talk to my students about writing. I had him scheduled to talk to one class, but he was so interesting he spent the entire day. He started by telling how he had spent most of his first seven years in solitary, or the concrete cunt as he referred to it, and how he was continually popping in and out of it.

One story the students dearly loved concerned how he had attacked a guard by sneaking up behind him with a blanket, throwing the blanket over the guard's head before he saw anything, and managing to tie him up and rob him without being seen.

The guard never did find out who had robbed him, and since there were no witnesses or evidence, no charges were brought against anyone.

This story had an appeal because it was told by a master storyteller in delicious detail; and it made a duck out of the man in authority.

After being starved, savagely beaten, left to rot in a strip cell, and after enduring all the other things designed to curb violent men for a number of years, he started, for the first time in his life, to think. Why was it he always saw the same faces in the hole? There was Chief, a wild Indian who prided himself he never took no shit from nobody, and the Greek who was meek for a while and then subject to violent eruptions.

"We all prided ourselves on our ability to stand up to authority. We were the men and the rest of the prisoners were gutless queens and snitches. Then I started thinking. We're not tough; we're stupid. We're programmed to get smashed down and lie in our own filth. We're trapped and if we don't use our heads we're never going to get out of here. The Indian has been beaten on the head too many times: his brains are gone. The Greek is crazy. He don't even belong in prison. He belongs in a mental institution. But me, I'm different. I got a brain and I better start using it."

Then Carter started telling how he had changed. It was after his trial for his life. He started analyzing his motives for doing things and he started developing self-discipline. At about this

47

time, someone introduced him to yoga. This was exactly what he needed. It gave him inner strength and self-control. Now he had found peace and could stand up to the badgering of any guard without getting upset with anyone.

He told the story of his trial and the woman juror who saved his life. And how, after the trial, they had corresponded and fallen in love. And how the authorities had discovered she was a married woman and refused to let her correspond with or visit him anymore, and how the woman then had procured a divorce so she could reestablish her relationship with Carter.

He described a touching scene. He'd had a visit from his sweetheart's former husband, who told Carter how much he loved his wife and what a rare, sensitive woman she was and that he knew Carter was a rare, sensitive human being, too, because he read some of the letters Carter had written to his wife. He even promised to hire lawyers and do what he could so they could be united. Carter described the man as "an angel" and said this visit had restored his faith in the decency and dignity of mankind.

Carter had everything going for him now. He had love and a new family; he was coauthoring a book; he had a job waiting for him with a yoga church when he got out of prison; and he had a plan for teaching yoga to inmates around the country that would revolutionize the penal system.

In a few days Carter handed in his story on the fruit harvest in the San Joaquin Valley. I set up an appointment to go over it with him the next day. I read it that evening. It needed editing and it wasn't written in newspaper style; but it had all the essential information.

The next day Carter showed up with a young inmate named Fleeson. I started to go over the article but he bridled.

"I think it's perfect and I don't want any changes in it," he said.

"You have a cross between a short story and a newspaper article; and you have run-on sentences; and you need to pull it together."

"Show me." he said.

I gave him an example of a run-on sentence.

"I did that for emphasis," he said. "I don't want anything changed."

"How about misspelled words?" I asked. I took a red pencil and ci led about eight or ten words on one page.

"I don't want you to censor what I write," Carter said.

"I'm not censoring you. I'm trying to show you how to tighten up what you've written. Your article praises Governor Reagan for providing a little extra money for inmates. We won't get into trouble for printing that. But I wonder if the state isn't providing scab labor. This undercuts migrant labor, lines the pockets of growers and forces a man to work for less than minimum wage while someone has a shotgun pointed at his head."

"It's all voluntary and it's better to let a man make a few bucks than to stand around all day doing nothing," Carter said.

"Fine, if that's the way you feel about it. I just don't want to make it look like I'm making the paper into a mouthpiece for the administration in Sacramento."

He looked crestfallen.

"Let me do some editing and we'll go over it line for line tomorrow," I said.

He left with Fleeson and I took the material home and worked on it.

He arrived after my last class the next afternoon, again with Fleeson. I had my neatly typed copy of the revised story and his heavily marked first draft in my briefcase and was prepared to give him an informative lesson in journalism.

However, I did not get the chance. As I opened my briefcase and was laying out my papers, Carter went to the venetian blind that covered the windows on one side of the room and, with a fingernail clipper, cut off a piece of white cord.

I tried to talk to him about his writing, but he slowly paced back and forth in front of me, snapping and twisting the rope in his hands.

At first, I tried to ignore this behavior. Carter was short, barrel chested, with sandy hair and cold blue eyes. He had long, thin arms and moved like a gorilla.

"Put that rope away and let's get to work," I said.

49

"Don't get upset, Mr. Campbell, I wouldn't hurt you. I just like to carry a little rope around with me because it keeps me from getting nervous. No harm in that, is there?"

This was it. The game was on. I didn't know what the rules were. But I had no choice. I had to play.

I watched him weaving back and forth in front of me. I was baffled. He was completely different from the dignified, powerful man who had talked to my classes.

Slowly he started to circle around me. I still tried to ignore him, but then I realized I had to do something. He was going to push me until he got a reaction.

The phone was within reach and I could pick it up and dial 333 and get the goon squad to take him away. Although, as yet, he hadn't done anything with which I could charge him.

No one was blocking my path to the door and I could have walked out. But that would be blowing my cool and was, perhaps, what he wanted me to do.

Fleeson, his fat young friend, was near the door. I was confident Carter didn't have any weapon except for the cord. However, I reasoned that Fleeson might have a weapon and, if I moved toward the door, he might move to block me, and they might try to take me hostage. Only, what the hell they would want to take me hostage for, I couldn't imagine.

Fleeson ignored me but looked closely at Carter, who nodded. Fleeson departed. I walked into the corridor and watched him go down the long hallway and disappear at the stairwell.

I went back into the room where Carter stood completely self-composed. The cord was coiled up on the desk. I picked it up and tossed it to him.

"Now," I said, "grab that cord by both ends and try to put it around my neck. There's no way you can strangle me when I have both hands free." The anger was rising in me. This man had stuck a knife in his last teacher and was now threatening me. I was ready for him.

He caught the cord and, holding one end by two fingers, slowly let it coil on the desk again.

"You are too smart to pull a stupid trick like this," I said, my

50

anger subsiding. "If you really wanted to snuff me, you would have tried to take me by surprise."

"You're naive. I mean you're blind. Things are happening around you; and you can't see them." Carter said.

"What are you talking about?" I asked.

"You really don't know what you did to me, do you, Mr. Campbell?"

"Truly I don't," I said. "I can't think of anything I could possibly have done to upset you."

"I'll tell you what you did. You made a fool of me in front of my *wife*. You don't do that sort of thing if you want to stay healthy in a prison. If you were an inmate and did something like that on the main line, you wouldn't last a day."

It took me some time to figure out what he was talking about. I had been critical of the newspaper article in front of Fleeson; and Fleeson was his wife. He had wanted to show off his new job in front of his young wife, and I had humiliated him. I hadn't been aware of his relationship with Fleeson. One of the reasons for this was that Carter had rapped about his romantic love that rivalled that of Heloïse and Abélard. Only, in the medieval tale, Abélard had been castrated and Heloïse banished to a nunnery. I was like a historian who has just unearthed indisputable evidence that Heloïse was a bull dyke and Abélard a hustling fag. I had been prepared to crack down on Carter, but he had taken me on another trip.

"You come to work with a grin on your face and everybody likes you, and you think you know what it's like to be in prison. But you don't know a damned thing. You're not locked in a cell; and you don't know what it's like to go nine years with 'no possibility of parole' stamped on your jacket. What the hell are you gonna do? Dream of the girl next door? There ain't never gonna be a girl next door. I mean even a pinup picture is ripped off the wall, by a bull. You discover the girl next door has a prick. And that's the way it's gonna be, forever. And the first year you deny it; and the second year you deny it; and the third year you deny it; and the fourth year, you start to look next door.

51

Jesus, there's no way you can understand how a prison messes with your mind."

"You led me to believe your romantic interests were in other areas," I said, attempting to phrase it as delicately as possible.

"Oh, you mean my love for Clarissa. She understands. I've told her everything. She accepts that I've been locked up for twenty years without a woman. Sometimes, when I think about getting out and living with Clarissa, I wake up in the middle of the night in a sweat. But Clarissa is wonderful. She'll help me through those rough times."

"What about Fleeson?" I asked.

"You have a tight, middle-class mind," he said. "You couldn't possibly understand. I know what you're thinking; a young boy like that, thrown in with a hardened criminal like me, an aging fag who'll rip him off. That is the way you and society see it. But it isn't that way at all. I have a beautiful relationship with that boy. I'm both father and mother to him. He was badly twisted before he came here. I'm very good for him."

"So you put on a big act and threaten me so you can look good in his eyes, is that it?" I asked.

"That's it," he said coldly. "I have to command respect in this jungle. When you rob me of respect, I have to do something about it."

"I didn't rob you of respect. I gave you some advice about editing," I said.

"You have a lot to learn about people who have been locked up for a long time," he said.

"I can't work with anyone that thin-skinned," I said.

"Are you going to fire me?"

"If you want the job, take it. I have a lot of other things to do, and I don't want to be looking over my shoulder every minute wondering if my editor is going to strangle me or stab me because I've said something to offend his sensitivity."

"I'll think it over," Carter said. "Are you going to report me?"

"There's nothing to report. You haven't done anything. As far as I'm concerned, I'd like to keep my mouth shut about everything. I'm sorry if I offended you, Mr. Carter. I admit I have a lot to learn about prisons. Take the story I worked on and go over it in your pad. We'll discuss it tomorrow."

He was in the newspaper room all morning and I dropped in on him briefly. He was making a paste-up of the articles we had already received from other reporters and that I had checked out. I asked him about the editing on his story and he said it was all right by him. In the afternoon I looked in the room again and all the material he had been working on was ripped up and stuffed in the wastebasket. This was Carter's way of telling me he did not want to be the editor.

I doubt he ever wanted the job. It was a dull, not very challenging assignment. He was delighted with the idea of being the editor. He could function beautifully in the twilight, fantasy world of his mind, but when asked to perform a specific task, he was in trouble.

There was no one among the reporters who wanted the responsibility of being editor, and I was half-convinced by Hugo Belson's charges that they were trafficking in contraband. I fired the lot of them.

I had a student in my morning classes, Barney Culligan, who was doing good work for me. Prison has a tendency to slow down or deaden everyone, for there is no point in doing a job efficiently. However, Barney had more nervous energy at his disposal than anyone I have seen in jail. It was probably this excessive energy that contributed to his criminal record.

He was in jail for pleading guilty to more than two thousand burglaries in the Beverly Hills area. Before he was apprehended the local newspapers had dubbed him "the Green Stamps Burglar" because a number of housewives, when they reported robberies, claimed green stamps were all that was taken.

He loved wandering around in the houses of the wealthy, nosing into things and picking up anything he could carry easily. He was not equipped to take heavy things like color TV sets or large appliances. However, he was extremely adept at ferreting out where housewives kept their cookie-jar money. He claimed he could be in and out of as many as twenty houses in a single afternoon.

He was never caught in any of these capers. But when he was apprehended for another robbery downtown, a number of Beverly Hills housewives who had spotted him roaming around in their houses identified him.

He hadn't committed every burglary with which they charged him, but since he had lost count of the ones he had committed, he agreed to plead guilty to all the unsolved house burglaries in Beverly Hills so the police could clear their records.

I don't want to create the impression he was just a nonviolent weird kid. He had a hold on his record from Arizona, where he was wanted for robbing a liquor store. When the owner of the liquor store reached for the phone, Barney blew the contraption off the wall with a shotgun blast.

He managed to beat this rap while he was in jail in California by claiming he was insane. At the time he bungled the liquor store robbery, he was an escapee from a mental hospital in Arizona, where he had been sent for observation. Since his last official address was a mental institution, he reasoned he was insane at the time, and an insane man can't stand trial.

He fought this out with a series of cleverly worded letters to the district attorney in Tucson and finally, since he was already serving time in a California prison, Arizona decided to drop the charges.

Barney was working as a phony hypnotist in a nightclub when he was busted. The amazing thing was he was only twenty-two years old. He was busy every minute he was on the streets.

I taught him the first period in the morning, and when he came to class the following morning, I showed him the sad state of affairs in which Carter had left the newspaper room. Barney volunteered to clean things up. At the end of the period when I went over to check on him, he had pieced everything together that Carter had ripped up and also had completed the paste-up. He was eager to do more.

Barney became my new editor on the spot. He learned quickly and did everything himself, so all I had to do was proofread the finished copy for him. We reported the news straight, without editorial comment. After a while Barney did write editorials, but

54

they were never about things that would conflict with the prison administration.

Mr. Draper supervised the final product. The only thing that interested him was that his picture be in the newspaper. Barney gleefully complied with this request. In one edition, there were five photographs and Mr. Draper appeared in every one of them. "Barney, isn't that overdoing it just a bit?" I asked.

"No, Draper loves to have his picture in the paper. If I had the juice, I'd do the same thing."

"I don't understand that mentality. I'm not at all eager to have my picture in a prison newspaper."

"You're a snob," Barney said. "Draper's greedy and a crook, but he ain't a snob. He was working in prisons ten years before I was born. He knows the scam. The joint is his life and he has bled it for a lot of dough; and it's been good to him."

After Draper was fired, Mr. Bianca, the assistant warden, was in charge of what was published in the newspaper. Bianca sent word via Hugo Belson he wanted to inspect the copy proofs before each edition was published. Bianca had been responsible for the ouster of Mr. Draper, and one of the things that had been a bone of contention between them was the newspaper. Bianca was the kind of man who could make or break people. It was rumored he was being groomed to take over a top spot in the state penal system.

The warden in our prison did not assert himself. He had come up from the ranks, starting as a guard, and was most concerned about a system that promoted security. He was not interested in power and delegated it to department heads. As a consequence, there was a lot of power floating around, and ambitious men like Bianca grabbed what they could. "If you cross Bianca, he will get you fired or transferred to an impossible post," the other teachers told me. We quailed at the thought of incurring Bianca's wrath.

Bianca was a short dude who wore glasses and had pointed purple ears. I studied those ears closely once when he sat in front of me at a prison high school graduation.

Barney and I both went over the proofs of the first edition we were to present to Bianca for his inspection. Neither of us could find anything that Bianca could possibly object to on political, ideological or moral grounds. The paper's only crime was that it was dull.

I called ahead of time to tell Bianca the proofs were on the way, and then sent them over by inmate messenger. We did not hear anything for a day, so I gave him a call again. We had the presses all ready to roll, I said, and asked him if he had checked the copy as yet.

"I'll let you know when I'm ready," he said curtly and hung up on me.

That afternoon he arrived in the education area and, with a wag of his finger, beckoned me to come into the hall.

"Dismiss your class right now, I want to talk to you," he said.

I was in the midst of something that was important to me, but I did as he requested. I saw no reason why I couldn't leave them unattended while I talked to him, but I didn't make an issue of it.

We went into the newspaper room, where Barney was working. Bianca had the newspaper proofs in a folder under his arm.

He handed them to me; I could see that he had gone over them carefully.

However, there were not many markings and we could make the corrections and have the presses ready to roll in an hour.

"You made a big blooper," he said. "You haven't been around prisons long enough to know how they operate, so I don't blame you."

"What did I miss?" I asked curiously.

He pointed to a picture on the front page. "Do you see anything wrong with that?" he asked.

I looked at it closely; it was a picture of the free people who comprised the clerical staff of the reception and guidance center. There were four men and three women. We had a story in the paper describing the function of this group and the photographer had taken their picture.

It was an unimaginative and amateurish photograph, but other than that, I couldn't imagine why he would find it objectionable.

"That picture has women in it. The inmates will lie in their

56

cells and look at it and masturbate. We must protect the women who work for us and not expose them to anything dirty or perverted."

I couldn't reply to this comment. I was willing to accept that some inmates might respond to this tiny shred of femininity. But it would be the sexually deprived but healthy inmate who would respond in this way, not the perverted one. The question that begged to be answered was: How can you hope to rehabilitate young men and send them back into society when you feel they will be corrupted by an ordinary office photograph?

"We'll kill the picture, substitute another, make the corrections in the copy and return it to you for your final approval as soon as possible," I said.

Mr. Bianca was like a man who was prepared to ruthlessly suppress a rebellion only to find there was nothing to oppose.

After he left, Barney and I worked together to make the corrections. The only available pictures we had were either of Mr. Draper or a hog from the prison farm. Since Mr. Draper had been forced into retirement, we had no choice but to use the hog.

Mr. Bianca approved our new edition without comment and Barney was convinced we had achieved great satire by making this substitution.

After this show of strength, Mr. Bianca never asked to check the paper again. He turned this job over to Hugo Belson, who also refused to do it. The reason for this was if anything did appear in the paper that offended someone, no one wanted to be responsible for it. In the rarified prison atmosphere, no one could predict what someone else might consider objectionable.

Barney kept the paper alive for a year. He withstood the snide comments of the other inmates, the uncooperative administration and the once-a-week searches of the guards. He did traffic in contraband and he did run games in the prison. However, he reassured me he did not use the education area for any of his activities and he did not use his office of editor to promote any of his schemes.

We had an honest relationship with each other. In religion, he was a fundamentalist and was always spouting biblical verse. If he had respect for something he would go to the torch for it. If he had no respect for something: Look out, he would destroy it without one twinge of conscience.

Once at Christmas time, I noticed he was a little glassy eyed and asked him about it.

"I've been smoking some weed in the unit," he said.

"How can that be? There's no way you can get marijuana in the prison."

"Do you really want me to tell you how it is done?"

"Yes, I do." I said impetuously.

"Do you realize that you are a free person and if I tell you anything that makes me a snitch and I can get killed for it? And if the law catches me, I can get at least ten years in the joint? That would make it pretty silly to tell you anything, wouldn't it?"

"You're right. I don't want that information," I said.

"A guy in the unit had his girl friend ship him a fruitcake," Barney said, deciding to tell me anyway. "Only, inside the fruitcake, it was pure marijuana leaves. There is a rule that you can't have a homemade cake; but you can receive a commercial cake. So all you do is take a commercial cake, unwrap it, substitute your marijuana cake, and you're in business. During Christmas, thousands of these cakes come in. It's impossible to check them all.

"This one contained exceptionally good grass. Do you want me to tell you how it's divided up and stashed in the units so the bulls can't detect it?" he asked.

"No, I don't want to know," I said, shutting him off. "I just want to make certain you don't bring anything up here or get the newspaper involved in your game running."

"I wouldn't do that to you, Mr. Campbell. I know you've helped me, and that would be a double-cross. I mean, I would die before I did that. Besides, I know this place is under surveillance and it's the last place I would hide or bring anything."

"There's one other thing," I said.

"What's that?"

"One of my duties is to impress upon you the correctness of

becoming an honest, law-abiding citizen, a man who has paid his debt—"

"Now you know that's a lie," Barney said. "How many times have you heard, the judges are crooked, the lawyers are crooked, your next-door neighbor cheats on his income tax, the politicians feast on dishonesty and corruption. Without dishonesty and corruption our entire system would collapse. Look around. You can't turn anywhere without finding the product of some corruption. Look toward the parking lot, at those cars out there. General Motors; want me to run down that trip for you? How many people were killed on the highways because those greedy bastards made faulty equipment and refused to tell anyone about it?

"Look in front of you. There's a copy of the *Reader's Digest:* a dandy magazine filled with the virtue of hard work and clean living. It doesn't believe in handouts or giveaways. Yet the backs of mailmen are broken every month carrying that magazine at one-tenth of what it costs the government to deliver it to millions of customers around the country.

"Why doesn't the government pay me a fortune to subsidize my business while I howl about the virtues of rugged individualism and independence? They're all liars, cheats and crooks and the little guy who tries the same formula gets beaten up, gassed, shot and locked away forever."

"Make sense, man," I said angrily. "What do you expect, the suburban housewife to greet you with a bed sheet, a laurel wreath and a bowl of Green Stamps, and the two of you do a libation dance on the front lawn before you scurry off to your next encounter?

"The rights of property are deeply ingrained in most human beings. When you mess with those rights, someone's going to take your head. And that's as true in the prison as it is on the outside.

"You are dissatisfied with corruption, so am I," I continued. "But that doesn't give you the right to do anything you damned well please and then cop out that you are no worse than the men who run the world. Show me how we determine who the bad people are, and who the good people are. Then show me how we punish the one and reward the other. These are the problems our civilization faces. And it takes education to figure out answers to these questions."

"I believe in education now," Barney replied. "Sure I do. Education gives you a license to steal. With that diploma, you can join the club and screw your neighbor. I tell you, Mr. Campbell, if I had your education and your knowledge, I wouldn't be in a prison with a bunch of horny, ignorant convicts. I'd be out there on the streets making $100,000 a year. I respect you, and I would never snitch you off or cut you down. But you're dumb; and I don't want to be like you—ever, ever."

Barney became fascinated by the process of writing and decided to write a book. He could type ninety words a minute and, in addition to his newspaper work, he managed to turn out twenty pages a day for me to criticize. He was not very inventive and would rewrite the same scenes countless times. Each time his writing became more polished; yet the story was such obvious fantasy it never came alive. He was describing how a group of prisoners took the warden hostage on a prison farm and, eventually, were all killed. It was a bloody mess.

I tried to tell him he could write a more interesting book if he dug into his own personal life. I threw questions and suggestions at him to get him to write something I wanted to read. Why does an intelligent, sensitive, energetic guy commit more than a thousand stupid robberies? Describe the scene when a Beverly Hills housewife discovers you with a hand in her cookie jar. What is it like to escape from a mental ward, rob a liquor store, and blow the telephone off the wall with a shotgun?

Barney closed his mind to my suggestions. I asked him to come to some of my classes when we were having discussions of ideas from Greek literature; he wouldn't do it. He was status conscious; it was beneath his dignity to sit in on a class once he was an editor.

I also taught creative writing and I wanted him to attend some of the sessions where the students discussed each other's stories. He was impressed by the work that was coming from my writing classes, but he refused to attend.

We were friends. I discussed my problems with administration and he went over his difficulties with his hold in Arizona. Yet there was always a distance between us. I admired his ability to make shrewd observations, but I could not get him to grapple with getting a wider perspective on things.

What disturbed him most about me was that I never opposed administration. For example, I didn't get Barney a special pass to cover events. Hugo Belson refused to authorize it because he suspected Barney of being a "wheeler and dealer." I could have fought this decision by going over Belson's head. But Barney *was* a "wheeler dealer" and so I didn't do it.

Mr. Bianca noticed that I had my students arranged in a circle when he came to talk to me about the newspaper. He requested Hugo Belson to inform me that it did not look good to arrange my class in this fashion and I should go back to the conventional arrangemement.

I was furious when Belson told me this. The circular pattern was ideal for the kind of teaching I was doing. Furthermore, Bianca was in charge of finance and officially had nothing to do with the education department. What right did he have to tell me what to do?

However, I was teaching on a shaky teaching credential because I had not taken the proper education courses and could have been dismissed or replaced by anyone with a valid California certificate. In fact, Draper had gone to bat for me and taken advantage of an emergency clause to make it possible for me to teach at all. I was in no position to play power games with anyone.

Barney wanted me to be a strong crusader for right and freedom and I invariably let him down. He would start to identify with me and then would become furious when I did not take a firm stand when administration hampered or frustrated me.

I tried to explain to him I had more freedom as a prison teacher than I did when I taught in public schools. I pointed out that teaching in public shcools was more hazardous, because you were always under the unenlightened scrutiny of parents and the community.

I told him of an incident when I taught in the public schools in Westchester County in New York when an irate mother called the principal and reported I was carrying on obscene conversations about naked women in my English classes.

When the principal questioned me, I had no idea what he was talking about. Upon investigation, I found I had told one of my classes about a Hindu sect called the Jains. The high priest of this sect was so dedicated to poverty that he ate only enough food to sustain life and wore no clothing. The Jains built a new temple in another part of town, and to shield their priest from non-believers' eyes, they formed a circle around him while he walked through the streets to his new abode.

One of my sutdents, when queried by his mother about what he had learned in school that day, replied, "Mr. Campbell spent most of the period telling us about a naked Jane." That did it!

I was able to clear my name with the principal but he did insist I get involved with less inflammatory material in my English classes.

After about a year of my running the paper, the decision came down from Bianca that Mr. Belson would take over its supervision himself.

I was relieved to be rid of the newspaper but Barney was crushed by this decision. Belson and Barney had been playing a cat-and-mouse game with each other and I didn't see how they could possibly work together.

I believed Belson would destroy the paper because he didn't want to take responsibility for what might appear in it. Barney had a problem. He could resign or he could compromise and try to work with Belson. I fully expected Barney to resign, but he didn't. He had worked so hard for that paper that he couldn't just give it up. He agreed to continue as editor under Hugo Belson.

It did not work out. Barney was fired after a few issues, and the newspaper expired with Barney's dismissal.

I didn't see Barney again until just before I was to leave the prison. By coincidence, we were both to leave at about the same time. He came back to the education area to tell me he had been granted his parole. He was subdued and that beautiful, wild spirit was no longer in evidence.

We talked and wished each other well, but we didn't communicate. I wanted to say, "Maybe you learned the wrong things from me, Barney. Compromise a little when the odds are solid against you. But don't compromise all the way."

But I didn't say anything.

CHAPTER 5

Prison is a place where you feel sorry for yourself.
Then you get disgusted with yourself for feeling this
way, then you get mad for feeling disgusted, and
then you try mentally to change the subject.
From a Student Theme

Before I taught in prison I had worked two and one half years
for The Great Books Foundation, where I sat down with people
all day long to lead or listen to discussions of the world's great
literature. I had trained more than 2,000 teachers and interested
adults in more than forty cities in the United States and Canada
in discussion techniques. I had worked with nuns in convents,
Junior Leaguers, cowboys in Montana, and had set up special
programs on an elementary level in Chicago, Oakland and Los
Angeles.

I had a degree from Harvard in English literature and had the
knowledge of a substantial body of literature at my command. I
knew what I had to offer worked. But I did not know if it would
work in a prison setting with the most hostile young men our
culture can produce.

It did work. I found that prison is the ideal place for trying to
figure out what it means to seek the good, and to search for

64

definitions for words like "truth" and "justice." A prison chains, but the mind is free to go exploring.

Prisoners are continually being told they are evil, corrupt, bad, nauseating, unfit for decent people to be around. If they accept this low evaluation of themselves, they are destroyed.

It would be easy to admit you are bad if you could look around you and see that only good people prosper. You could join the good people, give up your evil ways and live happily after. But prisoners see corruption and wrongdoing all around them and cannot accept the line that they are the only evil ones.

Frequently they are faced with moral problems the rest of us never encounter. They have to answer questions like: Should I snitch on a crime partner and serve less time in jail? Should I tell everything I know and implicate my friends, for a lighter sentence? Should I lie when the district attorney wants to get someone, and get preferential treatment for this action? Should I admit to a crime I did not commit and have already served time for, in order to get my release?

For instance, I had a student who had served three years on a rape charge of which he claimed he was not guilty. If he admitted the crime, the parole board would probably let him go. If he continued to deny it, they would probably hold him for two more years and perhaps longer.

How do you answer a young man when he comes to you and asks what he should do? You check his jacket at central files, including a transcript of his trial and all the other evidence of his past criminal record. You find he was convicted on very flimsy evidence.

He was a black who was convicted of raping a white hippie chick in the Haight-Ashbury. The girl was riding around the area in a police car when she spotted my student coming out of a dry cleaning establishment. My student had processed hair, as did her assailant. The police picked him up and found he had been in trouble before, not for rape but for stealing something from the back of a truck. He was busted for that crime and, later, when the district attorney found he had a previous conviction, he prosecuted him for rape. He was convicted on no other evidence

65

than the victim's identification. He had a witness who swore he was in another part of town when the alleged rape occurred, but his witness was also a juvenile offender and so the testimony was discredited. He got five years to life.

After the conviction, my student's girl friend managed to track down the girl who made the accusation. She confronted her and asked her why she deliberately put an innocent man in prison. The girl was, at first, belligerent. Then she broke down and admitted she made a mistake. She had a black boy friend and he split. She wanted to get even, so she made up the story and the police got involved and the rest just happened. However, she was afraid to admit what she had done because she feared she would go to jail herself, for perjury. The next day the girl split and there was no way of tracing her. She had dissolved into the transient-youth underground.

Any prison must have countless such tales of the miscarriage of justice. But most of my students were clearly guilty of what they had been accused of. Not many of them claimed they were bum rapped and frequently admitted crimes they had committed and countless others for which they had not been charged.

However, I was convinced my student was innocent. He was eligible for parole after two years, but when he came before the board and told them the story of how his girl friend had talked with his accuser and continued to protest his innocence, the board shot him down for another year and made it clear to him that only if he would freely confess his crime and be repentant could he prove he was ready to go back to society. They gave him another year to think over his decision.

It was at the end of that year when he approached me with his problem and asked me what I thought he should do. Should he admit to a crime he did not commit and go free? Or should he continue to deny it and serve more time? He was confident that if he were on the streets, he could raise the money to hire lawyers to reopen the case and get his name cleared, even though he had already served the time for it.

He was deeply troubled when he talked to me. I discussed it with him, but didn't know how to advise him.

He decided to maintain his innocence again, and was shot down for another year. I talked to him after his denial, and he looked me in the eye and said, "I'll not go through that soul searching again. I'll be in here until I die."

I did not use this story in my classes, because the protagonist was one of my students and I didn't want to embarrass him. Also, he had discussed the circumstances of his case with me privately and I would not exploit this privileged information. However, it is the kind of situation that is exactly suited for a discussion of values. What do you do when you are confronted with severe punishment for honesty? Should you lie or tell the truth?

These are questions to which there are no right or wrong answers. But they are questions that make you think and to which you must apply your own value system to find an answer. This kind of questioning is as old as civilization. Cicero set up hypothetical moral situations. There is a shipwreck. Two people are on a raft. The raft is only big enough to support one of them. Who should be saved? You pick the two people. Father and child. Teacher and pupil. Husband and wife. Who is more valuable to society? In any group, if you choose the two people carefully, this will lead to an interesting discussion.

To teach that there is only one right answer to any question, and the teacher has it, is to destroy the very purpose of education in the humanities.

There is a highly structured methodology to this kind of teaching, showing you how to prepare good questions, get everyone involved, stick to the point, etc. But the basic principles are devastatingly simple. As leader of a discussion, find a question to which you do not have the answer yourself, then do not ever give your own opinion. Make the students think for themselves.

This is, simplistically, the kind of approach my teaching involved. I wanted to discuss great literature because it contains ideas that have survived their own culture. Once you are skilled in identifying a universal idea, it is easy to get people of any cultural background to relate to it.

I started each new class by asking the students to answer the question: Who are you? This is an old parlor game trick, for it

67

isn't easy to define who you are and, in attempting to do it, you reveal much about yourself. I found students liked writing about themselves. and I could get a very accurate picture of their ability to do high school work from their essays. They were the academic spoor from which I could track the bumpy educational journey they had taken.

By leafing through the essays at the end of the period, I could quickly spot the students who were unprepared to do high school work. I would put aside a poor theme and keep a close watch on the student who wrote it. I would check with his other teacher, and if he were in academic difficulty in the other class we would make arrangements to have him transferred to elementary school. In this way, I weeded my garden. I don't want to give the impression that I taught only an elitist group. I just did not attempt to instruct students who were functionally illiterate.

Here are a few examples of themes from this assignment, with names and dates changed. I might add I carefully explained to the class before I made the assignment that whatever they wrote was private and I would not read to the class anything they wrote or question them about any of the material or give them a grade. I simply wanted a specimen of their writing about a subject they knew a lot about. I also mentioned it did not have to be personal and if they wanted to write on any other subject they should feel free to do it.

My students almost always chose to write about themselves, and no one refused to hand something in.

I am John Jones. I like wine and pussy. I can't get neither one because I am locked up.

This theme highly qualified the writer for work in my class. In three sentences, he had powerfully written who he was, where he was, and what he liked. Also, for those interested in literary terms, he has used an excellent example of synecdoche.

I was born in San Francisco, California and lived there all my life. I have been around the world twice and my most interesting hobbies are skiing and mythology.

I read extensively and I personally think European writers such as: Dostoevsky, Proust, Camus, Zola, Gide, and Tolstoy have no peers in American litterature.

I am a staunch admirer and follower of the late French existialist Albert Camus. Novels such as, THE REVOLT, RESISTANCE & REBELLION, and THE PLAGUE I believe are some of the best books written about 20th Century man.

We in this country have no way of understanding the true difficulties and pain of Civilization. One can hardly expect a young nation as ours which has been sheltered from chaos by two great Oceans to formulate an ideal mode of life for modern man. We have a lot to learn from our European fathers who have lived in constant turmoil.

These are my inner beliefs and I believe with European experience and American genius man could live in a more placid and amicable state.

This student is ready to do top-level college work right now. He writes that he has described his "inner beliefs" here. He means his intellectual beliefs. His inner beliefs are not in this theme.

Im John C. Randolph C for cannon. I was born in 1947 in Napoleon Ohio. Was raised there until I was 15 and was arrested for many various Charges until I raised a grand total of 19 arrests and one conviction. But I never did time because they (cops) felt I was basically a good guy.

At 14 the old man packed what he's stold from every sucker in town and for some reason hurried the whole family (which consisted of 5 boys, one mother and Pop.) off to a place called Coos, Oregon. But whith in 2 months I was arrested three times as started to racial riots, so the good people of that particular town ast the Randolph family to quietly leave. So we did. (Mom was glad of it cause the old man took up with this whore down the street from where we lived) But the rest of us was reluctant to leave this little paradise.

Soon we entered Calif. And was living with my uncle. they didn't want any more trouble out of me so they kept me on a ranch in a place called Redding. Everyone was shocked to finde I liked working. But one unexpected day I came up missing and so did the bosses pick up. It was merely a Quensidents (or how ever it's spelled)

Later I showed up in Ohio with a run away from a Juvinal hall in Calif. My old man came to pick me up, but soon every one understood I would run my own life. So I quit school. I worked a little and stold a little But got a long fine. I joined the Army to beat a stolen car rapp. Went A.W.).L. and got married, Robbed the mottor pool at Ft. Irwin, and a snitch crime partner got us caught.

I was put in Leaven worth for awhile an got a bad discharge and was living my normal way for about three years after that and my wife was allways around to bother me or snivle about moving or robbing something. Finally I nocked her up and split with a whore named June. I sold her for awhile but was busted again now I'm here. The wife had a boy and divorced me. At least in six months something will be accomplished, the Divorce will be complette.

Basically Im a very truth full person except when I lie a lot.

This gives the background, in his own words, of an ordinary inmate of a prison. I had this student in a previous class and he knew that I wouldn't embarrass him with what he had written. If he hadn't known me, he wouldn't have mentioned that he had been involved in racial difficulties on the outside. This could cause him difficulty if it were known throughout the prison.

The irresponsibility reflected in this theme is perhaps typical of many inmates. However, undoubtedly there is a certain amount of showmanship in his description of his life.

Divorce and loss of family are some of the most crushing events a person in jail has to go through. This writer is tossing it off as the one thing he has accomplished in his life. It is doubtful he feels this way. Having a stable family is the most prized thing an inmate can possess. I know of an instance where an inmate stole a photograph of a wife and two children so he could claim they were his family; although he had no one who cared about him. Prisons are places where illusion and delusion are necessary for sanity.

To correct the grammar, spelling or phrasing in this theme would be to destroy its value. The grammar is exactly suited to the subject matter. If he were writing a formal letter to the parole board, I would have worked with him to help him polish his work.

I tried to find something good in any work that was handed in. I also used excerpts to point out literary devices. For instance, using the previous theme as an example.

"I see the writer is a Shakespearean scholar skilled in the use of the oxymoron." I would go to the board and write "OXY-MORON" in large block letters. "No, it does not have to do with moron or that it is a stupid theme. Oxymoron means a mix of opposites. Observe how the author has done this brilliantly in his very last sentence. 'Basically, I'm a very truthful person, except when I lie a lot.'

"That is an awfully good use of that literary device. It is as good as Shakespeare when he talked about 'sweet sorrow.' Can you think of any other?

"That's right, I just used one!" Then I would write on the board "Awful Good." An insane oxymoron. If I could get something going we would spend the entire period on this literary device. If I couldn't catch their interest, I would let it drop. My teaching was a series of probes, and I couldn't do anything until I had them with me.

"Let's see if we can pick out some more. I remember in reading Dreiser's *American Tragedy* they referred to people in those days as 'good baddies.' Can you think of any others?

"Cool? One word all by itself becomes an oxymoron. Great, I

never thought of that. A cool person is actually a warm and friendly one.

"Black man? Yeah, I see what you mean. It used to be a term that would make people angry. And now it is a term that is used proudly. Black is beautiful. Very good."

From these responses I had the door open to get right into language and what it means. I could tell a story about how a few years ago our government and all the newspapers were talking about nuclear warfare. We were spending billions of dollars for defense. We built nuclear submarine fleets and silos where we could launch enough nuclear power to destroy the world. In fact, we even had a word for it: enough power to blow up the world became a "beach." And we debated why, after you had enough power to destroy the world ten times, it was necessary to create enough bombs to destroy it twenty times?

The point is, we called this defense. But it wasn't defense. Nobody ever claimed we had any defense against the enemy destroying us. We were building up tremendous offensive weapons, but we were calling them defensive ones. This is an example of a dangerous oxymoron at work.

At the end of the period, I would pick out one of the quieter members of the group and ask him to define oxymoron.

"Uh, let's see, I forget now," he would invariably say.

"Beautiful," I would reply. "It isn't necessary to clutter up your mind with obscure literary terms. But the concept is important for everyone to know. Watch what words mean. Sometimes they are exactly opposite of what they purport to mean. Sometimes they don't mean anything at all. Sometimes they are designed to put you into a trick bag."

If things were going right, I could teach semantics to my classes at the very highest level. You couldn't walk in and do this with just any class. You had to prepare for it. You had to open their minds to new ideas. You had to get ideas bubbling from them. You had to create a climate of inquiry before you could make a lecture work.

Once, a student made a duck out of me in front of the class.

The speaker, a guy named Hawk, had been a bronco buster in a rodeo; he wasn't very good at staying on the horses and had resorted to shortchanging people to supplement his income. He was explaining to the class how you set up your mark and operate as a shortchange artist.

The reader may question the morality of turning my English class into a training ground for criminal acts. But I was a curious person and wanted to know everything about every phase of their activities. Besides, I wasn't going to corrupt them any more than they already were. Shortchanging was something Hawk did well, and he wanted to communicate his skill to the rest of the class. I didn't question his sincerity and so I approved his topic.

His talk was colorful but technical and I couldn't follow all of the details. After he had finished, I thanked him courteously and added, "I don't believe you were successful because of your skill. You're a good-looking guy, and I believe you picked a chick and got her so flustered she didn't know what she was doing."

"I could do the same thing to you," Hawk said.

"I don't believe that," I said.

In a split second, the challenge had been hurled and accepted. Students ripped up pieces of paper and made a roll of phony bills. I was to be a clerk at a supermarket checkout counter and Hawk sidled up to me. His performance was superb. He was bowlegged and imagined he was wearing a ten-gallon hat. He started rapping to me about the rodeo and telling me about the special events—I watched him closely. After he made the purchase, he asked me to change a twenty-dollar bill for him. I counted out the money very carefully; then he decided to make another purchase. He gave me a ten-dollar bill to change for him again.

Again, I was careful, confident it was impossible I had been shortchanged. However, at the end of the performance, I counted my roll and found I was twenty-seven dollars short.

"It can't be true," I cried in disbelief. I started to count the money again.

How can I explain prison laughter? It is fantastic. It comes from deeply frustrated, humiliated men who day in and day out have very little to laugh about. Now it built and built until great waves of it overwhelmed the room. Men were doubling over and howling; tears were rolling down their cheeks.

Some students who were in the hall came by the window to see what was happening. I waved them away. When things had quieted down enough for me to get their attention again, I said, "OK, Mr. Hawk, I had that coming. I humbly apologize for questioning your skill. But, tell me, how the hell did you do that?" He took me through the transaction, step by step, and showed me where he had confused me.

The next day I came to class still smarting from my defeat.

"All right," I said, pacing back and forth in front of them. "You guys made a duck out of me yesterday because I didn't know what I was talking about. I thought I was smart and Mr. Hawk intellectually busted me in the mouth and proved to me that I was stupid. Well, I'm going to make ducks out of every one of you today. The only request I have is that you honestly attempt to answer every question I pose to you. I was honest with Hawk; I want you to be honest with me.

"My thing is language; it's communication. I want to show you some things about it you've never considered before."

I took off my coat and stood before them in my shirtsleeves. Slowly I unbuttoned my cuffs and slowly rolled up my sleeves. I was not wearing a tie because, mercifully, we were not required to—a tie could become a dangerous weapon and could be used to strangle if trouble erupted.

"See, I have no tricks up my sleeve. But I'm going to trick you with language. Watch every move I make. Did you ever consider language determines thought and all kinds of ideas are floating around we can't understand because we don't have the words to express them?

"Adding a word to your vocabulary is like adding a new piece of furniture to a room in your mind. I mean, if you don't have any furniture, an idea can wander in; but if it doesn't have any place to sit down, it isn't going to stay very long.

74

"If your intellectual furniture consists of an old deck chair and a birdbath, all you're gonna see is an idea flash a little water and be off. And you're going to be sitting there smoking dope or drinking a can of beer, watching it take flight."

"Wait a minute, Mr. Campbell, before you call me a bird brain," a student said.

"He didn't call you a bird brain, you bird brain," another student said.

That drew a laugh.

"All right," he said, reacting very personally to my description, "before he starts comparing my mind to a birdbath, then. I don't see any sense in having two words for the same thing. The other day I came across this word that means the same thing as 'horse.' What is that word?"

"How about 'equine'?" I said.

"Yeah, that's it, 'equine.' I didn't know what it was talking about. Why does there have to be more than one word for 'horse.' I know what a horse is, and you know what a horse is. Why can't the writer use just one word so everyone can understand it, and stop all that fancy shit? So I know two words for 'horse.' What's that gonna do for me? If I start rappin' that way around East Oakland, people are gonna think I am crazy."

"Good point," I said. "When you say "horse,' what do I think of: a racehorse, a cowboy's horse, a policeman's horse, something like that. But when you say 'equine,' that's a different matter. I immediately think of the earliest horse. It was called an 'eohippus' and it had a short neck and two toes on each foot. Through thousands of years its neck lengthened and it developed hoofs and, through a process of evolution, became a modern horse.

"I think of 'equine' in contradistinction to 'bovine.' 'Bovine' is like a cow. How is a horse different from a cow? This gets into theories of classification and goes back to Aristotle. He set up a classification of all natural things that is still in use today. It laid the cornerstone for biology, chemistry, geology, vertebrate and invertebrate paleontology, and science as we know it today. And it all started because Aristotle wanted to know the difference

75

between an equine and a bovine—a horse and a cow—and their respective families. So if you want to rap about an ordinary 'horse,' use that term or 'dobbin' or 'nag.' But if you want to get into a heavy discussion where you really want to get down with what a horse is, use the term 'equine.' But don't, in the name of heaven, plow the term under because it doesn't fit into the scheme of things in East Oakland.

"OK, so much for phase one, now let's get into phase two of this thing. Suppose you have the vocabulary and the other person does not. How, then, can you communicate? For instance, you and your wife are in your car, and it doesn't start. You know something about a car, but your wife does not. You look under the hood and determine there is something wrong with the distributor or the timing gear or the differential . . ."

"Hold it, you're going good, Mr. Campbell, don't blow it," a student said.

"What are you talking about?" I asked.

"The differential ain't under the hood. It's underneath the car and in the back."

"That shows how much I know about a car," I said. "But the point is you can't communicate with your wife about what's wrong with the car because she doesn't understand the terms and probably doesn't even care about knowing."

"I can understand that, but what's the point? What good does it do me to know that?" a student asked.

"Let me give you an example," I said. "Suppose you're a student of government and you understand something about how our government operates. We divide the power among three branches: the President, the Congress, and the Supreme Court. This means no person or one group can take over all the power in this country. It's called the balance of power or a system of checks and balances. Anyone who knows anything about government realizes this concept is a work of genius and to destroy the function of any one of these three could lead to tyranny and the destruction of our government.

"Suppose you're in a bar and a guy says, 'Crime on the streets has gotten out of hand. We should take every mugger and every burglar and shoot him on the spot. We should send everybody in prison to the gas chamber and get this country straight again.' So you reply, 'We can't do that because it is a violation of the Bill of Rights and the Supreme Court would declare it unconstitutional.' "

" 'Then we should abolish the Supreme Court,' the guy says. You can't communicate with him because he doesn't understand the basic principles of our government. If a person doesn't understand about spark plugs and differentials and doesn't care to comprehend what these terms mean, you can't talk to him about how a car operates. If a person doesn't understand terminology like 'balance of power' and 'checks and balances,' you can't talk to him about the legislative process. It becomes noise and nonsense.

"I know government is a great area for discussion, but I don't want to get into it now. The rule is: If you understand the basic vocabulary and the other person does not, you can't communicate. A hell of a lot of discussions are just shouting matches because the participants are not aware of this principle.

"Here is another, even trickier concept," I said. "Suppose the words don't even exist in the language; then you can't talk about it at all. For instance, they claim in Eskimo language there are seven different words for snow. Apparently, they watch that stuff very closely up there, and there are many different kinds of it. When Eskimos sit down to rap about snow, they can really get into it. We can't do that."

"Yeah, but we don't care about snow, so we don't need to know that much about it."

"That's right," I said. "James Thurber once reviewed a book about penguins and he said, 'This book taught me more about penguins than I cared to know.' How about this one, then. The Japanese have a word for something in their language that we don't have in ours.

"The word is 'u wakimono.' It means someone who is married to one person but in love with another. As far as I know, we don't have a word for that situation in English. The Japanese probably developed a word for this because they had a very strict culture that did not tolerate divorce; so many unhappily married people found themselves in that condition.

"Watch how you can use this word if it is common to your culture. Suppose you're a Japanese guy and you're walking down the main drag in Tokyo and you see a pretty girl at a sidewalk table. You go up to her and say, *'Sabishii desu?'* (Are you lonely?)

" *'U wakimono desu,'* she says. Immediately you have the scam and can proceed accordingly.

"Now suppose you have the same situation in America. You go up to the girl and say, 'Are you lonely?'

" 'No.'

" 'Well, is something the matter?'

" 'Yes, but I don't know how to tell you. You see, I have been happily married for five years, and then one night we went bowling and there was this guy in the next lane wearing a reindeer sweater and a golf cap . . .'

"If you're lucky, it will only take a half hour for her to get around to what her problem is, and chances are she won't even bother to explain because it's just too complicated. Whereas the Japanese lass can get down with the situation in one word. Now that's an example of where it would be useful to have a word like that in our language; but we don't. There are, undoubtedly, many other words floating around that would make our lives less complicated, if we knew them."

I was starting to blow their minds. Next, I went to the board and wrote in large letters, *"POINT."*

"Now then, how many of you think you know what that word means?" I waited a little while and eventually every hand in the room went up.

"Aha, I just made ducks out of every one of you," I cried. "What would you say if I could prove to you that word doesn't mean anything at all. Someone look that word up in the dictionary. The word 'point' has more than fifty different definitions. Point your finger, point of land, main point, point in a basketball game, grade point, or even the point you're trying to make when you're shooting craps.

"So, you see, you have no idea what that word means until you see it in context. It gets its meaning from the other words around it. Almost all words are this way, but point is an extreme example of it. Suppose we had fifty different words for each of its meanings: Would that be better? Or suppose we had more of our words do heavy-duty. Suppose we designed a language that had only a thousand words in it, but each word had fifty meanings. Could we communicate that way? Nobody knows because nobody has ever tried it. These are mind-blowing questions. Think about them sometime when you don't have anything else to do. Language is a very tricky thing and this explains why we are frequently misunderstood.

"Every society has secret or taboo words that are suppressed. The Jewish people have a secret word for God that at one time only the high priest or rabbi knew. And even today pious Jews never use the word. When praying they use the word "Adonai," which means the Lord."

"What is the word?" a student asked.

"I ain't a gonna tell ya," I said lapsing into my midwestern slang.

"Why not?"

"Because you ain't a Jew."

"Are you?"

"Of course, I am. I'm a Jew. I'm a black man. I'm an Oriental. You heard me speaking Japanese a little while ago, didn't you? I'm also a Greek; but let's get back to the subject. Our society suppresses sexual or lovemaking words. Although I admit the whole thing has gone a little crazy. Sometimes a suppressed word surfaces and it is so glad to be free that it goes running around, cluttering up everything.

"Take the good Anglo-Saxon word, 'fuck.' When I was in the army, this is the way we would talk: Today was my fucking day off and I didn't know what the fuck to do; so I went to the fucking PX. But I didn't see a fucking thing I wanted to buy; so I went out and bought a fucking can of beer and then decided to return to my fucking room and write a fucking letter to my

79

fucking girl friend. But I couldn't find a fucking pencil. So I said 'fuck it' and went to a fucking movie.

"Now this is an example of a taboo word that has gone insane. It isn't a sexy word or a naughty word here. It's a garbage word that clutters up speech and doesn't mean anything."

"Yes, it means something. It means the dude is horny as a mother and he ain't gettin' nothin,' " a student said.

"You're right," I laughed. "The prison society has taboo words that are violently suppressed. Can you name one?" They bombarded me with a string of words of sexual and defecatory connotation. I denied them all. I did admit 'good cop' might barely qualify, and took violent exception to the term, 'motherfucker.'

"How dare you claim that word is suppressed in a prison. Why, a prison is its palace, and it reigns as the king here. Most of you are its grovelling courtiers, paying it daily, nay hourly, lip service. No, I'm talking about a righteous taboo word."

"I don't believe there is a word I'm afraid to say anywhere, anytime," Hawk said.

"OK, Mr. Hawk, if I tell you the word, will you agree to go out in the yard when there are plenty of people around and shout it at the top of your lungs?"

"Sure I will," Hawk said.

"All right, the word is 'NIGGER'!" I shouted it.

Jesus, what a reaction. Everyone tightened up and I could feel the tense vibrations coming at me almost strongly enough to rustle the papers on my desk. It was like a summer day when an unexpected storm comes up and the thunder splits the sky wide open.

From the black section, a deep, disembodied, angry voice emerged, "Hey, radio that shit."

For a few seconds I thought I might have gone too far and the class could erupt in violence. Then the anger subsided and Hawk said, "OK, I apologize. You did what you said you were gonna do. You made a duck out of this cowpoke."

"Now you know what happens when you play around with a real taboo word," I said. "I don't want to get anyone upset or

80

have people going around claiming I am calling students 'niggers' in my class. I am just trying to show you something about language.

"I got such a hell of a reaction to that word, let me go into it a little bit more. I remember talking to this guy, and he told me he was living with this woman and they slept naked together. In the early morning, when he was sleepy and just waking up, she would pull the covers away from him and just look at him for a while. Then she would run her hands lightly over his body and bite him on the ear and whisper, 'Hello, pretty nigger.' "

I picked out a black guy who was horny and romantic and tripping out on the scene I had described.

"How about you, Mr. Purcell, would you get up and bust that woman in the mouth for calling you a dirty name?"

"Noo Waay! That is one beautiful woman. She is a fun-loving, stone fox. She is saying, 'I love you just the way you are and let's have a laugh at the whole world.' That is a beautiful thing to say. It shows she understands everything."

"Now we really have a problem." I said. "Here is a word so terrible the mere mention of it in this classroom could have led to violence. Not only that, but it wouldn't have stopped here. Eventually it would have spread throughout the entire prison, and heads would have been busted and people killed. A bloody, riotous mess could have occurred just by mentioning this one word.

"Yet here is a guy who claims, in a different context, the same word is the most beautiful thing he has ever heard. How do you explain that? You men figure it out. It's beyond my powers of comprehension. I've done enough talking for today. I'm going out to get a drink of water. I'll be back in a few minutes."

I rolled down my sleeves, buttoned my cuffs, put on my coat and departed. I walked down to the end of the corridor and looked in at the inmate john. There were no toilet seats there, so you couldn't linger very long unless you had legs of steel. There were two bits of graffiti on the wall. They wouldn't last long because the custodial crew cleaned the place every day. One said, "Lucky 13" and the other said. "I no want be lonely anymore." I

81

walked back to the middle of the corridor where the drinking fountain was, and took a drink. I decided to return to the classroom; but I was determined not to rap anymore. It was their show.

When I got back, the discussion was going hot and heavy. I took a seat at my desk and listened to them. I found myself taking notes as they batted ideas back and forth. The next time they solicited my opinion, I could no longer restrain myself.

"Here's the problem, as I see it," I said. "We have no vocabulary for deep emotions. We communicate this through vibrations and not language. For instance, we had a tense moment a little while ago. Not much was said, but everyone felt it. Language can't adequately describe these moments.

"Take the word 'love,' " I said. "We use it in a lot of different ways to describe everything from apple pie to freedom. 'A strong attachment for something' is the simple definition of it. But all of us know, sometimes it means more to us.

"The Greeks, in their language, broke 'love' down to a set of categories. *Episteme,* the love of knowledge, was the highest love. And there was *Eros,* which was romantic or sexual love. And there was the love of beauty and about five or six other categories. I can't remember what the others were right now.

"There was an ethical hierarchy about love built right into their language. Excuse me for the big words. It meant everyone was taught pursuit of knowledge was the greatest love, and pursuit of beauty was second, and a piece of ass was third or maybe even further down the line. So if a person had an attraction to something, he knew how high on the scale he was.

"But our language doesn't have the vocabulary to allow us to talk with ethical consideration about the highest kind of love. Each must decide for himself his greatest love.

"What do you suppose the highest order of love is in our society?"

"That's easy. It's why I got busted for jacking up a liquor store; and it's why you're teaching here. It's money," a student said.

"Right on," everyone agreed. We took a vote on the next two

categories, and it came out sex and dope, with sex winning by only two votes. Knowledge, beauty, family and religion weren't in the running.

"There is one thing I wrote a note on when I was listening to your discussion. Sometimes a person comes along with new concepts and a new vocabulary and allows us to talk about things we couldn't express before because we didn't have the language.

"Sigmund Freud did this when he created psychoanalysis. He invented words like ego, superego, id. Now that doesn't mean that Freud was right or even scientific about what he did. After all, nobody has ever performed an operation and isolated and discovered the id and the superego as if they were kidneys or livers. They may not exist. It's just that he created, through language, the possibility of talking about the human mind in a way we couldn't previously communicate about it."

"I'm beginning to see something," a student said. "I was reading once about an interview with one of those crazy guys who claimed he came from outer space. He said his advanced civilization wasn't any smarter than ours. He claimed their basic concepts were very simple. He compared our world to a tree and man was an ant trying to climb up the tree. If he stayed on the main trunk, the ant could easily reach the top of the tree. But he was always crawling out on a branch, thinking he was on the main trunk. The ant could do a fantastically brilliant balancing act on the tiny leaves at the end of the branch. But he couldn't advance because his sense of direction was confused. He had to retrace himself to the main branch again and start back up the tree. Or he could continue his journey along the branch until he fell again and would have to start all over again.

"I used to think this just meant scientific things. But now I see our language confuses us and starts us out on the branch. What we have to do is retrace our steps and get simple definitions for things."

"Yeah, and they have to be good definitions. They can't be words that mean fifty different things like 'point,'" another student said.

"And probably we need to discover simple new ideas that we can't think about now because we don't have the words for them," another student said.

"But don't forget, even if you did have this worked out, it wouldn't do any good unless other people understood it. Because, if you are the only one with the technical information, you can't communicate with the other person."

"Even if you had it all worked out, the older people would never understand. You would have to teach it to little kids."

"And you would have to give people LSD to get their minds opened up."

"Then that little bug could climb straight up the trunk of the tree."

"Yeah, but that will never happen."

At this point, the bell sounded, shattering our vision. It seemed for an instant, and quite by accident, we had received a staggering peek at the naked machinery that made our world go round. We had let our minds chase things until we had come to the wall. The boundary beyond which no human mind could penetrate without lapsing into insanity. It was scary.

"This thing has blown my mind."

"I just want to be alone so I can think things out."

"Aw, fuck it."

"What the hell does this have to do with teaching English?"

"I got shot down for six additional months, but I'm glad I did. It was worth it just to be in class today."

These were the comments I heard as they filed out for their break and the new class came drifting in.

I turned my next class on to seat work. I was no good for teaching the rest of the day. My mind was trying to figure out what had happened. I had started out playing a semantic game with them and they had started to make some sense out of my nonsense. They had started to put it all together.

I won't go into all the thoughts that were colliding in my mind. But I could see that ant crawling up the tree. It travelled for a while until it came to a place where there were several paths to take, all marked justice. It chose one path, using this concept:

A person who robs or willfully injures another person should be punished. We have judges, juries, prisons and parole boards to take the errant behavior that is nonproductive for the good of mankind and turn it into something that is good for all of us.

However, everyone even remotely connected with the legal system knows in many areas it doesn't work. Sentences are unevenly meted out. Money rather than morality determines guilt. Prisons are training grounds for crime rather than places where the damaged spirit is healed. The list goes on and on.

Imperfect as it is, no one has devised anything better. We're out on the delicate leaves, doing our intricate balancing act, wasting our intelligence tinkering with a system that is inherently bad.

So the ant goes back to where it started to look at justice all over again. The problem is that the ant, who I suppose is all of us, does not have a clear understanding of justice. Who can look at any man or woman and say with certainty that one needs three years in jail and the other needs five. Everyone understands an injustice, but no one clearly understands justice.

Our moral condition could be likened to a primitive society before the invention of the wheel. Civilization took a long time to discover the wheel because there was no precedent for it, no similar principle in animal or bird life which could be closely observed and imitated.

We have no precedent, historically, for a just society because none ever existed. We can't grasp this principle by observing nature, either, because with its hurricanes and earthquakes it slays or maims the good and the bad indiscriminately.

So what the hell is this principle that can change things the way the wheel did? It isn't the admonition to love one another or the Golden Rule. Both concepts are works of genius but inadequate for most of us who must function in an imperfect world.

We were talking about a principle that had not been discovered as yet, but very likely did exist. I had the strange feeling we had stumbled onto something the human mind was not supposed to comprehend. It's as if you once lived for a while in Philadelphia and a surgeon's knife removed all your memory of it. Since it was cut out and destroyed and there were no backup systems where it was stored, there was no way to recall it. And yet you were suddenly aware of the edges where it had been excised, and realized for the first time that something was missing.

The more I examined our discussion the more ways I found to interpret it, until I became confused. Then, like a flare over a battlefield, I perceived a truth. I could not solve these things because my mind was not profound enough. We had been approaching the strange and beautiful landscape where original thought can take place. But we were not there yet.

After school that evening, I went out the prison gate mumbling to myself, repeating a silly phrase, "Don't cut too many windows in my little house; or I will perish in the sunlight."

Late in the evening, I heard the howls coming from the men in solitary. I was lulling myself to sleep by the melody of their misery.

My brain throbbed from my concentration. I started thinking about Purcell and could guess what he was thinking right now. The black students were upset by the use of the word "nigger" when it was demeaning. I, too, knew what it was like to be demeaned. I knew what it was like to be scoffed at by those close to me; I knew what it was like to turn my head away from my superior when he uttered something I considered to be shatteringly untrue and scuff my foot and by my silence imply, "Yowsuh, Boss."

Like Purcell, I longed for the woman who understood these things, who could accept me "feathers and all" and could bite me on the ear and say teasingly, "Hello, pretty nigger."

But, no, the meaning of the day was something other than that. It was something that hadn't been mentioned. Yet it described man's condition more accurately than our cerebrations in the classroom.

It was my phrase. It was the phrase of the elderly lady living on welfare in a house trailer. It was the phrase of perhaps even the President of the United States, isolated and trapped in the corridors of power. It was a phrase so deeply felt that one guy, squatting over the toilet in a prison, risked being stripped naked and locked in isolation for several days, so he could give it a few brief hours on the shithouse wall.

The phrase was, of course, *I no want be lonely anymore.*

This thought brought peace to me; and I dropped off to sleep. In the morning I was all right. But I never attempted a lesson on semantics again.

CHAPTER 6

Prison is a place where you forget the sound of a baby's cry. You forget the sound of a dog's bark or even the sound of a dial telephone.

From a Student Theme

At first I listened to the students talk. I was like a benevolent district attorney, cross-examining them. Some had an enormous desire to communicate the wrongs that had been done to them. I did my best teaching when I first started, because I was concerned and curious. After a few months, I was familiar with what was disturbing them. I had heard so many stories of wrongdoing, of crooked judges, crooked lawyers, police brutality, ignorant unfeeling parole boards, careless stupid robberies, hostile destructive behavior that I turned them off when they started. "Don't snivel, do the best you can," I said when I didn't want to hear a retelling of an ill I had heard expressed a hundred times.

One law that was particularly offensive to them was the California system of indeterminate sentences. The design and purpose of this law was sound. A person was sentenced from six months to life. He could be released any time after six months if he showed he had straightened around and was capable of handling himself in society again. Thus the inmate had very real pressure to do the best job he could while in prison. However, in practice, the law meant a person could be kept in jail for the rest of his life for a minor offense. There was no way he could appeal.

If he were a political activist, the parole board could feel he was not ready to reenter society and could hold him in jail indefinitely. No prisoner was convicted for political activism and, indeed, it is not a crime. But activism can prejudice a parole board. They can be judge and jury, convicting a man and holding him in jail for his political views. Of course, no parole board would openly admit they do this. But they are human beings and are subject to prejudices. The problem is the system gives them complete power over a man's life.

As it worked out in California, the important black political activists brought enormous attention to themselves and, because of pressure from the outside, did get out of jail. It was the little guy, with sometimes nothing more than an independent point of view, who suffered the most.

Although not in the area of politics, here is an example of the power of indeterminate sentences. I had a student, Corrigan, who was convicted of a misdemeanor when he was fifteen and was eligible for parole after a few months. He was a hot-tempered kid, and when he went before the board they said something he didn't like and he picked up a chair and smashed it to pieces on the floor.

The parole board dealt with dangerous men all day long; they would not put up with that nonsense. They kept him in jail for seven years for that tantrum. Since he was a Youth Authority inmate rather than a convicted felon they were required to release him when he turned twenty-two. If he had been an adult he would probably still be there.

Personally, I liked Corrigan. He worked hard and had a good sense of humor. He would catch moths and conceal them in his jacket. He had some intricate device rigged up so he could release them one at a time. I would be watching him and, all of a sudden, a big moth would flutter out, circle around, and go out the window. One day he released seven of them. That cracked me up.

On the other hand, I had a student, Paton, who was very

bright and an excellent writer. He was in jail for killing a dope pusher who had "burned" him by selling "bad stuff." Paton was on the streets again in less than a year and, if he could keep out of trouble for a year, his crime would be reduced to a misdemeanor.

These two men were paroled at about the same time, and I was glad to see both of them get their freedom. Yet I found it difficult to equate the smashing of a chair as seven times worse than taking a human life.

Police brutality was another subject many of my students wanted to talk about. They claimed the standard procedure, if the cops didn't like you, was to force you to spread-eagle against a wall or car. Then after you had been frisked, a cop would kick the feet from under you, and as you tried to rise, a group of cops would beat the shit out of you with clubs. When you were beaten to a pulp, you would be booked for resisting arrest.

They also claimed in a certain district in the Los Angeles area that if the cops knew you and saw you riding in a car, they would force you to pull over and get out of the car. Then they would have you stick your head in the window and they would wind the windows up on your neck until it crushed your Adam's apple. You were helpless in this position, because if you threshed around at all, you could break the window and cut your throat. They would take their leisurely time searching the car. If you screamed and hollered, they would hit you in the balls with a billy club. When they didn't find anything, they would cut you loose with an admonishment to stay out of the neighborhood.

There were countless stories of various kinds of brutality, but I won't repeat more of them because all these stories, including the previous one, were unverified. However, I heard so many I can't believe they were all without foundation.

I was initially astonished at how many times some men were caught red-handed twenty or thirty times before they went to jail. They were put on probation, or the evidence was thrown out of court on a technicality, or a smart lawyer made a deal with the district attorney. Others were caught and sent to jail the first time they were apprehended. It was a very inconsistent pattern.

Most of them were incredibly inept. They left their fingerprints where they committed a robbery; they told their friends and neighbors what they had done; one kid claimed he had robbed a store in his neighborhood, and while he was scooping the money out of the cash register, the clerk looked at him and said, "Sammy, what are you doing to me? We went to junior high school together."

Sammy finished the robbery and went home to wait for the cops. Sure enough, they arrived in a few hours to cart him away. All they had to do to track him down was look in the phone directory.

After listening to a succession of stories like this, I went to the blackboard and wrote in block letters: "REMEMBER: WEAR GLOVES."

I thought if I couldn't teach them anything else, I at least could teach them something I considered essential to their chosen profession.

To my surprise, I got into a tremendous argument. They claimed the cops were too stupid to check fingerprints and their identification process was so screwed up that, even if they did have the prints, they wouldn't be able to match them with rightful owners.

I claimed this was an ignorant attitude and we got into a senseless shouting match. I was confident I was giving them advice that was in their best interest.

From this, I got a clue about teaching these men. Other teachers couldn't get into discussions with them because they came in with an authoritarian point of view. It didn't matter if the point of view was right or wrong, in their best interest or in their worst interest. The prisoners were violently antiauthority and would shoot down anything that was said in a positive tone because it came from the "man." However, if I only questioned them, I didn't give them a target to shoot at. With my technique, I worked at creating controversy within their peer group, and I was not involved. Consequently, they were begging me for my point of view, and I refused to give it. This is a very simple concept, but it is an important one.

The first story I chose to discuss with one of my classes was "The Most Dangerous Game." It is a story about a man who is a big-game hunter. He is jaded because he has hunted all the most dangerous animals. So he decides to hunt the most intelligent, difficult animal of all: man. He buys an island away from civilization and proceeds to do exactly that. Another big-game hunter is shipwrecked on the island and the story concerns how hunter and hunted stalk each other and the hunted eventually outwits and kills the hunter.

I asked each one of my students to read the story and then, after thinking about it, make out five questions that puzzled them. I made up a series of questions myself; then I studied theirs and was ready to launch into the discussion.

Things went beautifully. We got into the question of why the hunter, who was educated and wealthy, could get pleasure out of only one thing. From this, we got into the question of obsession. Some felt, to be good at anything, a person had to be obsessed with what he was doing. Others felt a man who took pleasure in only one thing couldn't enjoy life. It was a good question with a lot of play back and forth; we got into the hunter's character and looked at him closely.

Then I asked the question: Was it wrong for the hunter to kill other men for sport? A strange thing happened. Nobody could see anything wrong in that. The hunter had given the man a chance, and he was fair.

"Well, is it wrong for one man to kill another?" I asked.

"No, it's not wrong. We kill each other all the time. It's all a game of cops and robbers."

The more I bored in on them, the more tightly they wove their defense. Man has always enjoyed killing his fellow man. We're always involved in a war. Even the state kills with capital punishment. We drop bombs on women and children and enjoy it. We shoot people in riots. If you have a gun and somebody challenges you—waste him. We love killing each other. It's the best population control we have.

"The good citizen would love to catch a burglar in his house and blow him apart. He would get his rocks off doing that," a student said.

"Do you really believe that?" I asked.

"Sure I do. Just for stealing a piece of junk from his pad, the average guy, if he had the chance, would kill. And if some good guy kills a prowler, a sick dude with a habit, tryin' to make it, all the good guys jump for joy and get their rocks off, too. You know we're right, Mr. Campbell. It's just being honest."

I couldn't crack their arguments. I did get them to admit that you protected your own people, but beyond that they were willing to blow people away.

"If killing is not an evil, then what is evil?" I asked in desperation.

"A smelly dude is an evil," a student said. "I mean if you are funky, you cause pain to everyone around you."

"How can you compare the two?" I asked.

"You have to understand, we're packed in like sardines. If you have a funky cellie, it's pure torture. It can cause riots," another student said.

"Killing is the destruction of a precious human life, while being smelly or funky is a condition that can be changed. You can't compare the two, can you?" I asked.

"If you're a killer, somebody pins a medal on you. But if you're funky, nobody wants to be near you, unless you're a hippie. Why do you suppose everybody hates the hippies and wants to wipe them out? It's because they're funky."

"Did anyone here ever kill anyone? Maybe if we could approach this from another way, we could understand it better."

At first no one copped out, and then the sweetest, mildest, most open-faced student in the room said, "Yeah, I did."

"Do you want to tell us about it?"

"It was an old farmer. He chopped the tail off my dog, and I snuffed him."

"What?" I said, for a moment forgetting where I was and thinking he was making a joke.

"The neighbors tole me he done it. And then I seen the dog

come back all bloody. He was just an ordinary ole hound. But I got mad. And I took a shotgun and went after that old man. He didn't even want to talk. Maybe he was crazy. He charged straight at me. He was a big and strong old man, and I got scared. There's no way you're gonna do that to my dog and whup me, too, I thought. And afore long, that ole man was dead. I don't rightly recall how it come about. I was only fifteen at the time.

"But I agree with Mr. Campbell. There's no way you can compare killing a man with smelling bad."

I was grateful to him for putting things back in perspective for us. But I dropped that subject and went on to another question.

I was pleased with the discussion. The students were highly motivated. They were questioning each other, drawing from their own experience and opening up their minds.

The next thing I decided to discuss was *Antigone.* King Creon decrees the body of Antigone's brother be left unburied outside the gates of the city, as punishment for leading a revolution. He orders that anyone who attempts to bury the man be put to death. Antigone decides to defy the law and bury her brother, because she must obey a higher law than man's law.

I gave them some background on the play and told them the plot before we read it aloud in class. It was not a good translation; and the chorus was difficult to understand. I started to explain the complicated language to the students. I could sense I was turning them off by doing this. Finally a student said, "Don't keep interrupting us all the time, Mr. Campbell. Nobody cares what those words mean."

"OK, let's just skip the chorus and get into the action of the play," I suggested.

"No, I like the sounds of the words. I can trip out when I hear them. But that explaining is like a hammer that breaks up my thoughts," the student said.

From this, I learned something new about teaching. I was only interested in thought. The sound of the words was of no value to me. These students were in a different bag. They were children of the drug culture and hungrily grasped anything that would transport them into another world.

Their psychedelic poster art was designed to let the mind take a colorful, nonthinking trip. Words can do the same thing. Once in a while, I would get a student in my writing class who wrote sounds instead of thoughts. Here is an example of a couple of lines I still remember.

> Ak to molly to golly go sump
> De ump de yada yahoo

The poem went on and on, but I can't recall the rest of it. The students loved this sort of thing and nobody tried to interpret it. This kind of jabberwocky has, of course, many progenitors. Lewis Carroll was a genius at it: "Twas Brillig and the slithy toves."

My students finished *Antigone* and we got into a discussion of the play. By this time they were familiar with the rules of discussion and were eager to respond. My first question was: Did Antigone commit a crime?

To answer it, they had to define what the word crime meant. Nobody had ever asked them that question before. At first, we figured out that Antigone had broken the law. But is breaking a law a crime?

"She is obeying a higher law That is more important to her."

"Are there higher laws than man's laws?" I asked.

"Yes, there's God's law. That is higher than man's."

"Fine," I said. "Why don't we just forget about man's law and all obey God's law."

"That's a great idea."

"All right, suppose I am on the parole board and I think you are a dangerous man and I believe that God has revealed to me that you should be kept in jail for the rest of your life. So I obey God's law and lock you away forever."

"But that's crazy. That's not obeying God's law."

"Did Antigone obey God's law when she buried her brother?"

"Yes, she knew it was wrong to let her brother rot on the sidewalk."

"Yeah, but the king had to protect himself. He wanted to put down revolutions; and he had to make an example of the brother. He had to show he was the 'man' so people would respect him," another student said.

I had two people on opposite sides of the question. It was easy to get them struggling with each other and then pull other students into the controversy to see how they felt about it. "Can you run a government when people only obey the laws that please them?" I asked. "How can you determine what is God's law? Should you obey a bad law?"

"How about you," I said, pointing to a student who hadn't said anything. "Was it a bad law that convicted you?"

"I was busted for robbing a filling station."

"Do you think we should change the law so that guys who rob filling stations go unpunished?"

"No, the law is all right. I wanted some money and it was the easiest thing to do."

"Did you need the money?" I asked, hoping he would say, yes, so I could question whether or not he was obeying the higher law that a man should not starve to death in a land of plenty. But he took a different tack.

"No, I didn't really need the money. I wasn't starving. I had robbed before and not got caught. I was low riding and didn't give a damn about anything."

"That is a stupid, low-class crime," another student said.

"What do you mean?" I asked.

"You pull as much time for robbing a filling station as you do for robbing a bank. Only amateurs knock over a filling station, where they can't hope to get more than thirty-five dollars, when they could pull a big robbery and get a lot more money."

"How about you, are you a big-time robber?" I asked.

"I worked with a group and we used our heads. There is this town, Garden Grove, and it has only one police station. We had a dude go to the north end of town and shoot a shotgun into a federal bank. This set off the alarm and sent every police car in the city racing to the scene. Then the rest of us started hitting bars and liquor stores in the south end. In twenty minutes, we cleaned up and were out of town."

"How did you get caught?" I asked.

"I never did get busted for that. My girl friend snitched me off for robbing a jewelry store, and they searched my apartment before I had time to get to a fence."

Later I checked his records and found he was in for brutally beating a fifteen-year-old boy with a tire chain. He had a previous record of petty crimes, none of which were as exalted as robbing a filling station. It was very common for students to fantasize crimes or borrow crimes that appealed to them and claim them as their own.

The next day I wrote ten questions arising from the discussion on the board and instructed the class to write an essay on one or more of them. If they had a lot to say, they could spend the period on one question. Others could make an attempt to answer all ten questions.

I had every theme read aloud in class; the student knew that what he wrote would get a hearing in front of his peers. This gave him an added incentive to do his best. These themes reopened the discussion of the play or book. Sometimes the reading of one theme would launch us into a discussion that lasted the entire period. Other times I could read every paper in one or two days. Frequently a student had a very good idea but was unable to express himself clearly in writing. Under questioning, he would explain what he was trying to say, and I would reply, "Beautiful, just put down on paper what you told us and you will have the lead-off for a great essay."

I did not give grades on individual themes. I had them save everything they had written in individual folders, and at the end of the term I reviewed their progress and gave an overall grade. If a student messed up at the beginning but developed later on, I graded him on where he was, rather than where he had been. Their written work did not always follow a straight progression from bad to good. Sometimes they would write a good theme early in the term and do poorly on another theme later on. When they found something that interested them, their grammar and every other aspect of their writing improved. I had them revise the good themes and ignore the bad ones.

Antigone was a great winner the first time I tried it, and it worked in all subsequent classes. The play dealt with the big questions of the day. The question of whether or not we should bury a brother was one that none of us would have. Thus it was free of any emotional attachment and could be looked at objectively. Yet the decision we made in judging Antigone's case could be applied in any case where our conscience was in conflict with the law.

I was so encouraged by the response to Antigone, I wanted to take them through a course of the world's great literature. My problem was, I didn't have books. I did, however, personally own fifteen copies of the *Apology and Crito,* by Plato, which describes the trial and deathbed scene of Socrates.

The prison had a rule that all material used in the classroom had to be approved. I decided to ask permission of Hugo Belson to bring in my copies of Plato. My plan was to put on a demonstration that would be so good I could get monies from the school to embark on an extensive program.

When I asked Belson for permission, he replied, *"Apology and Crito,* what's that?"

"It's a Greek dialogue by Plato. It's one of the greatest philosophical works ever written," I said.

"You were hired to teach these jackoffs how to read and write, not to have them play around with philosophy."

"Exactly right," I said. "They will read the book, discuss it and write about it. I want to use it as an educational tool."

"Campbell, you're naive. You're working in a human garbage can. These guys aren't ever gonna accomplish anything. They don't need fancy things like philosophy. They need to learn simple things like how to count boxes in a warehouse, and how to read well enough to pass the driver's test."

"I'm teaching high school students. They can already do that. I want them to reach as high as they can," I said. Belson had worked for a number of years as an elementary school teacher in another prison and had no experience teaching on the high school level.

"They'll make a duck out of you," Belson said.

"I've already been working with discussion in my classes, and I know what I'm doing," I said confidently.

"Having students sit around and talk isn't education," Belson said.

"They're reading, writing and thinking," I countered.

"No, I can't approve it," Belson said, taking another approach. "Those Greeks were homosexuals, weren't they? We have enough problems with that here. We don't need to have you bringing in homosexual literature for them to read. The matter is closed."

I thought about explaining to him that the *Apology* was about a man who was on trial for his life because he refused to compromise his principles. It had nothing to do with homosexuality. But I knew it was hopeless. I shrugged my shoulders.

"Oh, another thing," Belson said, "I haven't been near your classroom. But sometimes when I've been on the second floor, I've heard loud laughter. I know you're handling it, because if you weren't we'd be pulling you out of there with a shank stuck in your back. I want to ask you a philosophical question. If some son of a bitch raped your daughter or killed your sister, would you want another son of a bitch to be paid a good salary to sit down with the dude and make him laugh?"

"I was hired to teach these men, not to punish them," I said. "I believe laughing is part of the teaching procedure."

"Think about it," Belson said.

"All right, I will." That ended my interview; I returned to my classroom.

I thought about my answer to Belson's question. I would not like it if someone harmed my loved ones. I might even kill to protect them. But I would not want the state to torture anyone so I could have vengeance. That is sick. Also, it creates sympathy for the person being tortured. Why shouldn't inmates in a prison laugh once in a while? If we didn't educate them or give them some hope for the future, they would go out on the streets to do the same thing again. This was exactly what was happening.

99

Furthermore I didn't believe Belson hated laughter, either. I'd seen him joke with inmates and, at times, show very real concern for their welfare. Belson was playing a game with me.

I thought about going over Belson's head, but that would mean going to Bianca. By this time, I knew this was useless. If Bianca found something orgiastic in an ordinary office photograph, Lord only knows how he would react to Plato behind prison bars.

I decided to break the law. I decided to smuggle in my copies of *Apology and Crito* and discuss them with my class. Once this decision was made, the rest would be easy. I could put the books in my briefcase and carry them into the prison without detection. We were never searched as we went through the gate, and even if, by some fluke, my briefcase was inspected by a guard, he would find no dirty words or pictures in my texts.

I discussed my plan with my students and explained that, like Antigone, I had decided to break the law because I believed there was a higher law that decreed I should try to educate them. They were intrigued by my crime and very willing to cooperate.

We worked out a scheme whereby if Belson did come into the room, we could conceal the copies of Plato and appear to be in the midst of a grammar lesson. We cut up pieces of paper the approximate size of the Plato books and had a trial run. When I signalled, they hid the sheets of paper and took out their grammar books, opened to page 37. I started to go into an explanation of the third sentence on that page. It worked perfectly.

"The plan is foolproof," I said. "There's only one way it can break down, and that is if somebody snitches on us."

"Don't worry, if any dude snitches on you, we'll off him," a student said.

"See what happens when you start a life of crime, Mr. Campbell? You have to worry about snitches and you have to back up your words with power, or you'll get into a world of hurt."

"OK, we won't kill anybody who snitches, but I want your promise that you won't tell anyone what we are doing. If there's

100

anyone who doesn't go along with it, I won't bring in the books."
I went around the room and extracted an individual solemn
promise from every student in the room.

The books were in San Francisco, and I had to wait until the
weekend to get them. On Friday, two days after I had made the
announcement to my class, I arrived at the prison gate in the
morning, simultaneously with Hugo Belson. We walked into the
prison together.

"Campbell, I want to talk to you," Belson said. He was in a
cheerful mood.

"I know you plan to bring those books in. It was reported to
me by three different people. They were practically lined up in
my office yesterday to snitch on you. I don't give a damn about
those books. I'm not going after you; but, if you get into trouble,
it's your neck not mine.

"The important thing is, you don't understand the mentality of
these men. They're sneaky and vicious. They've already sold out
their mothers, fathers, brothers, sisters and wives. Don't make the
mistake of thinking you're any better than the others they've
betrayed. Maybe it's a good thing this happened. Maybe it will
finally teach you a lesson that I have been trying to pound into
your head."

"I appreciate that you told me this, and that you didn't hang
me for it. I am going to bring the books in, and fully understand
that you're not responsible for the consequences," I said.

We walked the rest of the way together in a spirit of cordiality.
It appeared both of us had won our points. Belson was not out to
get me; he had enough other problems. Also, he was shrewd
enough to realize that if he nailed me, there was a real possibility
it would reflect more on him than on me.

I confronted my class with what Belson had told me, sparing
them nothing. They leapt to their defense, claiming no one in my
class had betrayed me.

"Everyone in this class knows you're trying to help us. A big
discussion started in the cell blocks about how you were risking
your neck so that we could get something besides rinkey-dink
things to read. Somebody who isn't in your class got jealous and

101

decided to get brownie points by snitching you off. The prison is full of weak-minded, sissy dudes like that."

"All right, let's forget about it. We're out in the open now and that's, undoubtedly, a good thing," I said.

The following Monday I brought in the books and we got to work. I did not have enough copies for every student, so I decided to have them read it aloud.

I had led thousands of discussions of the *Apology* and knew exactly how to handle it. We started out like Socrates, seeking a definition of wisdom. Socrates went to the artisans or craftsmen and found they had great skills, but when he discussed topics outside their skill areas, they had no wisdom at all.

"What does Socrates mean by wisdom?" I asked.

"Well, I think he means common sense."

"All right, suppose you don't have any common sense, can you acquire it by studying?" I asked.

"No, some of the most highly educated people are fools."

"Are you saying if you're born a fool, you're doomed to remain a fool for the rest of your life?" I asked.

We also got into an examination of the charges against Socrates. He was accused of being a curious person. Why was that a crime? Should it be a crime? Can you go to jail today for being a curious person? We also examined in the same fashion the charge that he "made the worse appear the better cause."

The student responses were good, but they were no different from the responses from any other class I'd had. Convicts, nuns, and college professors struggle in the same way with these problems.

Then I hit what was, for me, pay dirt. We got intensely involved with a question I had never, in all my previous discussions, raised before. Socrates mentions he will not bring his wife and two children to the courtroom, because he does not want to sway the jury with a sentimental appeal; he wants to be judged on the basis of reason and logic only.

I had a young man in the class named Flint who was in prison for selling narcotics to a minor. He had been convicted of selling marijuana to a twenty-year-old man who was only a few months from turning twenty-one. The penalty for selling to a minor is much stiffer than for selling to a legal adult. Indeed, he had ten years to serve before he could even appear before the parole board. If Flint had killed the young man instead of selling him marijuana, he would have received a mandatory life sentence, which means he would have been eligible for a parole hearing after only seven years.

Flint had a pretty wife and two young children. Flint's lawyer recommended he bring his family to court during the trial and put them right in the front row so the jury could see them. Flint refused to do this.

"What I did was my responsibility. Why should my children get involved in it?"

"Flint, you're a fool," a student named Jakes said. "You love your children, right?"

"I love them very much," Flint said proudly.

"All right, if you love them, it stands to reason you want to do what is best for them, right?"

"Right," Flint said.

"OK, now the best thing for your children is to have a daddy who can be with them and take care of them. You ain't no good to them, rotting away in a jail cell for ten or twenty years."

"I know that," Flint said.

"Then it's clear. If you love your children, you should do everything possible to insure that they have a daddy who can take care of them. You should lie, cheat, stand on your head, parade your kids in front of the jury—and anything else you can think of."

"You don't understand," Flint said. "They weren't party to what I did. I couldn't make them suffer for my crime."

"Fool, you make them suffer by being locked away. You're as useless as tits on a boar to them now. Look at it another way. Suppose you were the child and your daddy was on trial. Wouldn't you want to do everything you could to help him?"

"I'm a man," Flint said. "I can't hide behind their innocent

103

faces. I can't use them to get me off the hook. What kind of dad can I be if I can't look them in the eye? I don't want my freedom if I have to castrate myself to get it."

"Fool," Jakes said, boring in again. "Flint, do I have to tell you how the world is? It's not run by reason or high-mindedness. If you get into that bag, you're screwed. Look at Socrates. He tried a logical approach and they snuffed him. You're gonna have to learn that half the world is crooked and the other half is sentimental; if you refuse to go either route, you got nothin' goin' for you. That's why there are smart lawyers. It appears to me you had a smart lawyer and you pissed on him."

"It's like Antigoné," Flint said. "Sometimes there's a higher law and you have to obey it. Or it's like Socrates' 'inner voice.' When it says no, you got no choice.

"It's a funny thing," Flint continued. "When I was dealing, I didn't have any inner voice telling me it was a wrong thing to do. I was on hard stuff and about every other thing you could mention. I had money and was living well.

"I got too far into the scene, and I would never go back to it. But I never thought I was harming people. There must be a million people in this country who earn their living running bars, liquor stores and gin mills. There must be another million doctors and nurses who take care of the ten million people who are destroyed by alcohol. Just a few funny dudes who don't drink and don't get a cut in the profits complain about it.

"Furthermore, if drugs were legal, the politicians who scream about it now would be the first ones to buy up the franchises. There's a good buck to be made, it's legal, and the people want it. If you can't handle it, baby, that's your problem—would be their cry—just the way it is now, with alcohol. I'm not any better than those people. But I'm not any worse, either."

Abruptly, Flint's mood changed. "I'm just rapping. Jakes, I guess there's no way you can understand about how I feel about my family. I wonder, do you have any children?"

"I got no kids," Jakes said. "I wish the hell I did. I got no people at all. Flint, you dumb son of a bitch, I don't even know you. I got only a few months to serve before I get out again. I got no one waiting for me. If I could, I'd take your time—just stack it up and I'd walk it off for you, so you could get back with your wife and kids. My daddy was in the joint when I was a kid, and I know how it is."

"Jakes, you're dumber than Flint is," another student said.

I couldn't take it any longer. I got up and walked out of the room. I was cursing under my breath, with every foul word I could think of. I was cursing the pain of those dumb, hopelessly trapped bastards in my class. I was cursing the pain of those who had loved ones fouled up by drugs or alcohol. I was cursing the pain of babies born blind or burned by napalm. I was cursing the pain of people torn apart in automobile crashes. I was, in fact, cursing the human condition.

When I snapped out of it, I was out of the education area, past the main entrance and almost all the way to the cell blocks. I must have put a quarter of a mile of concrete between me and my classes. For a few seconds I didn't know where I was. When I looked around, I could tell that I was in a prison. What in hell am I doing here? I thought. Then it came back to me. I remembered the discussion in the classroom and that I had left the room. But how I got from there to where I was, I did not recall and cannot now remember.

I'm not crazy, I thought. I can make a good case that the world is nuts. But not me. I may be one of the few sane people left in it. Then I recalled that an insane person invariably thinks he is all right and the world is crazy.

All right, I'm crazy, I thought. I was driven temporarily insane for a short period of time. Why did I black out? I was trying to take the pain and misery of others upon my own shoulders, and I couldn't handle it.

I remembered the previous day, in another class, a student had brought me a letter from his mother and asked me to read it. He was about eighteen years old and was in jail for a series of petty misdemeanors. His mother had written: "When you were little, you stepped on my toes. Now that you're grown, you step on my heart."

No matter what, I'm not going to let these guys step on my

105

heart, I resolved, because if I do, I will be no good for them or anyone else. I will be a sorry thing walking around in a daze, talking to myself. When I returned, I do not believe any of the students realized I had been gone. I doubt I was away longer than ten minutes.

"You make it sound like a big deal," a student named Barstow was saying. "But it ain't. I had a lawyer tell me the same thing. I did bring in my kids and put them in the front row. It didn't do no good. I got long time, anyway. Juries don't go for that stuff anymore. They get their rocks off knowin' they have the power to make you suffer."

The discussion on this topic raged for the rest of the period and all the following day. I did not say a word in class for those two days. The discussion of the *Apology* was a great success. I had no way of communicating to anyone outside the classroom what had gone on. I could not prove it improved reading skills or that it made anyone decide to mend his evil ways and become a good citizen. There was later, however, some encouraging fallout from this discussion.

I remember the day Martin Luther King was killed. It was in April, and all of the sudents who participated in the discussion were long gone from my classroom. Big John, a black student who had been in that class, made a special trip from his unit to tell me ahout the assassination. It was about four o'clock in the afternoon, California time. I had just finished my last class and had not yet heard the news. Big John said, "You know, I never liked Martin Luther King, because he wasn't poor and didn't speak for black people anymore. I remember something in that book we read, that Socrates said. He said 'You can't harm a good man.' I understand what that means now. It don't matter that I knocked Dr. King or that some dude killed him. Neither of us could harm him. You taught me something about philosophy, Mr. Campbell; and that's why I made this trip to thank you."

It's a strange thing, but I don't recall we even discussed that point in class. Big John picked that up all by himself, and made it a part of himself.

I didn't do Plato again in another main-line class because my

106

books were stolen. I passed the books out without assigning them to individuals, and by the end of the discussion had, except for my own copy, lost every single one of them.

I made an impassioned plea to get them back. Four of them were returned, not enough copies for me to use in a full class discussion.

I toyed with the idea of having the guards search the men's cells for my books. But I could not send a man to the hole for stealing a copy of a dialogue by Plato. I knew I had won my battle because, in prison, no greater tribute can be paid to a book than to steal it.

CHAPTER 7

Prison is a place where hope springs eternal, where each parole board means a chance to get out, even if odds are hopelessly against you.

From a Student Theme

In addition to my English classes, I taught one course each term labelled Creative Writing. This was an elective, but was allowable as a full English credit.

When I was assigned the course, I made elaborate plans. I wanted to present a study of forms of literature and writing styles. I thought I would pick a topic they could all relate to and show them how several famous writers had handled the same subject. My first topic was violence. I had excerpts from Hemingway, Faulkner, Malcolm X· and many more.

I started out reading them a short story by Hemingway called "A Natural History of the Dead" which described in vivid imagery the rotting corpses on a battlefield. It was powerful, and I thought it would excite their interest. It bombed.

I started telling them about Hemingway and his fatal attraction to violence. They weren't interested. These students were full of their own violent material and did not want to be taken on somebody else's trip.

"All right," I said. "Tell me what you want to write about."

At first no one would admit to any interest in writing. Finally a young Indian student whom everyone referred to as Chief spoke up.

"I've just been voted secretary of the prison chapter of Alcoholics Anonymous. I want to learn to write so I can handle the newsletter we put out. I got no interest in dead writers or dead bodies on a battlefield."

"That's an excellent practical reason for wanting to write," I said. "But writing is more than hooking words together in grammatical sequence. It means you have something to say that no one else in the world can say any better. It's egotistical as hell. Let me put it to you this way. Years ago, when my niece was small, I would play a game with her. I would pretend I didn't see her and say, "Where is Cynzee?" Finally, in desperation, she would cry out. 'Here I is, wif pigtails.'

"That's what I want you to do when writing for this class. I want you to shout out, 'Here I is, wif pigtails.' "

"That's crazy talk. I can't understand any of it," Chief said.

"Let me demonstrate," I said. "There must be many things you can write about. Just being inside a prison is one."

"I want to forget about that," Chief said.

"What about what you're in here for?" I asked.

"I'm in for arson," Chief said.

"Arson," I exclaimed. "That's a fascinating thing to write about."

"No," Chief said sadly. "Arson is a stupid thing. And it's dull, too. I only did it for the money."

After some coaxing, Chief told us about how he had a family to support and a drinking problem. He needed money and someone put him onto a man who paid him five hundred dollars for setting fire to an abandoned warehouse so the owner could collect the insurance. From this, other jobs developed and he acquired a reputation in the business community around Los Angeles.

He described some of the methods he used in setting fires. To me, the material was fascinating.

"What you have just told us is an excellent theme," I said.

109

"I want to forget about all that," Chief said. "I want to spend my time in the joint doing something useful. I don't want to waste it copping out on what I done."

"I'm trying to show you that you have a wealth of material to write about," I said.

"Why are you so curious about what I done?" he asked suspiciously. "How do I know you ain't workin' for the 'Man' tryin' to put me in a 'snitch bag'?"

I understood his concern. At the time, there was a rumor going around that authorities had bugged the Catholic confessional at San Quentin. Some inmates swore that when they went before the parole board they were confronted with information that was revealed only when they were, supposedly, talking to God. Of course, information obtained in this manner could never be used in a law court. However, a parole board is not accountable to any rules of evidence and can interpret any information it acquires as it chooses.

Chief never did write about his past misdeeds. I made many mistakes with that first writing class. But I learned from them and developed a technique that worked.

I read and discussed only themes written by students in my class. However, once in a while, if I received an unusually good theme, I would read it to all my English classes. Relying on the imagery of my own rural background, I referred to these as "calf starters." This is what farmers give the young bull or heifer to get it away from sucking the mother's teat and onto ensilage or grass. I wanted to get them away from the sucking, sustaining pull of their own desperation and onto the lush grass of their own rich experience.

I read everything they wrote, aloud, in class. Thus the motivation for writing came from peer-group response, rather than from the grade they would receive. I rarely corrected spelling or sentence structure. I looked upon each paper as a personal expression, and to correct even the spelling, in most cases, would have been destructive.

I would not accept pornographic or "Hank" literature, nor personal attack on any inmate or free person in the institution.

110

This was not a difficult rule to enforce. Although students would be highly critical of certain free people who worked in the prison, they were reluctant to commit their views on paper. I explained these two rules at the beginning of each term. I do not recall having to reject any theme because of content.

These writing classes were beautiful. I could enter the room mildly depressed, as everyone who works in a prison atmosphere is from time to time, and at the end of the period be filled with an energy that was remarkable.

Sometimes I gave my own criticism, but usually I confined myself to discussing the ideas put forth in their writing. My students were not cruel in their comments, as public school students frequently are. We were all part of a growing, expanding, groping search for expression. Our minds were free and it was startling to contemplate that in a few hours the steel would clang and they would be standing by the tiny window in their cell door, waiting for the 4:30 head count.

I provided countless suggestions to get them started and rarely used the same ones twice. I wrote about ten topics on the board, ranging from "Describe the holding pen in a county jail" to "If a revolution comes in this country, how and where will it start?"

I found my most successful suggestions for theme writing came to me on the spur of the moment. I remember I once asked a group to describe the brutality in a prison without going into the conventional things such as beatings, stabbings, gang rapes, etc. I asked them to search for a way to make a subtle statement.

A student came up with a theme entitled: "Dead Man Walking." It described a scene he had witnessed in the yard at San Quentin. When a man on Death Row had to leave the compound containing the gas chamber for a court appearance, he had to walk across the yard, surrounded by six guards. The condemned man was dressed in brown, in contrast to the blue denim of conventional inmates. The condemned man walked with his head bowed as the loudspeaker boomed out repeatedly, "Clear the yard. Dead man walking. Dead man walking."

I encouraged students to develop their own writing projects, and if they got something going, would excuse them from regular

111

assignments. Many were capable of working independently. One of the best was a prisoner named Torch.

Torch was the secretary of the Hell's Angels in Oakland. He came into my writing class as a published author. He wrote poetry for religious magazines published in the Midwest. It was simple poetry, eloquently expressed, about his love for Jesus and the Christian faith. It was so good I expressed some skepticism it was his work. He promptly produced a number of letters from the poetry editor written on letterhead stationery and a cancelled check for fifteen dollars.

He started a book about his experiences in the Hell's Angels. He would describe a scene with remarkable sensitivity and then shatter the mood he had created with a grotesque incident. For example, in one chapter he told what it was like, in the early morning, to be riding along the highway in a pack. He loved the comradeship, the roar of wind and piston set against the backdrop of the big-bellied sun burning away the cloud cover and the early morning mist.

They crossed a bridge and stopped at a restaurant on the other side. One of the Angels called the waitress and asked for a saucer of cream for his kitty. He showed her the head of a small, furry kitten nestled in his jacket. When she returned with the cream, he dumped the kitten on the counter. It had been crushed on the highway and cut in half, and its entrails spilled out on the formica top, its clotting blood mingling with the spilled white cream.

Everyone roared with laughter at the vomiting waitress, and death became a wildly funny joke to them.

When I rapped with Torch, he told me how he got to be head of the Hell's Angels in his district. Torch was short and skinny and no one would pick him out as the leader of a rough group of men. He maintained his leadership because of his persistence. He told how another Angel, Rufus, had put him in the hospital three times. Each time, as soon as he was able to walk, he went after Rufus again. Finally Rufus gave up. He knew the only way to get Torch off his back was to kill him. Eventually Rufus defended him against all other challengers, and the word was out, "Hey, don't hassle Torch. The guy has guts."

It was this attitude that led to a bloody killing. Torch had a young, beautiful wife, Carmen. She was driving her convertible down the California highway and a dude, spotting a pretty girl, pulled in behind her and started bumping her car from the rear. At first Carmen tried to ignore him and then warned him not to cause trouble. He laughed at her and she started crying.

"Why are you crying? I don't want to hurt you. I think you are bee-yoot-iful," the dude said.

"I'm crying because I don't want to see you get hurt. You're a nice guy. But, poor baby, you're playing way over your head," Carmen said. "My old man is a leader of the Hell's Angels. If you follow me home, you're in bad trouble."

The dude ignored her warning and trailed her until she stopped in front of her house, where Torch was waiting for her. The dude crashed into her rear bumper again and careened down the street with a horrendous screech of tires.

Torch jotted down the license number as he pulled away, and a few days later he and some of his friends showed up at the house where the dude lived. They were not armed with knives or guns but did have bicycle chains. The dude and his friends inside the house had guns and started shooting at them. In the ensuing struggle, Torch was shot seven times, but he kept coming on. He charged into the house, wrenched the gun away from the dude, jammed it into his mouth, and pulled the trigger. He blew the dude's head apart.

Torch was so badly wounded it was six months before he was out of the hospital and ready to stand trial. He tried to beat the rap on the basis of self-defense. To Torch the issue was crystal clear. The dude had shot him seven times, so why the hell didn't he have a right to defend himself? He had come to the house unarmed. If the dude had apologized, Torch would have put his arm around him and suggested they go out and hoist a few beers together. But when the dude took a shot at him, forget it. One of them had to die.

Torch's attitude was, if he had been a lunch pail carrying member of society instead of a Hell's Angel, he never would have gone to jail. He believed the jury not only would have acquitted him, but would have praised him for having the "balls" to defend his own family.

Legally, of course, the problem is considerably more complicated. He did go to the man's house with a group of his friends and he did kick down the door, grab the smoking gun and kill his antagonist.

Torch was in jail on a murder conviction, but the killing was not premeditated and he would be eligible for parole after seven years. When I met him, he had already served three years and was confident he would make parole the first time he was eligible for it.

He was not interested in presenting any of his writing to the rest of the class for discussion. All our talks were held privately. I'm not certain any other members of the class knew about his background.

I did obtain permission from him to read his work in my other classes, where he was not a student. When I did this, some of my students claimed I was reading from a published author's work rather than from an inmate's written assignment. High praise from a critical source.

I asked him if the Angels would be upset if he wrote a book about them, telling it from the inside. He didn't think they would be and described various deals the Angels had made with outsiders who wanted to observe them. As long as they received a share of the profits, they welcomed investigation.

I tried to convince him he had a publishable book if he would complete it. However, I didn't convince him he had a market for it. He was interested in what paid him money and knew he could make ten or fifteen dollars a crack, writing religious poetry. To him, this was his market. The other writing was just messing around.

I had him as a student for eight weeks. Upon completion of my class, he graduated from high school and returned to the general prison population. I did not see him again.

114

Another interesting writer was a man named Banton, the heavyweight boxing champion of the prison. He was a broad-shouldered black fighter who walked with a swagger and was not noted for his friendly attitude toward other races. All the other students in Banton's class were white.

Banton was writing a novel about a "pimp and a player" who had a stable of beautiful girls, drove a pink Cadillac, had a pink stripe through his hair, and was affectionately called the Pink Panther. When the other students were reading or discussing their work, he was at his desk scribbling away, ignoring them. Sometimes I had to tap him on the shoulder after the bell so he could take a smoke break in the corridor.

He would roar with laughter as he read his work to the class and frequently would take up the entire period while the rest of us listened in silence. Banton was not receptive to discussion of his work and would not tolerate criticism. He was a god, manufacturing the perfect fate for his creation. His presence was powerful enough so no one attempted to change him.

The Pink Panther was married and had children by a wife who nagged him and mildly deplored his occupation. However, he always managed to win her back with sweet talk and lavish gifts. He was very good to his girls and never hit them or was cruel to any of them. They all loved him and it was "Daddy" this and "Daddy" that. There were plenty of swindles and con jobs in Banton's fantasy. However, no one was ever hurt by these capers and they always made you laugh.

He would describe how the Pink Panther would walk down the street in fantastic costume with several beautiful girls on a leash. They were wearing pink and grey dresses and slacks and had diamond-studded dog collars around their necks. They looked like elegant greyhounds and were laughing and dancing and jiving it up. After they had attracted a crowd and someone wanted the services of one of them, the Pink Panther would unbuckle the collar and the customer would purchase her as he would a gaily colored balloon. When she had been popped, she would dutifully return, ready to go again. And the "long green" would flow to him in an unending stream.

115

Banton wasn't the official heavyweight champion. The real champion was a handsome black student named Redbone, who was in another of my classes. He was the champion by default, because he was so good no one in the entire prison would volunteer to get into the same ring with him. I had an excellent relationship with Redbone, who was quiet, gentle, possessed enormous charm and was, of course, a magnificent physical specimen.

Redbone helped train and coach the other fighters, including Banton. Redbone wanted desperately to get a fight, but things did not work out for him. First a huge, blond exparatrooper transferred in and it looked like he was finally going to get some action. However, in a preliminary bout, a tough Chicano dude flattened the paratrooper and ended that challenge.

A bout was scheduled with the champion of another prison, but it never materialized. Next a match was arranged with a free person from a nearby town, who was also a Golden Gloves champion. Redbone was so anxious the day of the bout that I excused him from all his afternoon classes. I couldn't attend the bout myself because I had to teach an adult English class in town the same evening.

The next day I discovered the bout had been cancelled at the last minute because the boy's mother had forbidden her son to fight. Some guards talked about managing Redbone when he was out of the joint. But I doubt anything came of that plan, either.

Redbone wasn't a good academic student, but he had a fierce desire to learn. He told me he had a girl friend in the Berkeley area, a Ph.D. candidate who was in love with him and wanted to marry him. But he felt as long as he didn't have even a high school education, the relationship couldn't possibly work out.

I am certain my friendship with Redbone affected my attitude toward Banton, for I never quite forgave Banton for refusing to tangle with Redbone. When I asked Banton point-blank about fighting him, Banton looked me straight in the eye and said, "What's the point? The man is too good."

After Banton completed my writing class, I did attend a fight he had with another black fighter. It was an aggressive, bloody slugfest, which Banton won on points. No one could accuse Banton of lacking guts. As I look back on it now, I understand that Banton was a realist, a man who had come to terms with a violent world. But in his fantasy world there was no violence whatsoever.

To Banton and to many young people raised in our ghettos, the pimp has the best our land can offer. He is much better off than the titled English lord who lives in a stone-cold castle, drinks weak tea, and in the early morning, dons a blazing costume to chase after a shy, young fox.

The pimp is a better dresser and drinker; and after he catches the stone-cold foxes, he doesn't do them in; he harnesses them and puts them to work for him.

A third student writing a book was an Apache Indian, Ladbrook, who had been adopted when he was four from an Oklahoma reservation by white Protestants from Grosse Pointe, Michigan. Ladbrook was his adopted name; he didn't know his Indian one.

Growing up in a white suburb was difficult for him. He was handsome, but he felt he didn't look like the other boys in the neighborhood and was always getting into fights. This upset his adopted parents, who were instilling in him their own narrow religious beliefs, with an emphasis on nonviolence.

He tried to be the son they wanted and marched to school with the best of intentions. But as soon as someone taunted him about his Indian heritage, he was in trouble again. He wrote eloquently about one traumatic incident that had happened to him as a teenager. He got into a fight that ripped his new clothes and bloodied him. When he returned home, his stepmother, whom he loved and tried desperately to please, became furious with him and slapped him across the face, sobbing, "You're nothing but a damned Indian."

That slap dissolved every bone in his body, because he understood in a jarring instant that underneath her religious jargon she was both violent and deeply prejudiced, and that she, too, hated him because he was an Indian. After that slap, he knew he was never going to make it in Grosse Pointe and was

117

furious with his adopted parents for taking him away from his Apache background, where he could have grown up with some sense of identification. He left home and returned to the Oklahoma reservation where he was born. This culture was strange to him by this time and he could not identify with it, either. It was at this point he went on a tear that led to stealing, looting, juvenile detention halls in a number of states and, eventually, a prison in California where he was my student.

For him, the book was emotional therapy. He was reliving his tortured and traumatic childhood with adult perspective. He wrote with great simplicity and tenderness how his adopted father used to hold him in his arms when he was small and tickle him. He loved to be tickled and it was enormous fun when they laughed together.

He described with great intensity the fundamentalist religion that he hated, rejected, yet clung to, because it was the only thing he had.

He was his own psychiatrist, asking himself the pertinent questions and putting his answers on paper. By now Ladbrook had the maturity to better understand the people who had hurt him, and he was in control of the hatred and painful need for love which had previously overwhelmed him.

Most of the writers, of course, were far less ambitious. I remember one short story about a worm. The writer described how the worm woke up in the early morning and looked around. It was a beautiful day and he was overflowing with tenderness. Right next to him he spied a lady worm and fell in love with her. He reached over, embraced her and found, to his horror, he had fallen in love with his other end.

This story is what the inmates call a bummer.

The funniest sessions occurred when I had my students write commercials. I found many of them were experts at writing clever, bright, lively copy. To maintain self-respect, everyone in prison is forced to do a cosmetic job on his past. And most had a crazy vision of the world and loved making up lies.

Commercials are more familiar to these students than any

other kind of communication and they are, of course, firmly rooted in a fanciful concept of the world that has fists coming out of washing machines, thinking men with painfully narrow tastes, talking animals of every description, etc. The effects of this looney, highly profitable business on some is profound. I remember walking down the long prison corridor to my job and encountering a young man coming down the other side with a tattooed black eye and, indelibly tattooed on his cheek, "I'd rather fight than switch."

I found it was an illegal tattoo, performed in prison, and the authorities had ordered him to have it removed. However, it could not be removed without a medical operation, which he refused. Since the operation might lead to permanent scarring or damaged eyesight, the matter was dropped. It wasn't clear whether he had the slogan tattooed because of a desire to advertise a product or to show his sexual preference. But it was clear that he was willing to donate his face as a billboard for permanent graffiti.

I started my students out by demonstrating how to distort the truth without telling a single lie. I told them to write advertising copy on one of two subjects, warned them they could embellish, exaggerate, omit, slant to their heart's content, but they were not allowed to make any statement that was factually incorrect.

I would go to the board and write in large block letters:

1. DESCRIBE THE PRISON SO SOMEONE WOULD LIKE TO ATTEND IT
2. DESCRIBE A BROKEN LEAD PENCIL WITHOUT AN ERASER SO SOMEONE WOULD WANT TO BUY IT.

When they read their work aloud, the laughter and foot stamping was so great I feared the bulls of the goon squad would come rushing down the hall, thinking a riot was in progress. From time to time, I suppose, Hugo Belson would peer through the window and try to fathom what was taking place. But he never came inside and he never questioned me.

119

I didn't save any of these advertisements. But I do recall some of the pitches: Free swimming pool with plenty of healthy, handsome young men lounging around with nothing better to do than cater to your every whim. Free gymnasium providing boxing, weight lifting, volleyball, basketball, etc. No taxes to pay. Sumptuous meals served absolutely free. No tipping allowed. Guaranteed protection against burglars from the outside. (In the entire history of this resort, no one has ever attempted to break in.) Concerned attendants to escort you around the spacious grounds.

One ended this way: If you desire additional information about this Garden of Eden, contact your local police officer and show him you are interested. He will be delighted to accommodate you in any way he can. *Remember now—act quickly—only a limited number of scholarships are available.*

I thought about writing to an advertising agency in New York and asking them to let me show them what my students could do. But I never got around to it. I wonder how Madison Avenue would react if they discovered prisons are an excellent training ground for their craft. I can see the personnel interviewers saying: "You went to Harvard, Yale, Princeton—no good. Sing Sing, San Quentin—you're hired."

I have included in this chapter some themes written by my students. When I left the job, I picked a pile of papers from my desk and put them in my briefcase. This is the best of that lot. So they are not specially selected, but they do represent what a teacher might receive on an average day.

A couple of them were written by a student who held the local record for time spent on parole, *five minutes.* He slugged someone in the prison parking lot while he was waiting for the bus to take him into town. See if you can identify which themes are his.

THE ART OF LONELINESS

What Lies within these prison walls No one really knows until he has experienced the feeling of being shot off from the World in which he was born. Being shot off from the world that he was

120

once a part of tends to change his whole view of life. His personality will obviously change because of the different environment he must adjust himself to. Life will never be the same as it was before he was committed. The main reason that life won't be the same is because Now this man have had the chance to experienced the Art of Loneliness. Of course there are many other ways of experiencing this devastateing Art. I suppose evry man in some way has felt the unpleasant feeling of loneliness. From time to time I encourage Myself by keeping in mind that life isn't full of all pleasant things, so to make it easy I just look for the worse and expect the best. What make loneliness such a distinguish Art is that it comes in so many different forms. It doesn't pick it's victims nor is it particular about the damage it causes. To some people loneliness would vanish if he had a considerate amount of money. But, what is so sickening is, people that have more money than they can spend are complaining and also comitting suicide. I imagine there will never be a solution to solve our many frustrating problems that causes loneliness. So I guess that it is just one of those things in which we have no alternative but to live with it.

LITTLE OLD LADIES I HAVE KNOWN.

Slowly I crept up on my unsuspecting victim as she toddled down the sidewalk. As she reached the curb I broke into a run and, grabbing her purse, shoved her into the path of an oncoming diesel that was trying to beat the light. As I pushed I felt a change coming over the old lady. Was it fear? For a split second I felt guilt, pitty and remorse then I realized that she had snatched her purse back and dropped into a karati stance. As I went flying towards the front of the truck I wondered sadly why it always had to be me.

First there had been the little old lady that I had tried to role in an alley one night. This didn't work out so well as she had a large doberman pincher with her who seemed to like nothing better than to chew on parts of my body. That was the first but not the last. There was the old dame who thought she was Anney

Okley, I still carry two thirty eight slugs in my left leg from that one. Then some near sighted old gall short changed me while I was trying to do the same to her. There were more too but their memories are painful so I will not mention any more.

It will be sufficient, I believe to mention some of the changes that had come over me in the last six months. I went from one seventy to a scrawney one eleven. My suites, formally the best the salvation army had to offer, are now rags. I no longer eat hamburger every day but I do find a half full can of greavy train now and then. My life was a wreck and now the final blow.

As I pulled myself off the grill of the truck at the next stoplight and clawed my way over to the gutter I knew that this had been my last caper. Yes from now on I decided to put my experience to good use and become an English teacher.

THE PERFECT GIRL

My idea of the perfect girl is as follows:

I'll call her Bridgette Annalee Devine, because when I got through with her, her initials would fit, B.A.D., bad.

She would have Sophia Loren's eyes, Bridgette Bardot's nose, Elizabeth Taylor's lips, Audrey Hepburn's neck, Vanessa Redgrave's body with Jayne Mansfield's breasts, Angie Dickinson's legs, and my 16 year old cousin's vagina.

She would have Jackie Kennedy's clothing tastes, Princess Ann's grace, Queen Mary's class, Greta Garbo's smile, Ann Margret's hair and laugh, Sandra Dee's complexion, Tuesday Weld's sex drive, and Christine Jorgenson's morals.

She would come from a country farm in Tennessee or Oklahoma, have an accent like Wanda Jackson, own a colonial mansion in Venice, a winter cottage in Switzerland, a summer bungalow on the French and Italian Rivieras, a penthouse in New York, as much money as Fort Knox, A Rolls Silver Cloud, and XKE, a Cadillac El Dorado, a Buick Riviera, and a Maseratti or two for low-riding.

I would love this girl until bankrupt do we part.

This girl would have love only for me and praise the ground I walk on. My every whim and wish would be her command, and if I decided to pimp her she'd strap on a Sealy Posturepedic, if I wanted to smuggle dope she would keister stash it, and last but not least, she would commit suicide when I tired of her.

EDUCATION

School is a farce, no jive. It's just a place to keep you out of trouble until you get a job. I mean, what better way to prepare you to face a hard job than to make you sit on your can day in and day out for twelve stinking years.

Fuck the world!---

Who cares about Bonaparte's Retreat or that Chris discovered the U.S. Big deal, he could have done it a hell of a lot faster if he had waited for Wilbur and Oliver Wright. And even they were crackpots. Why did they fly those unsafe rickety planes when they could have built a slew of X 15s and conquered the world, we'd have no wars now.

Live right with L.ovely S.ort of D.eath---------------------------

G. Washington was the Father of our country. Boy was he a fool. Yet in church they say Jesus is. Whose to believe what?

Things go better with White Port--------------------------------

So big G. was our first president, I don't give a fuck about yesteryear. Who is Mr. P. now? If it's another Abe, send him to the grave.

Girls are for reproduction. Fatbutt boys are for fun! -------------

So everyone's had a war or two, we need them to decide who is bossman.

Long live Hitler. Sieg heil!--

Who cares about learning to plan for the future. Live for today, tomorrow you might be dead. Why worry about the future gererations, they aren't worried about us.

Use 45 automatics, they have sex appeal! ---------------------------

What for are we fighting in Viet Nam. Let them fight their own battles. So Russia wants to dominate the world. It might be better who knows.

Down with Up!--

123

Yeah, school is waste. Send me back to the flower garden and let me geeje on acid. I burnt my draft card, set in the streets in protest, live in my one room bath, drive a skate board, lost my citizenship, and don't give a fuck.

Vote for dope and perverted sex!---

The Yanks won the Civil war. Big deal! If they had lost there'd have been no Watts rioting. Abe's for slaves. So what, remember the Alamo, who cares who gets Texas. I'm sick of those Texas jokes anyway.

Eleanor Roosevelt is a hophead!---

The rate of violent crimes is rising. So what, I believe in the Golden Yardstick, "Do unto others before they do it to you."

Christine Jorgensen for president! ---

VIOLENCE—A RELEASE OF INHIBITIONS AND ANXIETIES?

In our society, one reads, hears and sees through motion pictures that "America—The land of the free, Equal opportunity, free enterprize etc." This is a fantasy for children and foreigners who are not aware either through maturity, or just the cold facts of working for a living.

The democrats through President Johnson, voice a platform of "You never had it so good." Yet, a block away "Americans" are protesting the war and numerous other issues. True—we are fortunate to be one of the best paid peoples in the world. But, the cost of living is so high that many people are over drawn or paying interest on a loan they could not afford.

This is one of the many aspects of the "free-American" way of life. The news media of today is fantastic. This indeed forms public opinion and as such is fairly truthful in most eyes of Americans. It is commonplace today to see on the news a situation as I will describe: Till a short time ago, few were informed to the Biafarian Struggle in Africa. CBS News on TV showed a commentary on the spot of a suspected Biafarian soldier who was just captured. Under British rule this portion was of

English speaking people. In the brush country, it shows the captor, captured and newsman.

The captured, hand bound speaks in broken English, he is in his teens or early twenties.

"No, I am not Biafarian soldier, I look for my father and mother. No kill me. No kill me."

News commentator talks to captor and tells captured: "Do not worry, he will not kill you, you are a prisoner, do not worry."

"Sit down on the ground" shouts the captor.

"Do not kill, Do not kill" pleads the captured.

Two men bind the feet of the captured! You see the shadow of the captor on the ground as he raises his arm. The barrel of his rifle comes into view as he fires a short burst. The prisoner is dead.

Beads of perspiration built upon my hands as I watched this murder on television. There was no script, no dress rehearsal, just murder. A hate for authority immediately arroused in the pit of my stomach. For after all, I am the captured and custody is my captor.

This happens in America, names and places change, but conditions do not --

WIVES

What are some of the advantages in marriage? Hell, that's what I'd like to know. So far the only thing I've liked is the small club we joined, called S.F.M.S. San Francisco Mate Swappers.

l don't like coming home from work or the races to go through the lipstick, perfume, longhair on coat inspection. I don't like the breath test. I am a member in good standing of the Boozer's Forever Club and have to drink socially to uphold my membership.

I have on several occasions, been notified that the little lady has slightly ($156?) overdrawn. Les Vogel's Chevrolet has called to say our car is fixed and would we like for them to deliver it. Who did she claim borrowed it for a week?

125

What I really appreciate is coming home from work to an empty home, getting settled with the TV and have next door neighbor call to let me know she has the baby and the little lady is downtown shopping.

Or I go to park in the garage and the little lady is entertaining guests who decide its safer to park in the drive.

But what is the most invirgorating sight of each day is bright and early in the morning. Upon waking I generally gaze at a short wave receiver set attached to the top of the little lady's head and a dark blue and snow white thing she calls her face. It takes willpower, nerve, and a strong stomach to crawl in the sack with that.

THE STRANGER

I stepped out of the taxi, paid the driver, and stood on the wet pavement while the car pulled away from the curb. As I looked up at the face of the biggest apartment house in New York, I realized how small and unimportant I was. It was early March and the weather man had been promising fair weather, only to be proven wrong by the vicious and angry clouds, which keep the city in darkness 24 hours a day.

I started to climb the steps that lead to the main entrance, when a cold lashing wind made me stop in the middle of my ascent, to gain support from the hand rail. I pulled the collar of my overcoat, so that it would help protect my flushed face, which felt as if it had been slapped. The sudden blast of air died as quickly as it had risen.

I continued up the stairs a little faster than I had before. I felt myself grow more tense as I neared the top, I felt as if I was in flight from an evil force, and I could only be safe when I had reached the front door.

I reached the top of the stairs and entered the building. Once inside I felt the warmth of the building as a baby feels the warmth of his mother's womb. The building seemed to penetrate into every pore of my body. Slowly the numbness, brought by the bitter weather, was replaced by a languished warmth.

I took off the wet overcoat, which seemed to be the only part of me still holding on the cold and wet brought on by the storm. As I gave it to the check girl at the cloakroom, I heard the great clouds crash and thunder with all the fury and wrath of God himself.

I walked over to one of the front windows, and was looking at the outside, when the whole city lit up as if it had been a miniature city in a box, and someone decided to check on it.

When the flash had passed the rain began to fall once more, the only difference was that now I was safely concealed from the cold dampness, the evil enemy which had chased me up the steps and lost. I was warm and inside a shelter, watching the storm find more victims to prey upon.

HOW TO GET ALONG WITH WOMEN

Getting along with women is really quite easy. Women are very demanding creatures. They demand your time, your attention, your affection, and most of all your money. The first rule in getting along with women is never let them think their making you do something you don't really want to do.

Once a woman finds out that she can make you do thing against your better judgment your cooked, She'll do one of two things; she'll use you to any extent, or she'll find someone else more dominant. Most women seek security although they don't show it. They like to feel that their in safe care, many times they'll put up arguments, but as long as your set in your ways you'll never have trouble with them.

Some women will purposely irritate men too see which one has the most patience. If they are to have any children they want a man who'll be a good father.

Remember at all time that your a man, your the strong sex. At all times watch yourself, women scrutinize men very carefully, every where you go and at all times. In a sense your on 24hrs observation, their always watching your habits and traits, and you must be sure to show the best side of your personality.

First appearance is always something to be very careful of. If your out to win friends you don't run around with your hair unkempted, perspiration stains on your shirt, dirty pants, and stale breath.

Your physical fitness is another great asset. A man who can't keep himself in good condition surely can't help someone else. You must at all times be polite and show good manners. When you first meet a woman you must be sure you don't fall all over yourself. Women love praise and thrive on men looking at them in awe. But very seldom will they fall for any of the worshippers. On your first aquaintance with a woman be polite in the introduction but show little or no interest in the woman or women.

Like any other intelligent animal, women are curious, more so if I may go as far as to speak my personal feeling. The more curious you can make a woman the more she's going to lower her defenses. If you play your cards right, she'll make a pass at you, which is a whole lot better, and in many cases saves a man's ego.

Your most important test will be in bed. Most women will go to bed with a man because he has made her curious, she would like to see how good of a lover or mate this particular person is. If a man can satisfy a women in bed, she is very likely to over look his little faults. The bed is one place where you can make a woman feel secure. If you are able to make her reach her climax, she is immediately your friend. The more exciting you make the act of love in bed the more stimulating you become to her.

Reading all this won't make you a Rudolph Valentino, but with practice, it will make you very successful with women, and with them is better than against them.

UNTITLED STUDENT PARODY

It was the night before Christmas and all through the pen not an inmate was stirring in the cellblocks so grim.

The keys were all hung and the cons were locked up tight in hope no fool would try to make a break this night.

The guards in the towers held their guns in their hand, waiting for a convict to use a fool-proof plan.

While me and my hand-book and my cellie on my lap we had just settled down for this long winter nap.

When out on the yard there arose such a bang, I rose from my bed using all kinds of slang.

Looking out of the window at the new fallen snow, I gazed in wonder at two running objects below.

In the towers they were shooting, it was a deafing sound, then I saw the two escape runners come down with a bound.

The guards drove out to where the two bodies lay, and threw them in a truck like a man bailing hay.

But as the guards turned around the bodies arose, and they both laid their fist by the guards' fat nose.

I heard the cons exclaims as they drove out of sight, "So long suckers, I'm going home this Christmas night."

IS IT ANY USE

Life, that is so quickly over, is of little use. When we are gone who will remember us? Sure, for a few months or years people will say.

Yes, he was a good old boy, or I wonder what he's doing now.

But it doesn't take long for the microscopic gap that is left by our passing to be filled with other things and other people.

Even so with iron door closed behind us It wouldn't be *too* bad if we knew to where we are going.

Can death be compared with going to the Joint?

Do we know where we are going?

I don't. My plans for the future are constantly changing. What I want and like battle in me against what I know is right. But is it right? What is right for John Doe Citizen may not necessarily be right for me.

Didn't I fill a need in society? Without the criminal how many people would be out of work? Let's see, part of the police force some insurance personel, some lawyers, private dicks, and alarm company employees to name a few. Also all of the C.D.C. people and others who live off of them. Does this justify a life of crime?

CHAPTER 8

Prison is a place where you hate through clenched teeth, where you want to beat and choke and scratch. But just often as not you wonder if the psychologists know what they're talking about when they say you actually hate yourself.

From Student Theme

After Draper was forced out of the office of superintendent of education, the department was run by Mr. Bianca. As far as I could determine, there was no reason why Bianca should have been in charge of the education department. However, the warden delegated authority, and when power was loose, the most ambitious assistant grabbed it. Bianca was busy with his other duties and rarely paid a visit to the education area. However, anything involving decision making was referred to him. The job of administration was in the hands of Hugo Belson, who, as acting superintendent, didn't have any authority. Draper had accumulated nearly one year's sick leave during the twenty-seven years he had been in prison work. No new superintendent could be appointed until his sick leave ran out.

Belson would have liked the job of superintendent but was unable to pass the written examination for the job. Even though Belson was an ambitious man, there was no chance he could move up the ladder. In fairness to him, he was in the unenviable position of being the scapegoat if anything went wrong and unable to capitalize on his achievements if things went well.

Belson's response to this situation was to turn over the running of the education department to an inmate named Petoskey. This was, I believe, a brilliant thing for Belson to do. Inmate Petoskey had a genius for administration. He ran the daily routine like a maestro conducts a symphony. A phone call to him solved any problem.

Petoskey was a most unusual man. He had charm, wit and the ability of a top executive. He was thirty-six years old and was serving his first prison term. He was released from the service when he was twenty-four years old, and during the intervening twelve years he had never filed income tax or earned less than forty thousand per year. He was a con man extraordinaire.

In his early days in the education department, we were close friends. However, as his influence increased, mine diminished, and by the time he achieved his release we had only a nodding acquaintance. Although, I confess, he always treated me fairly and I never had any difficulty with him. He knew what he was doing. He ingratiated himself into the power structure and obtained his release from prison in one year, on a rap that could have cost a lesser man five to ten years.

When I first knew Petoskey, he was recently assigned to the job of clerk in the education department. He first approached me with plans to write a book about his experiences. He had already completed about twenty-five or thirty pages about a caper of his that had been chronicled by·a major syndicated columnist.

Petoskey managed to infiltrate the John F. Kennedy presidential primary campaign in California. Petoskey forged a pass and very easily became an important part of that political machine. He managed to get his picture in the *San Francisco Chronicle* walking right beside John Kennedy, posing as one of his trusted aides.

He gave briefings on certain aspects of Kennedy foreign policy to visiting congressmen, well-wishers, and contributors. He was also in charge of collecting a few thousand dollars in campaign funds, that went directly into his pocket; and he spent an entire evening on the town, entertaining Senator Smathers of Florida without mentioning there was a hold on him in that state for cashing a bad check totalling several thousand dollars.

Petoskey explained to me he loved that role more than any other he had ever assumed. He was an Irishman named Eddie with a sense of belonging, spirited conviviality, and power. Everybody loved him. He stated that he started out acting but later became the character he was portraying.

"If you felt that way, why did you steal the campaign funds?" I asked.

"I had to maintain the ethics of my profession," he said innocently.

A television producer offered him six thousand for the rights to dramatize this incident. He showed me the letter and the contract they offered him, and asked my advice about what to do. I advised him to sell it to them fast. However, he was reluctant to do this. He didn't need the money because he apparently had enough stashed away. Too, the state would claim 25% of any money he received, and he considered that a monstrous rip off. I don't know what he finally did about the offer, but I doubt the incident ever appeared on television.

He could write intelligently, and I thought a book by him could be sold to a publisher, using this story as the lead item. We spent the hour after my last class, which ended at 3:30, discussing the material he had assembled, until he had to go back to his unit for recall and count.

Petoskey was raised by two maiden aunts who spoiled him outrageously. He served in the marines, where he started running crooked dice games. After his discharge, he spent two years at a small California college. However, his acquisitive nature and curiosity were not whetted by academic life. He had a desire to operate beyond the law. He was a talented and complicated man and it was difficult for me to understand why he deliberately chose dishonesty.

For instance, he described how he would frequent the bars in the Los Angeles area looking for a married woman on the prowl.

He would take the woman to a motel and, after making love, when she was in the shower, he would go through her purse and take money, jewelry, watches, everything she had. He would wait for her to come out of the bathroom, and then he would confront her with what he was doing. The response was invariably the same, and it came in stages: disbelief, anger, a threat to call the police or husband.

He would pick up the phone and graciously hand it to his betoweled victim, "Fine, call your husband or the police and explain everything."

The woman, of course, could not do this, and he got his kicks out of watching her squirm. He openly admitted it was a twisted and vicious thing to do and attributed the pleasure he derived from this act as a very satisfactory ventilation of the hatred he had for the self-righteous women who had brought him up.

He was without remorse, and felt he was more effective in pointing out the evils of adultery than Billy Graham. He was quick to assert his primary desire in these encounters was not money, and that later he outgrew his need to indulge in this kind of behavior.

Petoskey had a compendious knowledge of banking procedures. He read banking journals and kept up with changes in the industry. In one scheme, he would go to a major airport and spot people who were paying for their tickets by check. One quick glance would give him the name, address, numbers on the check.

When he had collected information on a number of people, he would drive to Las Vegas, where he knew a printer who specialized in making false identification, including drivers' licenses and credit cards.

He would then go to the cities where his marks lived to check out how much money each had in the bank. He called the bank where his mark had his checking account, posing as an airlines clerk. He claimed the mark wanted to write a rather large check and the airlines would accept it if there were sufficient funds in the bank to cover it. If he was clever enough, he could get the exact amount on deposit at the time. If there weren't sufficient funds to cover his stated amount, he would put the name aside

134

and try it later in the month after additional deposits had been made.

After he had the identification and knew how much was in the account, the rest was easy. He simply went to a branch of the bank where the account was and showed his identification, invented a story, received an interbranch check and cashed it. He claimed he never was apprehended during his operations in this field, which was limited only by the preparation and hard work involved. In a good week, he could make five thousand dollars. Of course, he did not work every week. He claimed that people are caught when they duplicate a pattern, lose confidence in themselves, or become careless. Also, banks, from time to time, change their procedures. When new precautions were introduced, he had to come up with alternative methods of circumventing them.

The cashing of interbranch checks was his bread-and-butter income. However, he perpetrated many different swindles and frauds. He unquestionably enjoyed living by his wits and assuming many different identities. At one point, he even took a legitimate job selling aluminum siding. He threw himself into this job with characteristic zeal and quickly became a top salesman, earning approximately twenty thousand dollars in a little more than four months.

When I asked him why he quit, he explained he had used false credentials to get the job, but had been forced to fill out income tax and social security forms and was afraid of being discovered by the Internal Revenue Service. He also claimed he became tired of that identity and wanted another change. He simply picked up his last check and walked away.

He described how he once swindled a Mafia chieftain in Chicago out of $25,000. I questioned him closely about this, wondering if he didn't run the risk of being killed. He claimed not. The man was too embarrassed to want to admit he had been taken. He claimed Mafia people were not sharp and were easily tricked.

I speculated a publisher might be fascinated by the incident, but wondered if publicly gloating about it might not bring a

135

violent end to his illustrious career. His first reaction was to deny it would cause any difficulty; however, later he showed some anxiety and decided to tone it down.

I questioned him if he had ever done anything that made him feel guilty. He claimed he felt no remorse about any of his criminal activities, but he had done one thing that made him feel ashamed. At first, he wouldn't tell me what it was.

"I'm not your psychiatrist. Don't tell me anything you wouldn't want published," I said.

A few days later he decided to tell me of his evil deed. When he told me about it, he was in a state of high agitation, unusual for him. He had decided to marry a Catholic girl from Chicago. He was not a Catholic himself, and rather than go through the lengthy and difficult conversion process, he assumed a new identity and forged baptismal papers, confirmation, and all the other things necessary to qualify him for a wedding in the Catholic Church.

I, at first, did not comprehend why this forgery was disturbing to him. He explained that in every other incident he'd had contempt for the people he ripped off. In his mind, they were always greedy or dishonest themselves. In this case, however, it was not the priest or any church official who was damaged or punished by his actions. If there was any injury, it could only be to himself.

He was arrested for the first time shortly after his marriage broke up. He had been drinking and was driving erratically when a policeman stopped him on the Oakland Bay Bridge. The policeman checked out his driver's license and found it was false. His car was searched and several checks and false identities were found.

After consultation with his lawyer, Petoskey decided to plead guilty to one minor charge, in exchange for the dismissal of the many other charges against him. For the first time, there was a picture of him, and the California police were able to close their books on many forgeries.

Petoskey talked freely about his escapades and took great pleasure in relating the intricacies of his operations. Even the judge remarked he was the cleverest man he had ever encountered. Since it was his first arrest and conviction, he received a six-months-to-life sentence.

Petoskey gave the impression of great honesty and sincerity. He was, of course, by conventional standards, an outrageous liar. Petoskey claimed he was never caught in a lie and, in fact, did not lie.

Most people, when they lie, are caught in a maze of contradictions. This did not happen to Petoskey, because he became completely submerged in the character he was playing. When his marriage broke up, he lost his confidence and could no longer function well in his profession. He found it impossible to assume other identities.

He was new to prison, vulnerable and easy to talk to when I first knew him. As his confidence returned, he gradually took over the education department. He had a genius for getting along with people, and since he was an inmate, there was no chance he could threaten Belson's job.

He made up class rosters and assigned men to classes. He handled all complaints and transferred students on his word alone. We teachers had the right to go over his head and discuss his decisions with Belson. But Petoskey was always reasonable and, to my knowledge, no teacher ever found it necessary to dispute him. He reorganized the control system so that absent students were tracked down and accounted for immediately.

He designed an efficient system for filling out records and putting on grades. We had two days allotted at the end of each term for compiling these records. Before Petoskey, it was not long enough to get everything done. We were forever standing in line and spending hours hunting down missing files.

Petoskey came up with a system whereby we announced beforehand when we wanted to put on grades. At the appointed time, an inmate appeared with all the records in a cart. Petoskey even arranged for inmate assistants to help us. He reduced the two-day task to a two-hour one, and the rest of the allotted time was like a holiday.

Petoskey also became interested in Title I funds, and he and an administrator from the nearby high school district drew up a proposal that would have allocated $150,000 in funds for the prison education department.

Belson and Petoskey got along famously. Petoskey had his chance to play with "big money" again, and Belson could gaze vacantly out the window, confident his carefully chosen helmsman would properly steer the ship.

Belson did go to bat for Petoskey and it helped with the quick parole. We had a little party for Petoskey in the education department the day before his release. Belson produced a large cake and we all had a fruit juice punch.

At the time, there was a story in the newspapers about a California woman, mother of seven, who was given the same sentence Petoskey received for writing a $70.00 check with insufficient funds. The journalist who wrote the story pointed out the cost to the state in child support payments and incarceration would cost more than $20,000.

I discussed this case with Petoskey at his going away party. To me, there was a discrepancy in justice that allowed a woman who bounced a check in a supermarket when she was trying to feed her family to get the same sentence as a professional bad-check artist who had ripped off the banks for hundreds of thousands of dollars.

When I mentioned this apparent injustice to Petoskey, he clasped his arm around me and said, "Mr. Campbell, you have no conception of the way the world is. You stubbornly cling to the mythology of the way it should be. The best of your kind must be put on the cross, forced to drink the hemlock, or take a bullet in the head."

This was part of the genius of Petoskey; he flattered me by placing me in such exalted company. While, at the same time, he demolished me.

"You have to understand the nature of bankers," he continued. "They are the pederasts of the body politic. They are greedy, vicious, cruel and self-righteous. But they understand the world and how to operate in it. Don't get me wrong, I like bankers. I understand how they think, and that is why I could operate successfully beating their system.

"Look at it this way. Where do banks lose their money? To professional operators who at great risk to themselves surgically extract sums of money from them? Certainly not. We, in fact, provide a service for them. We continually test their systems, just as you place a boat in water to see where it needs caulking. If the leak is small enough, they don't even bother with it, because it would cost them a hundred times the amount that dribbles out to stop it. For example, adding the salaries and pension plans of three new security guards would cost them more than I ever received from them in any given year.

"Eventually, they catch us anyway. We grow careless or soft and they have to develop a new crop of con men to help them evaluate their security systems. No, the person who costs them the most money is their average customer, the inefficient, careless housewife who blunders against their tidy record keeping.

"It's this woman they despise. She can't be bought off, like a rates commission or a fat politician. Almost every lawmaker in the land has his campaign financed by a banking institution. Is this because banks care about justice? They don't give a fiddler's fuck about justice. They care about the bottom line—profit.

"They can't ignore or deny this pitiful housewife, because they need her money, multiplied 30 million times, to practice usury on the home owner, and to finance giant corporations to rip off people throughout the world.

"Bankers are beautiful. They terrorize their customers from whom collectively they derive their power. Why, if they had their way, they would rip the housewife's tongue out, cut her arms off, and have her stand like a scarecrow in front of their largest lending institution, writing with her toes this message, 'Forgive me, Mr. Bank President, for I have sinned. My desire to feed my children was so strong that I wrote a check for insufficient funds against your great institution.' It would clear up 85 percent of their delinquent accounts immediately.

"Bankers don't hate people like me. We understand each other.

139

I could, upon release, go to almost any bank in the country and offer my services to improve their security system. They would accept me immediately, with great relief and joy, and pay me well to have me on their side.

"As for that lady on welfare, when she gets out of jail do you think the bank will welcome her back? They won't even let her open an account with them. They hate her guts."

Such was the swollen ego of Petoskey, the best damned school administrator I ever served under. He left our prison for a federal joint on Treasure Island, where he had to serve an additional month. Several months later we got a postcard from Florida, announcing he was happy and prosperous and inviting us to visit him if we ever had the money to take a trip to Florida.

Petoskey's inmate assistant, Barnstable, was a handsome, soft-spoken young man who had spent one year in theological seminary before he went to prison. His prison-tested IQ was the highest among all the inmates in the institution. He was an intellectual, musically talented and a devoted Christian.

He was in jail for the ax murder of his mother, father, brother and two sisters. He had spent more than a year on Death Row before getting his sentence commuted to life imprisonment.

Ronald Reagan had campaigned strongly in favor of capital punishment. Governor Brown reviewed the sentences of the more than seventy men on Death Row and commuted a handful of sentences to life imprisonment before his term expired. Barnstable was one of these men. Because of his youth, he was not sent to Folsom Prison, where most long timers were housed. It would be several years before he was ready for that environment.

Barnstable stopped by to talk with me from time to time. Although we were never close friends, I did enjoy these chats. Barnstable was fascinated by Martin Luther and his theological views. He was also much interested in Luther as a composer and considered him a genius in the field of music as well as theology.

I encouraged Barstable to write, but to no avail. He had a precise mind and was not given to flights of fancy. This explains why he worked well with Petoskey. The one had the idea, and the other worked it out in complete detail.

140

I suggested he write what it was like to be on Death Row. He replied that it was boring and had already been described by Caryl Chessman. He had no interest in reliving this experience.

He was always considerate and cheerful. He did not back away from a discussion of his crime; although, since he had no memory of it, there wasn't much information that could be gleaned. I did read his arrest jacket in Central Files and this, as I recall it, is the story.

Late one afternoon Barstable pulled up in front of his house with his girl friend. He left the girl in the car and went inside to change his clothes. He walked into his parents' bedroom and surprised them in the act of making love. At this point he went berserk, grabbed an ax and chopped to death all the members of his family. He then appeared at the door, ax in hand, and walked into the yard, his clothes spotted with gore. When the police arrived he was in a daze.

Initially he confessed to the crime and described it in detail. The psychiatric reports were primarily concerned with establishing his sanity. There was the conventional scenario that he had suppressed a deep hatred toward his family; and, when it surfaced, he lost control. Perhaps an extensive psychiatric study of him had been done, but it wasn't in his file. Since he was sentenced to die in the gas chamber, no psychiatric examination was given to him once he went to prison. Why study a dead man?

After his sentence was commuted to life, he was fed back into the prison population, where he functioned without difficulty. No further examination was necessary.

I did not attempt to deeply probe his mind because I was certain I was not qualified to judge his reactions. Most people can be helped by facing their problems realistically. But is this true of someone who has committed patricide, matricide, fratricide and sororicide?

"Did you hate your family?" I asked.

"No, I loved them," he said. "We were a happy family."

"You're familiar with Hindu philosophy," I said. "Was it like Siva the Destroyer coming down and laying everything waste?"

141

"No, I am a Christian. I don't believe in such things."

"Could it have been a demon?" I asked.

"No. I don't believe so. I know you will find this difficult to believe, but I'm certain I didn't commit this crime. I have no memory of what happened. The entire episode is blanked out. There's no way I can retrieve what happened."

"You confessed to the crime, didn't you?"

"Yes, I did. I guess I was horrified when I saw what had happened and my mind played tricks on me."

"If you didn't do it, then someone else did. Do you know who the person was?"

"Yes, I do."

"Are you shielding someone?"

"I'm absolutely certain I never killed anyone," he said, refusing to answer my question directly.

"OK," I said, dismissing the subject.

"I have discussed the matter with my minister, and he, too, is convinced of my innocence," he said.

"What about a psychiatrist?" I asked. "Have you talked to one since you've been in jail?"

"No, not since before the trial."

"Would you like to do that?"

"I wouldn't mind," Barnstable said.

Later I talked to a counsellor about getting a psychiatrist for him.

"Why bother?" the counselor asked.

"What do you mean, why bother?" I asked.

"Why bother," he repeated. "With a crime like his, he's never going to get out of jail. He functions beautifully in a prison setting. Why poke around with his mind and get him all upset?"

"He's bright and he's perceptive. Maybe a psychiatrist, by working with him, could learn something about how the human mind functions. Maybe the psychiatrist could discover how to identify people like Barnstable before they pop off, and stop some completely senseless crimes."

"They have enough to do, working with men who are getting out of jail."

142

"Hell," I said, "I used to meet a lot of graduate students getting their Ph.D.'s in psychology. They were always making out questionnaires on trivial subjects, passing them out to hundreds of people, and then codifying and classifying the responses. Why don't they stop that silliness and come into our prisons and study men like Barnstable?"

"That's not the way the system operates," the counselor replied.

Barnstable was present at the going-away party we had for Petoskey. There, Belson put his arm around Barnstable and said, "I want you to know this young man is the bravest person I have known." Then Belson went on to relate how, a few months previously, Barnstable's life had been threatened if he didn't agree to falsify some academic records. Barnstable had mentioned to Belson he was under heavy pressure but wouldn't reveal who was trying to intimidate him.

If Belson called in the person who had threatened Barnstable and dressed him down, it would mean death for Barnstable. If Barnstable were clearly identified as a "snitch" who went to the "Man" when he was pressured, eventually he would be killed. Probably the murder wouldn't happen in this prison, but if he were transferred to Folsom, his "snitch record" would follow via the grapevine, and someone there who didn't know him would be appointed to "take his head."

Belson had some options open to him. He could transfer Barnstable out of the education department, so that he no longer had access to records and couldn't possibly alter them, or he could arrange a transfer to another prison. However, Barnstable liked his job and elected to stay on. Eventually, the crisis passed.

It is doubtful the threat was as serious as Belson claimed. Belson had the habit of overdramatizing every incident. He did not verify assertions. If the story fitted his prejudices, he accepted it without question. No amount of logic or factual refutation could force him to change his mind.

Early in my prison teaching, he was concerned I might be bringing marijuana to my students. The young English teacher I replaced readily admitted to his students he used marijuana

143

himself, and Belson was convinced he used it in prison. There was no evidence to support this; and yet Belson persisted in telling undocumented stories.

Although Belson never directly accused me of bringing in marijuana, I did pick up "snitch rumors" from time to time that he believed I didn't have disciplinary problems because I was using pot as a pacifier. He had made comments to other teachers that there was no way anyone could make him believe I kept my classes in good order by having them sitting around discussing Greek philosophy.

Belson didn't come in to my classes to observe what was taking place. Countless times, I extended an invitation to him, but he always found an excuse to stay away. Very honestly, he admitted English was his weakest subject. He thought teaching students how to diagram sentences was the most marvelous thing an English teacher could do. When I pressed him to tell me why, he replied, "Because I never learned how to do that myself. If some English teacher had grabbed me when I was a kid and rubbed my nose in a grammar book, I might have learned something. Then I wouldn't be stuck in a hellhole like this ..."

I didn't know where to begin to counter this argument. I felt like a doctor who has made an incision and found a terminally cancerous condition. The only thing I could do was sew up the incision and silently shake my head. Undoubtedly, my attitude infuriated him.

My room was searched by the guards at night almost every week. Once, in a surprise raid, all my students were stripped naked and the classroom was thoroughly searched. There was nothing I could do to protest this because, in prison, custody rules. What distressed me was that no one in authority was willing to even entertain the thought that I might be educating my students.

Belson suspected me of trafficking in marijuana because of an incident that happened a few months after I had started teaching.

Mrs. Svenson, another English teacher, who was hired at the same time I was, discussed the possibility of having a debate

144

between our two morning classes. Her classroom was on the first floor near the administration offices, and right next to a large room that was used as a projection room and for meetings. It had a raised platform with a piano on it. All we had to do was move the piano to one side, and we had an ideal stage for our debate with plenty of seats for our combined classes.

We approached Belson for permission to use the room for our debate. Mrs. Svenson, who was more diplomatic than I, presented our case. Debate was a worthwhile educational tool taught in most high schools throughout the country. By allowing us to have a debate, he would enable us to upgrade the curriculum and create a healthy spirit of competition between our two classes. Belson could take pride that he was encouraging innovation in the classroom.

Belson responded favorably to our request. His main concern was that combining our classes might lead to an incident and he would have to explain why he allowed the debate to take place.

We explained to him classes were combined when films were shown, and the students were in a darkened room. Our debate, of course, would be conducted in a full light. Mrs. Svenson and I willingly agreed to take full responsibility for the conduct of our classes. Belson, who only recently was acting as head of the education department, agreed to the debate.

There was high interest in it. Our classes made up a list of twenty topics and by class vote decided on two: "Resolved: Marijuana Should Be Legalized" and "Resolved: Crime Does Pay."

My class had the affirmative on both issues. Since no prisoner would openly say marijuana should not be legalized, I had some concern about developing a good debate around the first topic. However, the students quickly grasped that a debate was not a search for the truth, but a con where the cleverest person won. Both of the young men arguing against the legalization of marijuana had been busted at one time for using it. Neither of them had seen the error of their ways, but they saw a chance to win an argument by confounding their opponents and took pleasure mouthing arguments contrary to their beliefs.

Much good-natured kidding sprang up between the two classes, and my students were determined to clobber the opposition. They managed to accumulate a staggering amount of material to support legalization. They wrote letters home, and mothers, brothers, wives, girl friends did legwork for them; the documentation flowed in.

They had medical reports, statements from judges, lawyers, doctors and celebrities. They collected several hundred pages of research material. They even came up with a pamphlet issued by the government printing office under the imprint of the Department of Agriculture that showed how to plant, cultivate and cure marijuana. It was distributed, upon request, to anyone in the country.

I outlined the procedure for the debate, allowing time for presentation and rebuttal. I also offered to help the team sharpen their arguments, but they resisted my aid.

The morning of the debate, the participants wore their highly starched denims and spit-polished shoes. We met in my classroom, where I checked the roll, before repairing to the debating room. I gave them a little speech, complimenting them on their hard work and wishing them well. I also pointed out they were breaking new ground and that, if things went successfully, debates could be included in the curriculum on a regular basis.

When we arrived, Mrs. Svenson's class was already there. They were seated on the left side of the room, and my students took the right side. It was assumed Mrs. Svenson and I would serve as judges for the debate. However, I was overwhelmed by such a feeling of partisanship for my students I knew I could not function as a judge.

I bolted out the door, raced up the stairs, ran down the corridor to the newspaper room, where I confronted Barney and recruited him to judge the debate for us. I explained all he had to do was to judge on the basis of how the debaters presented their arguments, rather than on his personal beliefs about the issues involved. He agreed to do this.

After a brief consultation, Mrs. Svenson made the announcement that Barney Culligan, the editor of the newspaper, had

146

agreed to be the impartial judge. The debate began on the first issue: "Resolved: Marijuana Should Be Legalized."

My affirmative speakers ran into difficulties in their opening remarks. One speaker was cut off by the timekeeper in the midst of reading a longish article from a major magazine. This debater was an expert in the field of marijuana, but he had too much material at his command to function well in the highly stylized arena of debate. The rebuttal went much better. My men tore apart the arguments that it should not be legalized and, I thought, won the debate.

The second debate immediately followed and was a different story. I had no idea how my debaters would handle the topic "Crime Does Pay." James Arthur Barkham had agreed to take the affirmative on this issue. Barkham was a loner, a shy person who made no attempt to get along with his peer group. He was soft-spoken and from a cultured background. His father was a lieutenant commander in the navy and his mother, I believe, had been a schoolteacher.

He had been involved in many scrapes with the law and was presently serving time for parole violation. He was brilliant, and it was difficult to imagine why he had not received a high school diploma. He wrote well and had a keen, analytical mind. Many of his short written pieces I used in my classes for discussion.

One story he wrote, which always generated a good discussion, concerned a group of young men and women, all high on LSD. They were hungry (apparently this drug increases appetite) and they wanted someone in their group to get food for them. They had money, but their problem was, entering a market to purchase food was like entering a brightly lit, crazy forest. All the gaily decorated packages made them trip out, and they became trapped in their surroundings.

One woman finally agreed to make an attempt at it. She walked into the store, moving like a mechanical robot. Once inside, the colors proved too much for her and she got lost. She threshed around and finally managed to stumble outside, where she collapsed under a large neon sign. She had a peaceful, spaced-out smile on her face and every time the sign flashed on

147

she pulled her skirt over her head and said. "Awk." When the sign went off, she pulled her skirt back down again. Her friends split, leaving her to face fate.

The scene was well written, and the incident was real. Whenever I read it to a class, some students thought the people who ran away were rats. She had risked much to help them, and they had abandoned her. Others felt she was a dumb broad and there was no obligation to rescue her.

He wrote another story after a discussion about mercy killings and extermination of undesirables in institutions. We were talking about people who cannot feed, dress or take care of themselves—people who are no better than vegetables. We discussed whether humans like this should be put to death. Most of my students were opposed to taking human life, no matter how hopeless the situation was. This is understandable when you realize that when a nation starts killing its undesirables, men in prison are candidates for extinction.

We had an interesting discussion and Barkham wrote his story. It concerned a person who could neither talk nor hear, who led a vegetablelike existence in a hospital.

Although the vegetable couldn't communicate with the people who took care of him, he developed great affection for them. He had a superior brain and learned how to extract all kinds of scientific data from the way sunlight filtered into his room. He also observed the stars at night and had determined things about their orbits that would have changed man's fundamental concept of the universe. However, there was no way he could communicate his findings to those who were taking care of him.

At the end of the story, the vegetable senses they are going to destroy him. His great mathematical brain cannot comprehend why they would. If they took care of him for a number of years, why would they suddenly change? He can only comprehend that something terrible had happened in their world, but he can't figure out what it is. He goes to his death, wondering why these strange creatures whom he loved and who, he thought, loved him must destroy him.

I was impressed with the story and made an attempt to send it to someone in the Department of Corrections who was planning a literary magazine for California inmates. It had to be approved by prison officials before it could be submitted.

The story bounced back with Bianca's signature. "Obviously copied. Don't let students make a fool of you. Permission denied."

Barkham's entire life was like this. No matter what he did, no one would give him recognition. It is difficult to describe him. I would have to go back to the 1950s and James Dean for an example—the confused, ineffectual rebel without a cause, who didn't seem capable of accomplishing anything. However, give him a cause, and he could stagger you with his dramatic power.

When Barkham delivered his debate, it was as if he had sucked up all the frustrations, and putdowns, and sanctimonious sons of bitches, and humiliations, and feelings of inadequacy, and helpless cryings in the night, and self-images rusted out and smashed worse than old jalopies in a junkyard, as if he had ground it all up in his belly and finally spat it all out, giving a new perspective to those who our society says, over and over, are lower than dirt and doomed to stay that way.

I will try to put down the words as I recall them. But what I can't duplicate is how a skinny, introverted young man put on a dramatic performance a skilled professional actor could never duplicate.

"Mr. Chairman, my worthy opponents, esteemed fellow students. We have before us today, the question: Does crime pay? Let there be no doubts in any of your minds. *Crime does pay.* It pays crooked judges, crooked lawyers, crooked policeman, G-Men, FBI men, deputy sheriffs, narc agents, parole officers, prison guards.

"It pays manufacturers of burglar alarms, pick-proof locks, safes, iron bars, tear gas, mace, pistols, billy clubs, patrol cars, lie detectors, handcuffs, the list goes on and on.

"Crime is the biggest industry in this country today. A crooked judge, appointed by a crooked politician, makes forty thousand per year. How many of you gentlemen ever made forty thousand in your entire career? Not one. The combined total of all the crimes committed by everyone in this room does not add up to forty thousand. One year's salary for a judge.

"That kind of money would be enough for you or me. We're all small-time hustlers, cheap crooks, and dumb bastards. We're only thinking of a few good things like a suit of clothes, a new car, a place to live, or a need to shake the monkey off our backs. But the judge is smarter than we are, and he is tougher than we are, and he strips us and our families of everything we have.

"How many of you, when you had the money for a lawyer, heard him say, 'If you can get together one thousand, two thousand, three thousand—I can make a deal with the judge and get you off without a sentence.' And if you got the money up, remember the scene in one of those expensive restaurants near the justice building. The judge and your mouthpiece pull out the information written on the back of an envelope, and when your case comes up on the docket, they say some mumbo jumbo about honesty and a second chance, and you go free. Does crime pay? You better believe it.

"And you think you're pretty big stuff yourself, because you got the judge in your pocket. The truth is, when you paid the money to the shyster, you got taken over by a pimp. You do the hustling, and he gets the money, and splits it with the judge. They're dishonest, and they're shrewd, and they're greedy, and they got no mercy at all.

"When you got no dough, and pull a public defender, the handcuffs bite into your wrists, and you get the bus ride to the joint. When you got too many busts, you're like a used-up whore, nobody is gonna touch.

"We are their crop—the bleeding bastards from the ghettos, and fucked up families. They make certain we're hungry, desperate, and ignorant. They don't want to drain the swamp because the swamp rats that come from it provide them with the fancy clothes, and the big money. They drive their 'hogs' to their estates, and have contempt for the scum they suck the life out of.

"Let's talk cold fact. You clean up the ghettos, you feed the people, and educate them, and you put them out of a job. You reward honesty, and punish dishonesty, and you put them behind

150

bars; and they ain't gonna have it. They got their license to steal; and they're going to keep it.

"You think that multibillion dollar crime industry wants you to straighten out your life? No way, man, no way. They throw you into the joint, where the losers teach you how to commit other crimes. When you learn from losers, you can't be a winner.

"Let's talk statistics. Eighty percent of us who walk out that gate walk right back in again. The twenty percent who don't come back are killed on the outside, or die of an overdose, or manage to escape to another state, where they get busted and appear in another state's statistics. We're nearly one hundred percent sure of becoming permanent raccoons in their expensive zoos. How's a man going to make it on the outside? Learn a trade in prison? Train on a printing press that was obsolete thirty years ago? Where are you going to get a printing job when you're out? In a museum?

"Who's going to hire the ex-con? You give a man fifty dollars, and a brown suit, and a parole officer who treats him like a piece of shit, and expect him to make it when he doesn't even have a job? No way, man.

"They know what they're doing. We're going to bounce right back through their courts, and keep them rolling in dough. That's the way they want it. It's like smearing turpentine on a dog, and cutting him loose. Hell, even the bitches won't go near him. Then they find him starving in the bushes, sickened by his own smell; and the dog catchers beat him, and haul him back again.

"They know what they're doing. There are always the same number under lock and key. When it's easy to make the busts, they open the gates and let us out. When arrests slow down, they hold us in a little longer. It's all planned.

"There's no way you can beat their system. There are thirty thousand people in jail in California. Suppose we all disappeared, would that end their crime problem? You know it wouldn't. They'd have the joints filled up again within a week. They might have to start bustin' drunks until they got into full production again. But don't worry, they would retool in a hurry.

151

"Crime is big business—and, it is a crime. The newspapers start headlining a few muggings on the streets, and what happens? They beef up the police force with uniformed thieves, who, systematically, shake down every shopkeeper in the precinct. When they do catch a mugger, they let him go. They need the boogey man on the streets, scaring hell out of the people, so they can continue their ripoff.

"I could go into dope, and how the police and politicians grow fat on it. It's raised in Turkey; and it's processed in France, right outside of Marseilles. The federal government could bring pressure to bear to close up those plants, any time they choose. They don't want to do it. They'd rather scream about how terrible it is and get their cut of the action.

"Crime does pay. That is the trouble. We all know people who do wrong should be punished; and people who are sick should be cured. Everyone agrees justice should be served. When an honest lawyer tries a case before an honest judge, justice can be saved. When society wants all its citizens leading productive lives regardless of the cost, then justice can be served. When judges, and policemen, and prison people, and politicians stop *making* money, and start *losing* money when crime is committed, then justice *will be served.* Then jails will become hospitals, and schools and counseling centers; and poverty and ignorance will disappear.

"Don't hold your breath. It isn't going to happen. The big crooks who put us here hate our guts. They despise us because they despise themselves. They know if they ever turned honest they would lose everything, and be worse off than we are.

"Does crime pay? Aw fuck it. You know the answer!"

James Arthur Barkham returned to his seat on the platform, amidst cheers from both sides of the room. The other speakers pointed out, in a conventional way, that robbery was no way to make a living.

Barkham's interpretation of the question had taken the opposition completely by surprise. Since nothing that Barkham had said was in dispute, the rebuttal was waived.

Mrs. Svenson went to the rostrum to congratulate the participants on an excellent debate, and I went over to Barney to get his decision. He looked scared when he handed me his score sheet.

"Mr. Campbell, you're not gonna like this," he said. He had judged Mrs. Svenson's class the winner of the debate on marijuana, and my class the winner of the debate on crime.

"Jesus," Barney said. "How did I let you suck me into being a judge? I could get shanked."

"You won't get shanked, but I should fire you," I said. "My team won that marijuana debate by a country mile."

"I judged it exactly the way you told me to do it," Barney said.

When I announced that the team arguing against the legalization of marijuana had won, a great cheer went up from Mrs. Svenson's class. My students were glum. When I announced that the winner of "Crime Does Pay" was the affirmative team, everyone cheered.

At this point, the bell rang and the students filed into the corridors on their smoke break. I went over to congratulate Mrs. Svenson's debaters: the lead speaker against the legalization of marijuana was shaking his head in disbelief. "If I write home and tell my mother I won a debate speaking against the use of pot, she won't believe it. She'll think you people beat me up or tortured me," he said, obviously enjoying his victory.

Mrs. Svenson and I were delighted by the success of our debates. They had gone better than either of us had anticipated. A few days later Mrs. Svenson and I were talking in my classroom when Belson paid us a visit.

"I have just heard some shocking stories about your debate," he said.

"What have you heard?" I asked

"I was told the students were making obscene gestures, fights broke out, and everything was in disorder."

"Why, that's not true," Mrs. Svenson said. "The students behaved themselves with perfect decorum. In all my years of teaching, I never saw a group conduct themselves any better."

"I heard they said lewd things to you, Mrs. Svenson, and neither you nor Campbell did anything about it."

153

"What's that?" I asked angrily. "I don't like being falsely accused."

"I don't know the specifics. I heard it was out of control and a chaotic mess," Belson said.

"That's not true. In fact, I believe our debate on marijuana was the greatest triumph of integrity I have ever witnessed."

"What's that?" Belson snapped. "You had a debate on marijuana? My God, why is it that English teachers are always all mixed up? It isn't your duty to tell these guys the law is right or wrong. You were hired to educate them, not encourage them to snivel."

"Wait a second," I said. "We didn't encourage them to use marijuana. The legalization of marijuana is a legitimate problem that our society must consider. They're part of society; and they have a right to debate the issue, same as anyone else."

"No, by God, you're wrong. These men have no rights at all. That's why they're in here. It's our duty to have them respect the law, not encourage them to believe the law is wrong."

"Listen to this," I said, changing my tack. "The men who argued against the legalization of marijuana won the debate. What do you think of that?"

"So you and Mrs. Svenson shot them down. Do you think they aren't able to see through that? Do you think that is going to educate them?"

"We didn't judge the debate. Barney Culligan did," I said.

"Culligan," Belson said incredulously. "It gets worse and worse. I shouldn't tell you this, but Culligan is the biggest wheeler and dealer in marijuana in the prison. For months, we've been trying to get the goods on him. But he's sneaky and clever as hell; and we can't catch him. Those people are just making ducks out of you."

"Barney wasn't running a game on me. It took integrity for him to make that decision," I said.

"You don't understand what this job is all about," Belson said.

"Just a minute." Fury was mounting in me as I spoke. "I'll tell you what I do understand. You came in here and repeated rumors about obscene gestures, disruptions and chaos. None of

154

these occurred. Nor were there any lewd remarks addressed to Mrs. Svenson. You have our testimony on this. Go down our class roster and check it out with every single student. They'll tell you the truth."

"I didn't hear it from an inmate," Belson said.

"Then you didn't hear it from anyone who was an eyewitness. What you picked up was a latrine rumor. I think you have an obligation to track it down and demolish it. You know prison is fantasy land. You have told me yourself not to believe the stories I hear. That's good advice. I advise you to follow it. Otherwise it's slander; and I don't want to be slandered.

"I realize that training in basic skills is important for these men. But education is much broader than that. Education is also to teach people to think. It's a search for the truth. You have an obligation to find out the truth. It's wrong for someone to wait until he hears something that fits his preconceived notion, and accept it without question because it coincides with his own prejudice. It's wrong!" I said, practically shouting.

"I didn't accuse you of anything," Belson said. "I just told you what I heard. I'm not going to investigate anything. You've already told me worse things than were reported.

"Let's put it this way," he continued. "This is the last debate we'll have. There are more risks involved than value that can come from it. Forget the other things. I don't care who's right. I just don't want to hear about it. I know you think I don't understand, but I do understand—too damned well. That's the problem. I know you're sincere about wanting to educate these guys. But you don't understand the kind of people you're dealing with.

"And, Campbell, I want to tell you something for your own good. You have a nasty temper. You blow up with your students the way you did just now with me and you can get yourself killed. Though you don't understand it, part of my job is to protect you."

"Incredible performance," Mrs. Svenson said, after he left. "I suppose we should have insisted he attend the debate, so he could judge for himself."

155

"No that would have been a mistake," I said. "We might have passed muster with the marijuana debate, but I hate to think what would have happened to Barkham. Belson probably would have sent him to the hole, or washed his mouth out with soap."

That ended our debates. A short time after, Mrs. Svenson resigned. She got into difficulty with a big, angry stud named Mexico, who had a couple of unpremeditated murders to his credit. Mexico dropped his pencil on the floor; she ordered him to pick it up. He refused. She insisted. Mexico started shaking and moved toward her desk. She kept her cool and managed to calm him down until she could slip out of the room and call the goon squad. They yanked him like a sore tooth. He protested he had never raised his hand against her, which he hadn't. But she felt, for a fleeting moment, she had confronted death. She went to Central Files and read Mexico's jacket. The next day she handed in her resignation.

Barkham stayed with me for several terms. When I first taught him, he was weak in language skills, but he improved dramatically as his interest increased. He could write an excellent essay, starting from a premise and logically building a case. I used his early essays on Antigone to demonstrate to other classes how you started with an assertion and developed your argument by fact, logic, and quotation from the text. I looked forward to his written work because it always contained a discussible idea.

He lived closely within himself and did not make friends. He despised authority and had a talent for tearing apart any system or institution.

Strangely enough, after a while he developed a protective attitude toward me. I believe this was a new emotion for him, and he didn't always know how to handle it. For instance, administration allowed everyone to smoke in class, so I brought in my favorite pipe. When I had to leave the class for a moment, I carelessly left the pipe on my desk; when I returned, the pipe was gone.

Initially, I was angry about its disappearance, but I recognized it was my own fault. I could have called a guard and had the students searched on the spot. But the idea of all my students stripped naked was more painful to me than the loss of my briar. I could have given my class roster to the guard captain and requested all their cells be shaken down that evening. But the person who took the pipe would have hidden it somewhere else, and my attempts at recovery would only lead to humiliation.

I explained these alternatives to the class and then dismissed the whole thing. "I know what I should do," I said. "I should run down to the principal and report that I think someone in my class may have criminal tendencies. That will disappoint him."

Barkham, however, exploded. "God, I hate prisons and all the stupid, slimy vermin that infest this swamp. Don't you realize," he said, addressing the class, "that here is a man trying to help you, and all you can do is, in a cheap way, rip him off. Don't you have any self-respect? Don't you have any pride in yourself at all?"

I looked at Barkham in disbelief. It startled me to see an anarchist dissolve into a law-and-order freak before my very eyes.

In a little while I had occasion to go out of the room again; when I returned, the pipe was on my desk. I didn't comment or ask any questions.

However, I lost that pipe again, the same day, in an afternoon class. This time I didn't even mention its disappearance. The next day I purchased a corncob pipe identical to one they could purchase in their canteen for a quarter. This pipe was never stolen from me. Inmates, like everyone else at heart, are snobs.

Barkham was protective of me in other ways. From time to time, I lectured to my students. To my surprise, these lectures were always enthusiastically received. As a student, I had hated lectures and considered them the lowest level of instruction. My lectures were combined with discussion, and no sensible educator could possibly have approved of them. My two most popular ones were on Graeco-Roman literature and the Renaissance.

I told them about the myth of Sisyphus and described how the guy would continually try to roll the stone up the mountain, knowing full well as soon as he got it two-thirds of the way up, it would come tumbling down again. I asked the class if they could think of something in our society that was similar. Someone came

157

up with the example of the workmen who paint the Golden Gate Bridge. As soon as they finish painting it, they start over again at the other end; so they spend their entire working lives painting one thing.

I then posed a question: If they were promised immediate parole, how many of them would agree to spend the rest of their working lives painting that bridge. I stipulated their commitment would have to be absolute; they could not use it as a way to escape. They would, of course, get union wages and holidays and could lead normal lives. Out of that class of twenty, only one student claimed he would accept those terms. His name was Freddie Fernandez, and two weeks later he was in the hole for stabbing a Chicano dude in his unit.

Another lecture was on the Iliad. One of the inmates drew a Trojan horse; I picked the paper up from the floor where it had fallen. The horse had a silly expression on its face and several arrows sticking in it, one of which pinned its penis to its belly.

I took the drawing back to San Francisco with me and, at a party, showed it to a young woman who taught art in the public schools. She burst into tears. To her it represented loneliness, deprivation and ruined masculinity. I was astonished, because I didn't believe anyone on the outside could possibly care about those crazy bastards I taught and, in my own peculiar way, did love.

I talked about Pompeii and mentioned the Romans had less puritanical views about sex than we did. I pointed out that American schoolteachers, when they visited this reconstructed city, were shocked to find that the public road markers were in the shape of a penis.

The teachers had to keep their mouths shut about what they saw, because if they went home and told their students the ancient Romans, "let it all hang out," the school board would be on their case fast.

The artists in my class had a field day with this, and drew some funny cartoons with phalluses as signposts, pointing the way toward everything from the ancient city of Herculaneum to Redondo Beach.

When I gave my lectures, I talked from notes scribbled on a piece of paper. When the class asked me for specific dates, I could be off sometimes as much as two centuries. This historical inaccuracy on my part upset Barkham. I remember once I had been talking about the Renaissance in France, and Rabelais. Mankind had developed great literature, art, sculpture, elegance and philosophy during the Greek and Roman times.

Then for hundreds of years, the Dark Ages came, and man was little better than a grunting beast, without expanding thoughts about himself or the universe. Monks preserved the wisdom of the ancients in manuscripts tucked away in cold stone churches. They worked far into the evening, copying these texts by candlelight and getting stoned on barley wine. They argued about how big an angel was, and how many of them could dance on the head of a pin, and whether or not Joan of Arc really saw Jesus, and whether or not he was naked when she saw him, and if he wore clothes, who his tailor was.

Rabelais was born at a time when man was rediscovering the past, digging into monasteries and translating the great works of a lost way of life. He had an enormous appetite for everything; liquor, song, women, learning. He knew Latin, but he wrote in French. He listed in one chapter six hundred things a man could use in lieu of toilet paper; among them a door knob and the neck of a goose. His philosophy was: Do what you will. He was a crazy, wild man with unbelievable energies, but he made the French language interesting and eventually it became respectable.

A man like that couldn't survive in our society. Today he would be put in a blue smock in a mental institution and given electric shock treatments until the nerve endings were burned out of his brain cells.

When I told a story like this, I mixed inaccurate dates and historical references into a crazy mishmash. Barkham took copious notes of everything I said and then went to encyclopedias and checked on me. He presented me with a list of my mistakes.

"Why do you do that, Mr. Campbell?" he asked. "Most of what you say is true. But when you make mistakes, it looks like you're just taking us on a trip; and we can't trust what you say."

159

"When I was talking about Rabelais, I was talking about Renaissance man. They were interested in self-discovery. I don't want to break up learning into little plastic bags and hand it to you. I want you to dig in and find out things for yourself. I'm delighted by what you're doing."

"It wouldn't cost you much effort to do research and get your facts straight," he said.

"I talk off the top of my head. I never know what I'm going to say next," I said.

"It makes you look bad," he said.

"Oh hell, you're referring to Barber," I said. Barber was in the class. He was smart in that he had a quick, retentive mind; but dumb in that he had taken his shovel and bashed in the head of a green security guard who had tried to force him too close to a fire they were fighting in the Santa Cruz mountains. Barber also checked on my lectures and delighted in pointing out to the class how stupid I was.

"I've gotten Barber's nose in a book more than any teacher he ever had; and I am damned proud of that," I said. "I don't get a kick out of proving to you men how smart I am. I get my kicks out of seeing your minds grow and expand."

"You're worse than any of us. You're a God damned incorrigible," Barkham said. But there was warmth in his voice when he said it.

Just before his high school graduation, he got into a fight with his cell mate. Barkham picked up a chair and cracked him with it. As punishment, he was sent to the hole for ten days. The inmate he hit wasn't hurt; but the trouble occurred about a month before Barkham was due to report to the parole board. Since he was in on an indeterminate sentence and had violence in his background, they shot him down for two years before he could appear before the board again.

I managed to see that Barkham got his high school diploma, but he never did appear in the education area again. I ran into him returning from his job in the welding shop months later, and told him they were offering college courses in the evening and that I would like to see him enroll. He looked at me sadly and said, "Mr. Campbell, I know you tried to help me, but I'm through with education.. It gave me aspirations that I can't handle." I never saw him again.

Much later, a student who had been in one of Barkham's classes said, "Remember that dude Barkham, the one you thought could write better than any of the rest of us? Do you know why he hit the dude and got busted and shot down for two years?

"He was a strange dude. The way I heard it, Barkham was rapping with his cellie, and he told him that he loved you, Mr. Campbell. His cellie started razzing him and calling him a faggot, and Barkham went crazy and chased him into the cell block and clobbered him over the head with a stool, right in front of a guard."

"That's a lie," I said. I doubt the story was true, but I was becoming like Belson. I did not want to find out the truth.

I did not get into a hassle with Belson again until Christmas Eve. This holiday is a very depressing time in a prison. I invited a folk singer to bring his guitar and sing songs to my afternoon classes. Belson spotted the singer walking by the education office and confiscated the guitar. Then he came to my classroom and explained he had protected me. He explained that if it got out I was serenading my students instead of teaching them, my job might be on the line.

It was during this Christmas period I had trouble with an eraser thrower. Every time I turned my back on the class, an eraser zinged over my head and bounced against the blackboard. Sometimes it hit me. It didn't hurt, but it made me furious. It was the kind of thing you might expect of a junior high school class, and these were all, supposedly, men. It happened in a good class, where I couldn't detect any hostility against me. I was mystified.

The class ignored these incidents and, for the most part, so did I. However, I was determined to put a stop to them. At first, I

161

tried turning to the blackboard and quickly wheeling around, but the thrower was much too clever to be caught by this method, and I made myself look ridiculous.

I next responded by removing all erasers from the room. Then when I turned my back, a pencil clattered against the black-board. Since this was a more dangerous instrument, I returned the erasers.

I discussed my problem with my newspaper editor, Barney. He knew who the thrower was, but it was against his code to be an informer. However, he did suggest that I have another teacher, by prearranged signal, walk by a small window that allowed a full view of the students. This would give me a free person as a witness, and I could proceed to throw the book at the offender.

A teacher down the hall from me willingly agreed to be my spotter. Our room clocks were synchronized. We agreed that exactly at 2:30, I would turn my back to the class while he was watching through the window. The hall was darker than the room; it wasn't easy for someone in the class to see outside.

At exactly 2:30, I turned my back and started writing on the blackboard. Splat. I got an eraser right between the shoulder blades. What a beautiful sensation it gave me.

When I turned around, I saw the teacher give me the victory sign and disappear. A few minutes later I left the room, ostensibly to get a drink of water. The teacher was standing in front of his classroom, grinning broadly.

"I got your boy," he said. "Just give me the word and I'll write him up. Since the eraser hit you we can hang an assault rap on him, if you want."

"Thanks a lot," I said. "I'm going to enjoy this." He had written the name on a piece of paper.

I returned to my classroom, where everyone was busily at work. I picked the eraser from the floor and flipped it into its box. Then I sat down at my desk and unfolded the paper. Ronnie Kinsella. I was surprised. He was a lean, intense, very contained young man. But he wasn't even on my list of suspects. I decided to wait until the end of the period to inform him that I was going to have him written up. I didn't want to make an example of him in front of the class because I realized that any show of authority on my part would create hostility among the other students. I had the goods on him and I intended to let him have it in a very precise, unemotional way. The news would get around soon enough that I was a cool dude and not to be messed with.

Just before the bell rang, I said, "Mr. Kinsella, please stay around after class. I'd like to talk to you."

He came to my desk after the bell and eagerly handed me a theme. "I want you to look at it. I think it's the best thing I've ever written."

"Sit down," I said, casually glancing at his paper. "This theme is typewritten; you couldn't have written it in class."

"Yeah, I know," he said disarmingly. "I can't think good in class. I wrote this theme at home, in my pad. It's a make-up theme." I thumbed it, then gave it a closer look.

"Oh my God," I exclaimed. "This is an authentic Martin DeGraaf." Martin DeGraaf was a professional writer who had spent most of his life in prison. When he was a young man, he had published a few novels extolling the virtues of family life and clean living. He wrote articles for magazines edited for teenage boys. Sentimentality and innocence were the hallmarks of his writing style.

He was an aging man now, wrinkled and balding, who worked as an X-ray technician in the prison hospital. He was also a homosexual, and unflaggingly willing to comfort, counsel and copulate with confused young men.

"What do you mean, Martin DeGraaf?" Kinsella asked weakly.

"You know exactly what I mean. Don't con me. You don't need that old man. Your writing is just fine. Much better than that 'Lawrence Welk with a hard-on against society' theme you just handed me."

"Oh God, I hate DeGraaf," he said. "He's old and he's ugly—"

"Fine," I said. "Stay away from him and you'll be all right. Believe in yourself. You don't need anything that man has to offer."

"That's easy for you to say because you're strong. But I'm not. He's a very smart man, and has helped me, Mr. Campbell. He's

163

gone over every assignment you've given me and explained it to me. He's my boxing coach, and he really knows the fight game. I'm third in the welterweight division because of him. He believes in me; he thinks I can become a champion."

"He's sucking your youth and your innocence from you, like a vampire sucks blood," I said. "Stay away from him."

"Oh God, I'm confused. If my mother knew what I was doing, it would kill her. I want to die. I want to kill myself," he said, and he started to bawl.

I almost said, "That DeGraaf should be put in jail." But I realized the absurdity of my thought. It was exactly where Martin DeGraaf didn't belong. Jail was his flower garden.

I didn't mention to Kinsella that I knew he was my thrower. He was pleading for help, and I had only the power to punish him.

The next day I got a call from Petoskey stating that Kinsella had requested transfer to a chemistry class. Kinsella had told him he had nothing against me as a teacher, but he needed the science credit for graduation. Petoskey checked his records and found his claim was accurate. In fact, Kinsella had lied about his course requirements to get into my class. Kinsella had heard I was a good teacher and thought he needed my class more than he did a high school diploma.

"OK, Mr. Petoskey, transfer him and give him my best wishes," I said.

I did call his counsellor. The counsellor was fully aware of Kinsella's relationship with DeGraaf. There was nothing that could be done unless they were caught *in flagrante.*

"Why can't you transfer Kinsella to another prison?" I asked.

"That wouldn't do any good. There are Martin DeGraafs everywhere. Kinsella has to conquer himself."

At least, I muttered to myself, I won't be getting hit in the ass with an eraser anymore. Prisons, like the rest of society, can drive a sensitive man insane. I was pleased I was an insensitive lout.

I learned about DeGraaf early in my prison teaching. An inmate who was not one of my students brought me a story to read, claiming it was his own. It was a skillfully written tale about a tender-hearted horse player. I was impressed by it and closely interrogated its purported author. He fell apart and admitted it was written by DeGraaf. When I questioned others about DeGraaf, I got the story. One of his first approaches to a young student was to establish his credentials as a writer and offer to help with his English assignments.

His game didn't work with me. However, many times students tried to slip me one of his compositions. I became an expert on his literary style and offered an A+ to anyone who could fool me into accepting a Martin DeGraaf composition.

I read themes aloud, and when I came to one that had a phrase in it that couldn't possibly have been written by an inmate, I would toss it aside and say, "Thank you, Martin DeGraaf."

The students were amazed I could invariably identify his writing. It was easy to do. For instance, in Kinsella's theme there was a sweetness and light motif that made me suspicious; and when I hit the sentence, "I think a lot of my mother, she is the dearest person in the world to me," I knew I had an original DeGraaf.

By coincidence, I still have this DeGraaf theme. Undoubtedly incidents like the one described in it do occur in prison. But this particular story is not true.

CHRISTMAS IN THE JOINT

I was instructed to write about Xmas in the joint, and this before Xmas had arrived, that is I was supposed to submit the article before I had ever experienced a Xmas in the joint. Now that I have delayed the writing, I have a little bit to write about. Before, I had nothing, so I hope that our instructor will take this into consideration when he grades this latepaper.

I arose at the usual time and went to breakfast. It was a fair breakfast. I returned to my room and went back to bed, where I remained until twelve o'clock noon. at which time I was awakened by the officer calling my name, to inform me that I

165

had visitors out there waitning for me. I dressed and reported to control for my visit. Upon going into the visiting room, expecting to see my mother and father, I was confronted by my father, my brother Charlie, who has just returned from almost four years in Vietnam and my young sister Pam.

My father told me immediately that my mother was in the hospital and that he was afraid there was very little likelehood of her recovering, that they could not stay long as they wanted to get back to the hospital. Some Xmas present. I think a lot of my mother, she is the dearest person in the world to me. I can't adjust to the thought that she may not be here long. I won't accept it.

My father said that my mother had sent me a X'mas package but that they would not let him leave it, as the rules called for the package being mailed he had already tried that and the Post Office was closed. He also told me that my mother had made him promise that he see to it I get the package. He thought it was pretty rotten of the officers that I was not allowed to have the package. I was forced to agree with that.

Then, on X'mas eve I was sent a slip which read, Package at mail room, do not call for, Contraband. I did call for it that same evening and was told it was home made cookies from one of my girl friends and that I could not have it. I was not allowed to see it. However, I wrote her and told her that the Package had arrived and that I appreciated it very much. I did not tell her that I had not been allowed to have it.

Merry X'mas! Some one must be kidding. In the joint there just is no such thing, believe me. I know! I wish that X'mas would be like the 29th of February, come around only once in every four years. I will remember X'mas in the joint for a long long time and I assure you that my memories will be anything but pleasant, and I defy any one to show me why I should feel different. However, if my class mates were to take up a collection of Wham-Whams and Zoo-Zoo's to compensate me for my two lost packages it might just help a little to ease the pain of a painful X'mas.

CHAPTER 9

Prison is a place where you find gray hairs in your head, or where you find hair starting to disappear. It's a place where you get false teeth, stronger glasses, and aches and pains you never felt before. It's a place where you grow old and worry about it.

From a Student Theme

I was determined to prove to myself that my system of teaching literature worked and, like a laboratory technician, was continually taking it apart and tinkering with it. I knew it worked for me, but I was trying to develop a system any teacher could use, and if it was successful only with teachers with specialized talents, then it was of limited value.

I started training students to lead their own discussions. This also worked beautifully. Some students were better at it than others. I remember two who were outstanding. One was a tough teenage Mexican American who had been busted for robbing a McDonald's hamburger establishment. His partner had been killed in the encounter.

It was a bloody scene. His partner clutched a plywood statue of Ronald McDonald and fired a handgun while the police, in a stakeout, riddled him with bullets, his blood staining the replica of that commercial clown.

167

My student, Gonzalez, escaped during the excitement but was picked up a few hours later at his home. Gonzalez had excellent reasoning powers and was a logical, incisive questioner.

We became friends. He brought to me the court record of his trial (under California law, all prisoners are entitled to copies of their official trial record) and showed me where the judge, upon sentencing, had referred to him as a vicious, hardened criminal and requested that he be sent to an adult prison. The judge's phrase was: "To put this young man among juvenile offenders would be like placing a tiger among pussycats."

I encouraged students to give speeches and at the end of the term Gonzalez asked to address the class. Usually these talks lasted from five to fifteen minutes. Gonzalez took the entire period. He started out by describing the crime for which he had been busted. Then he went into his background, a conventional tale of how he had started using dope and sacrificed everything to his habit. He drew a laugh when he told how he had kissed his mother-in-law good-bye when she was leaving on a trip and later that night sneaked into her house and ripped off her color television set.

Then he described how he had come home with five hundred dollars in his pocket that he was going to use for a fix and his wife had told him his son needed a new pair of shoes. He denied her request by saying the boy could use adhesive tape to patch up the holes in his sneakers. Gonzalez burst into tears when telling this story.

To most people it may seem natural to cry about something you have done wrong. But in a prison setting it is foolish. It is equivalent to someone swimming in piranha-infested waters slashing himself with a knife, hoping the fish will be aghast at the wounds. Every inmate has caused suffering to loved ones. Every inmate has to handle the problem of guilt.

I didn't know what had gotten into Gonzalez. Highly emotional confessions did not take place in my classes. This was the unwritten law. If a man had to cry, he did it with a close friend or alone.

Inmates did cry and snivel, but they did it in front of juries,

168

parole boards and counsellors. It's cool to cry in front of free people. They dig that kind of stuff. But don't do it in front of your peer group. They've been the same route. They know the game.

I was aware his talk wasn't going over with the other students. I was embarrassed for him and wanted to take him off the hook. I was waiting for some comment from the group that would break the spell and allow me to step in and terminate the speech. But there was only silence.

All kinds of things were going through my mind as I listened to him rap. He was coming on strongly and honestly with what had happened to him. If he had been addressing a group of free people, he would have had his audience in tears. But he had picked the dumbest place possible for his confession. Maybe when you start to educate a kid like that, you damage him, I thought. Maybe it's wrong to civilize a tiger when he still has to live in the jungle.

After class, when the others had gone, I talked to him. He was glowing with pleasure. "I let it all hang out today," he said proudly.

"You didn't tell them what they wanted to hear," I said.

"Damned right I didn't. You know what prisons are like by now. Every dude in the joint will think I've gone weak and will try to move on me. Let me run down to you how that happens. A soft dude comes into the joint and he's scared. He doesn't want to cause any trouble; he just wants to get along. You can smell the fear in a dude like that. You get behind him in the canteen line and rip his tickets out of his hand. 'Thanks a lot, punk, for the gift' you say. If he backs away, then you've got him. You see him around after that, and he's all messed up, and you work on his fantasy. You come on as a friend. 'Look, I heard something you ought to know. The iron pushers are out to get you. Those big dudes who lift weights in the gym. They got eyes for you. They want a new pigeon. If they get you in a trick bag, you better pray. You know what you better pray for? You better pray they have the courtesy to use that hair oil they sell in the canteen as a lubricant. Because if they don't, they'll tear your asshole out. You

169

need protection, baby. We'll get together soon and talk about it.'

"Then you wait until he is alone in his cell and you come at him. He is scared and it's sexy as hell. It's like his balls dissolve and the woman part floats up. And she's trembling and her eyes are wide with fear, and she is confused and wants protection—and you score."

"Gonzalez, don't you realize what you have described is sick as hell?" I asked. I was thinking that the judge who assigned him to the joint instead of putting him in with the pussycats was absolutely right.

"It's the truth," he said defiantly. "I'm not concerned anyone is going to turn me out. What hurts me is what the other Chicano dudes in the class are going to say. 'Chico,' they'll say, 'you talk better than a white man. But you made a fool of all brown people when you got up and sniveled the way you did today.' "

"Gonzalez, you make no sense. If you had all that insight into the situation, what in hell made you get up and make a confession? I know it didn't come off the top of your head."

"You're right. Except I didn't think I'd break down. That surprised the hell out of me. I've done some things in my life I feel guilty about. I wanted to punish myself. Prison is your punishment. It isn't mine. Locking me up may have saved my life because I was on a tear when I was busted. I could confess to a priest. But if there's a God, which I doubt, he already knows what I have done. I could confess to a free person or the parole board, but that's copping out. That's trying to use my guilt to my advantage. I had to confess where it would hurt me the most, to a bunch of cons who would hate me for it."

"Gonzalez, you have good reasoning power, but you're crazy," I said.

"I've done a lot of thinking since I been in this class. I like the smell of the truth. It's crazy, but I do. You say to me, 'Go to college and get an education.' What should I become, a lawyer? They're all crooked. An honest lawyer couldn't make a living. I really don't want to lie, steal or cheat anymore. I'm a good worker. I was always able to hold a job. Even when I was busted,

170

I was working as a plumber's assistant. I was better at that kind of work than anyone I know. Also, I can set up a wholesale outlet, selling to plumbers, and make a good living.

"I see the value of an education, but you can't go to college to get it. They're all too busy turning out rip-off people for the establishment. I'm not like you. I could never be a teacher. If I get an idea in my head, I have to act on it. I can't just play around with it and sit on my ass and go on to the next idea. I don't have that much patience."

A few weeks after our conversation an inmate reported Gonzalez was knifed. I asked a guard in his unit about him, and he said, "There was a little trouble around here a few days ago. But it didn't amount to very much. Just a couple of Chicanos fighting among themselves. We transferred one to Quentin and the other to Soledad. It happens every day."

Hamilton, the other discussion leader, was very different from Gonzalez. Hamilton was the all-American boy. He was tall, handsome, weighed 220 pounds and was captain of the prison football team, where he played fullback. He was white, and the majority of the team was black, so the fact that they had voted him captain was a tribute to his capabilities in that sport.

Hamilton was also a singer and had sung professionally with a nationally known group. I met him before I had him as a student, when Mrs. Svensen had wanted to hear his voice and had made arrangements with the guards to use the organ in the chapel. She needed someone to chaperone her and asked me to accompany them. We received some baleful looks from the guards when the three of us walked down the corridor to the prison chapel.

There was something a little eerie about that scene in the poorly lit prison church: this big, hard-muscled, handsome stud, with the courtly manner, was standing in the pulpit, singing his heart out, accompanied by a portly middle-aged organist over-flowing with maternal tenderness. It was as if they were both auditioning for the Metropolitan Opera; yet I was their only audience and my function was to see that the singer didn't rape or inflict bodily harm on his organist. He had a professional-quality voice and sang the only thing they both knew without sheet music before them. *Ave Maria.*

After the performance Hamiltion went back to his unit and Mrs. Svenson and I returned to the educational area. She was praising his talent, and absolutely sick about the system of justice that had put him in jail. He was a brilliant, sensitive young man in jail on a marijuana bust. I asked her if she had checked his records, and she had not.

I asked another teacher about Hamilton and his comment was, "Oh yeah, that guy is too good to be true."

The next day I went to Central Files. Everything the state knows is kept in Central Files. This includes history of arrests, psychiatric examinations, mental tests, letters from family members and acquaintances, and anything else that might be pertinent to shed information on what makes its subject tick. These files are open, upon request, to any free person in the institution. Inmates are not allowed access to them. They are, of course, inordinately curious about their contents because the parole board bases its decision upon them.

I flipped through Hamilton's file: it was an extensive one. He was in on a marijuana bust, but he had a rap sheet that was more than two pages long. A rap sheet is on yellow paper and contains a record of the number of times a person has had a skirmish with the law. I didn't examine his record closely. I had determined that it was extensive, and since he then wasn't my student, any further investigation by me would have been an invasion of privacy. I was convinced he wasn't simply a misunderstood, nice guy.

When Hamilton was assigned to one of my classes, he responded beautifully in discussion and picked up the technique I was using after only one session. When he volunteered to lead the group, he did everything well. He could draw out the quiet ones, bring the conversation back to the central point when it was going astray, and break the discussion down to clear-cut questions to which everyone could relate.

I had expected he would try to con me or ingratiate himself

with me, as I suspected he had done with Mrs. Svenson. But he didn't. He was always aloof and formal. He never told me he played football, and I didn't realize he had this talent until he was called out of class one morning to attend a meeting. When I questioned him about it, he admitted he was the captain but was quick to add, "I'm getting old. I'm twenty-four and I have a trick knee. I'm not interested much in football anymore. It's just something I can do."

A plan formed in my mind. I knew the director of admissions at Harvard, who had been a classmate of mine. With some hard prepping, I was certain Hamilton could cut it, academically, at Harvard. They could use a good fullback for their football team and a singer for their choral groups. Also, I was curious about their reaction to his prison background. Even if they didn't take him, I thought they might have some suggestions for his future.

I didn't tell him about my idea because I didn't want him tripping out on something that might not materialize. I did call him in to talk to him about going on to college after he got out of prison.

"No, I couldn't do that," he said.

"Why not?" I asked.

"I'm married. I have a wife and small boy. I'll have to take care of them."

"They're making out now without you, aren't they?" I asked.

"They're on welfare," he said. Then he started rapping about his background. He came from a broken home and grew up on the streets. He busted out of school when he was fourteen and was married when he was sixteen. He had been upset by his disrupted family life and had been in constant trouble with the law. He had a loveless marriage with a girl who worked as a waitress and was also a high school dropout. They separated shortly after their son was born. He auditioned in Los Angeles with a singing group and was accepted. He made television appearances and went on tour with them. The group was busted in San Francisco on a marijuana raid and, since he was the only one with a record, they put the others on probation and sent him to jail.

He had nothing in common with his wife who was an illiterate. Yet, because of his broken family life, he felt the most important thing he could do was provide a stable home. He planned to do this by getting a laboring job when he got out.

"If you and your wife don't have similar interests, perhaps it's better to get a divorce and start a new life," I said.

"No, I have to try to work it out," he said.

Hamilton graduated from high school and came up for parole. Just before his hearing, he got into trouble. He was working in the gardening department. Ordinarily, this would be considered an easy assignment. Mr. Krauss, who was in charge, was a mild-mannered man with a degree in horticulture and was considered very competent.

Apparently, in front of the gardening class, Hamilton pointed out a mistake that Krauss had made. Krauss was furious and wrote a bad report on him. The report maligned Hamilton's character without mentioning any incidents of misconduct. I spoke briefly to Mr. Krauss about Hamilton, and he said, "He's a very arrogant young man. He's tricky and deceitful and I don't believe he's ready to go back into society."

"I found him to be an excellent student and had no trouble with him," I said.

"You don't understand these men as well as I do. I've taught inmates for fifteen years. They know how to con you into believing anything."

"I guess you know he's coming up for parole and a bad report can damage him," I said.

"I've expelled him from my class. I don't think he's ready to get out of jail at this time," Krauss said.

Hamilton had glowing reports from me, Mrs. Svenson and his counselor. He was denied parole for one year. The parole board does not give reasons for their decisions. There is no way to protest denial of parole.

I can only surmise why he was shot down. Good reports can be discounted if they come from people who are not competent to evaluate inmates. Good recommendations are ignored if they emanate from weak-minded people who are susceptible to a con job.

Hamilton was in great turmoil after he was turned down for parole. He wanted to go back to Krauss and get things straightened out. But Krauss refused to talk to him or even let him in the area. Hamilton wanted to apologize to Krauss but, in a Kafka-esque way, didn't comprehend what he should apologize for.

I abandoned my plans to seek a college scholarship for him. There was the possibility that if he was going from prison to an Ivy League college, he would never get out of jail. Prisons can't tolerate winners. Everyone is put down. Guards can't move on to become policemen. Administrators are not welcomed by private enterprise. Prisons breed a superstitious, psychological leprosy that infects both the keepers and the kept.

Not all my classes were successful, and I don't want to give the impression that I had all my students joyfully eager to overrun the paths of learning, restricted only by the academic limitations that were imposed upon me. I was prison-wise and had things going for me when I got into difficulty with one of my classes.

It was in the class right after lunch. When a class shuffles in with full stomachs, it's difficult to whet their intellectual appetites. In my early days of teaching, I would fire questions until I caught a spark, and then I would work like hell to fan it. I was a little wild-eyed, because I felt if I could intellectually motivate a group of lethargic captives, I could motivate any group. I usually did manage to get something going, but it was hard work, and I was exhausted by the sessions. Later I learned to pace myself and tailored my teaching to my emotional needs rather than their intellectual needs. For instance, if I had been lecturing all morning, I would assign the early afternoon class seat work and sit down and read a book.

I had been teaching more than a year when I was assigned a class of students who had recently arrived in the joint. Most of them were juvenile offenders who had been in Youth Authority prisons and had been removed because they were troublemakers.

175

They had no experience in a real joint, but of course, had heard tales of how rough things would be.

I didn't notice that the class was almost entirely students who had never been in a joint before. On the second or third day of class, something happened that unnerved me. I was driving to the prison early Monday morning from San Francisco. A police car pulled up beside me and the driver waved at me. I waved back. Then the police car dropped behind me, and a few seconds later its siren began to wail. I was baffled. I knew I wasn't breaking the speed limit and was confident I had broken no laws. I turned around; the policeman was gesticulating wildly. I was in the fast lane and, for some unknown reason, thought a convoy was coming through and the policeman wanted me to pull over. Stupidly, I came to a dead stop. The policeman screamed at me, "You God damned fool, get the hell over in the slow lane!"

I pulled over on the other side and stopped again. The policeman pulled up behind me and came flying out of the cruiser.

"You stupid fool, you tried to kill me. Look at that, my hands are shaking so badly I can't hold the book to write you up," he said.

"What are you talking about?" I asked, completely perplexed.

"Get out of the car, I'm going to throw the book at you!" he screamed.

I got out of the car, completely bewildered, "What is it, officer, what have I done?" I asked.

"You came to a stop in the fast lane of a superhighway when I was right behind you. Do you realize, cars come along ninety miles an hour in that lane? Christ, I was a sitting target. I could have been smacked all over the road."

I had a New York driver's license, since I had not gone through the nuisance of getting a California one. He booked me for driving without a valid license, stopping in the fast lane of a superhighway and going fifty miles an hour in a sixty-mile zone. He had been waving at me to get me to speed up or get out of the fast lane. He did calm down some when he became convinced that I wasn't deliberately trying to kill him.

176

When I related the tale to my morning classes, they thought it was hilarious. They tripped out on the idea of my car smacking into the police car and killing the cop, while I pulled away from the carnage, having committed the perfect crime.

When I told the story in my early afternoon class, the reaction was completely different. I had a new student there named Daniels, a stocky, sandy-haired kid who played on my fears. "Mr. Campbell, they'll send you to the joint for what you done," he said. I questioned the other students in the class about my crime and received the correct advice. If I got a California driver's license before I came to court, the first count would be thrown out; and if I acted contrite, I would merely have to pay a fine. I did get the California license and was fined only ten dollars.

The next day Daniels went after me again and, although I managed to cut him off, he did get the class laughing at me. I was a duck. The following day I knew something was wrong as soon as I entered the room. Everyone was quiet; I could sense the tension. As I was checking the roll, by a prearranged signal, probably given by Daniels, each inmate removed his belt and started snapping it between clenched fists. I stood there watching them in disbelief. A few students were holdouts but, eventually, every student in the room was participating.

My first reaction was to laugh at them. If this had happened to me in my early teaching days, it would have upset me. But I knew the score now and probably had spent more time in the joint than any of them.

Then I started to get angry. But I knew that was what they wanted—to get a rise out of me. By the time I could summon anyone, they could replace their belts and look as innocent as angels. My accusations would make a duck out of me. Once the teacher is afraid or off-balance, the prisoners can manipulate him. It is the way they are manipulated, and it is the way they manipulate.

I could lecture them or threaten them, but this was the way they had been treated all their lives. It would do no good. I knew I could not show my anger; I had to match their game with my game.

177

I walked to the window and looked out, ignoring them. There was a pretty girl with a pass in her hand, walking from the main gate to the administration building. She was undoubtedly on the way to the visiting room to see a loved one.

After a while I turned around. They were moving their belts very slowly, as if they were playing accordions in unison.

"What's the matter, Mr. Campbell, don't get scared. We're just relaxing after a big meal. Our guts are so full, we had to take our belts off," Daniels said.

"Mr. Daniels," I said calmly. "I would like you to take your books, go outside, and wait for me. I would like to talk to you."

If he refused to leave, I would call a guard and have him remove Daniels from my classroom. I had my scapegoat. I was following Belson's advice. When you have difficulty, pick one guy and bust him. However, I did not have to call a guard, because Daniels complied with my request. I walked to the door and said in a low voice that still could be heard by everyone in my class. "Please make yourself comfortable on a bench. I'll be with you in a few minutes."

I returned to my classroom and, sitting on the edge of my desk, slowly opened a grammar book and formally addressed the class.

"I want you gentlemen to open your grammar books to page 36. There are ten sentences there under section C. I want you to copy each sentence and put in the proper punctuation. The rules for punctuating these sentences are on page 34. I suggest you copy the sentences first, then read the rules and get to work. I'll be back shortly to answer any questions you may have."

I left the room to talk to Daniels. I had him walk down the corridor with me, so that we wouldn't be in earshot of the class.

Daniels was all set to argue with me, but I cut him short.

"Don't bother to defend yourself, because I'm not going to accuse you of anything. I just don't want to teach you anymore. For a year now, I've been accepting rejects from other classes. You're my first reject. Go on back to you unit. I'll find a new teacher for you tomorrow."

"I tell you I didn't do noth—"

"Shitcan that talk," I said, using their language. "Get out of my sight and don't snivel."

"What about a pass?" Daniels asked.

"I'm not going to give you a pass. If you're not smart enough to get back to your pad without being stopped by a guard, you deserve to get busted."

"I made a mistake about you. You're a cool dude, Mr. Campbell," Daniels said as he went down the hall. There was respect without hostility in his voice.

When I returned to my classroom, everyone was quietly and busily at work. They didn't know what to expect next. They had been prepared to play on my fears. Now I had the opportunity to play on theirs. I reached into my desk and pulled out two stacks of forms. One was a pile of yellow forms and the other was a pile of gray forms. The gray form was 415. This was a disciplinary form. If I filed one of these, the subject would have to stand trial before a disciplinary court and could get up to fifteen days in the hole for the offense. However, it didn't go into his jacket in Central Files. If the inmate was not convicted, it was torn up. The yellow form was the sneaky one. It was a performance report. It was confidential and did not require any disciplinary action. Inmates didn't see the contents of this report. However, it went directly to Central Files and would be perused by the parole board when the inmates came up for a hearing.

If I wrote that an inmate had taken off his belt and made threatening gestures with it in the classroom, this could be an extremely difficult thing to explain to a parole board. A parole board member could ask a leading question about a particular class. If the inmate didn't supply the information or claimed there had been no difficulty, then the member would read the report and bear down on the incident. By skillful questioning, a member could get an inmate to confess to many things that were not in his file at all. Some gullible young men were left in shambles after a parole hearing. The standard rule for anyone going before the board was: Never cop out to anything.

The fear and the frustration in that room was rising. I took a stack of performances forms and gave the appearance of scribbling away on them. I made the dramatic gesture of finishing one report and placing it onto another pile. Then I would gaze about the room and start writing again. I would not, of course, have busted any of them for their game. But I was angry. They had tried to make me squirm, and now I had them.

Finally the tension became too much and one guy, in the corner by the window, burst out, "Jesus, I know you're writing me up. I don't care if you write me up. Just let me see what you're writing about me. Say anything you want, but just let me see what you've written so I'll know what to expect when I have to face the board."

I hadn't even noticed the student who made this outburst. But he made me aware of my self-righteous sadism.

I tore up the forms, which were blank anyway, and threw them in the wastebasket. "I haven't written any of you up today. You all start clean with me tomorrow." Shortly after this the bell rang.

The next day Daniels showed up early. He had given up his lunch to talk to me.

"I want to stay in your class," he said defiantly.

"Thanks for reminding me," I said. "I'll go down to the education office right now and arrange for your transfer."

"No, I mean it, I want to stay," he said.

"Look, I'm not going to snitch on you. I'll arrange it on some technical ground."

"I want to stay in your class."

"I've taught school for a number of years," I said. "Second chances never work out. Do you know how many school systems have been wrecked because guys like you want to horse around? Prison is about the only place left for someone who wants to teach without having to kiss the ass of the students, the principal, the parents, or the combined forces of the PTA."

"Now you're really getting down with it. That's why I want to stay. I like the way you handled me. When you got tough with me, it was just what I needed. I believe in discipline. My old man used to let me do anything I wanted. He never once cracked down on me, even though I needed it. I mean he was a nice guy, but he was a weak dude, and I couldn't stand him."

"Don't snivel," I said "Don't cop out on your old man. I don't want to teach you. I'm not your dad, and I don't want you running games on me, like you did on him."

"Everybody snivels once in a while," he said. "Even you. Why do you think I organized that thing with the belts? You were up there sniveling your head off because a cop gave you a ticket. Hell, what did you expect us to do, feel sorry for you? I got seven years to serve before I even see the board, for killing a dude in a barroom fight."

"OK," I said. "You made your point. Stick around today, and if things work out, you can remain in my class."

Daniels did remain and became a model student. I arranged for him to take the high school equivalency test, and at the end of the two-month term he had enough credits to get his high school diploma. I kept a tight reign on that class the entire time.

About a week after I let him back, Daniels showed up in my other afternoon class. When his name appeared on my new student roster, I looked at him and said, "I didn't do a very good job of getting rid of you, did I. It reminds me of the story about camels. The Arabs claim if you ever allow a camel to poke his head under the tent flap, you discover shortly thereafter the entire camel is inside the tent with you."

Sometime during the term, Daniels approached me before class with a boyish grin and claimed he had something he wanted me to see. He handed me about eight wallet-sized photographs of nude men and women performing various acts of heterosexual love.

"What do you think of these?" he asked expectantly. I suppose if some student in public school had handed me those photographs, I would have returned them with the comment: "Grow up and get yourself a girl friend." But this was the joint and there was no opportunity for heterosexual outlet.

"That'll keep your mind occupied during the rare moments when you're not concentrating on English grammar," I said flippantly.

181

"I knew you would like them," he said warmly. "Look through and pick out the best one for yourself. I want you to take it as a gift from me."

In prison, one survives by interpreting vibrations. I thought he was trying to reach out to me. The only thing he had to offer me was a pornographic picture.

I treated him gently. He handed me the pictures one by one, and I carefully looked at them. I picked out one of a skinny girl and sheepish-looking man in fellatio posture.

"That's the best one," I said. "But I can't take it from you. Enjoy it, but keep it out of sight so you don't get busted with it."

"Yeah, I like that one, too. We got the same taste," he said. "Go on, take it."

"No, I don't want to get busted with it in my possession," I lied.

He put the picture back in his wallet. "OK," he said. "Don't worry about me. I know how to take care of myself."

Later that afternoon, I was in the teachers' lounge, listening to Hugo Belson tell a story to one of the other teachers. It concerned a shop teacher at another prison where Belson had taught. The teacher was in the habit of offering his students a cigarette from time to time. This was against prison rules and cause for dismissal. One of his students collected ten cigarettes. Instead of smoking them, he inked in the exact time and date of each gift on each cigarette. He then presented these cigarettes to the captain of the guards, and the shop teacher confessed and was fired on the spot.

That evening when I returned to my room, I thought about Daniels. I'm a fool, I thought. I let the guy set me up. Daniels may have been given those photographs by one of the guards.

I left my fingerprints on each one of those photographs. What a damned fool I was. Daniels could claim I brought the pictures into the prison. Even if he couldn't prove this, he could establish that I had looked at contraband material without confiscating it, and this alone would be sufficient for dismissal.

Or perhaps he would try to use these photographs with my fingerprints on them in a blackmail attempt. I even thought about letting Belson know about the situation so I could cover myself. I was convinced I was in trouble. Daniels finally succeeded in making a duck out of me, I thought.

The next morning I went into the newspaper room to talk to Barney about my problem.

"Relax," Barney said. "I know that dude Daniels. He likes you. In fact, you're probably just about the only thing he has going for him right now. Being in prison is like being in hell. It takes a while to get adjusted. He is in on a bad beef and has long time. His wife is divorcing him and will not allow him to see his little girl. He lost it all.

"Don't listen to Hugo Belson," Barney added. "That story about the cigarettes is probably a lie. It's just his way of keeping all you teachers off-balance. Suppose you went to him and told him what you had done about those pictures. He'd back you against the wall and he'd bust Daniels for sure. Daniels has a short fuse and if he thought you had snitched him off, somebody might get killed."

"You mean you think Daniels might try to kill me?" I asked.

"No, he wouldn't do that. But when you're just starting to trust again and the whole thing blows up, it smashes all the wiring inside and you got nothing to fall back on.

"He wouldn't even be particularly mad at you," Barney continued. "It's just he would think you ain't any different than anyone else. Prison is chaos. Another dude in his unit might make a remark or look funny at him and boom—the blood flows. If he's lucky, they both get sent to the hole for a few days to cool out. If he's unlucky, somebody gets offed. If he is the survivor, he gets room and board for the rest of his life and they transfer him to Folsom to let him shuffle the corridors till his heart stops.

"Don't let Belson play his game with you. It's fun for him; but it ain't no fun for us, because us dudes in the cell blocks are dancing in the middle of the court in the dodge ball game. When you free people fuck with the mind of a fucked up dude, the cons are the ones who get jumped and pay the price for it."

"Barney," I said, "you're better than a psychiatrist. I thank you for setting me straight."

183

"Let me give you some more advice," Barney said. "Don't get involved with a dude like Daniels. He's not very bright and he's not going anywhere. He's latched on to you because there ain't anything else available. There's no way he can ever understand what you're trying to do, or where you're coming from. Forget about him, and do your teaching just like you have been doing."

"Now you sound like Hugo Belson," I said.

"I hate Belson," Barney said, "but he does understand prisons." Barney, of course, was right about the pictures. Daniels didn't try to run a game on me.

After graduation, I heard he attached himself to a strict, by-the-numbers guard named Kirk, whom most of the other inmates hated. Kirk became his father image and Daniels never came back to visit me.

CHAPTER 10

Prison is a place where you lose respect for the law because you see it raw and naked, twisted, and bent and ignored, and blown out of proportion to suit the people who enforce it.

From a Student Theme

Prison riots occur almost every summer. They start in one prison, spread to others, and newspaper accounts of them invariably claim they are racial in origin. They are perpetrated by physically healthy, frustrated young men who see the flowers blooming outside the walls and experience the degradation of confinement inside them. Many sources can be quoted on the causes of prison riots, and many contributing factors exist. There is no way, however, to deprive men of freedom and at the same time guarantee their docility.

Prison authorities are prepared to cope with riots and can systematically withdraw such privileges as yard time or television viewing until the ultimate in confinement is reached. This is achieved when all inmates are locked in their cells and are fed from trays of food which are pushed under their cell doors.

The first step in riot prevention is to identify and isolate the troublemakers. This is done with the cooperation of prison informers, or "snitches," who report them to the prison authorities. The troublemakers are then sent to other prisons, where their influence over other inmates has not been established. During the summer buses move every day, carrying their cargo of shackled men. It is reminiscent of the game of Hearts, in which each player passes unwanted cards to his neighbor. No charges are brought against the men who are transferred, although a record of frequent movement does not stand a man in good stead with the parole board.

The men who are moved are usually highly intelligent and, if they are agitators, can easily start their activities in the setting of another prison. Indeed, it could be argued this bussing creates a cross fertilization that spreads riots. Certainly it opens up channels of communication between the various prisons in the California system.

Rumblings of racial unrest could be sensed in May of my first year in the prison. At this time a black inmate named Chamberlin was transferred to my class on the complaint of another teacher who claimed he was inciting other black inmates to riot by writing themes on racial topics.

My classes had become the dumping ground for undesirable students. I never protested this practice, as many of my best students had come to me as rejects from other teachers. I found an undesirable student was usually a young man with an independent mind who had low tolerance for the society that had rejected him. Using my discussion technique, I gave him a chance to articulate and defend his point of view. As I refrained from giving my opinion, he found himself arguing with his peer group rather than with me.

Chamberlin flourished in this atmosphere. He was a handsome young man, with woolly hair, sensitive brown eyes and gun-metal blue skin. He walked flat-footed, with a "don't tread on me, motherfucker" air.

Because of tension in the prison, I avoided all racial topics in my classes at this time. We discussed *Antigone* and whether or not a person should obey a bad law. Chamberlin dug into the play and demonstrated a remarkable grasp of its subtleties and contradictions.

In his written assignments he at first turned in themes outlining the injustices suffered by the black man. They were good themes, eloquently expressed; yet they were derivative, and I wanted him to reach more deeply into his creative talent. I explained to him that while I was in no way critical of his work, I felt his talent lay in description and character development rather than in polemics.

He became an enthusiastic student and once told a rigid-thinking joint-converted Black Muslim student who questioned the value of education, "I used to think like you, but now I know different. There's a lot in a book if you can read it and think about it and come to your own conclusions. Running games doesn't lead to anything but death and destruction. From now on, I'm going to spend my time getting an education."

"Hold it, Mr. Chamberlin," I said stopping him in the middle of his speech. "I don't believe you."

"What's the matter, you believe those things, don't you?" he asked.

"Yes, I believe them. But I think you're trying to con me. You're going before the board in a few months, and I think you're trying to make sure I give you a good report. Don't worry, I'll give you the best possible recommendation. What I want from you is the truth, not my party line."

He looked at my sheepishly and said, "How did you know that? It's frightening. I get the feeling you can see right inside my head."

"You're conning me again," I said.

After this, Chamberlin started doing excellent written work. He wrote a short story about his experiences in Vietnam, where he had served for two years. His story contained sensitive description of the Vietnamese countryside and told how the Vietcong promoted racial trouble in the U.S. Army, exhorting the black soldiers to fight on their side, as they were all fighting for the right to their independence.

When we discussed the story after class, Chamberlin told me of another incident he hadn't written about. While in Vietnam he had made friends with a white southerner he called Snowdrop. While on a forward patrol, the Vietcong had infiltrated their position and slit the throats of all the sleeping white soldiers. Snowdrop had been killed, while none of the black soldiers were touched. Chamberlin was confused, because he was bitter about the unfair treatment black people had suffered and the death of Snowdrop had clearly demonstrated that whites could lose their lives because of their color.

I suggested he write a story about his relationship with Snowdrop, but he replied he couldn't, as it would work against the best interests of black people. He told me he had never discussed this with anyone else and asked me not to repeat it. I felt this time he wasn't trying to con me.

The original story Chamberlin had written about Vietnam impressed me so favorably I read it aloud to my other classes as an example of good writing.

A white student came to me after class and said, "Mr. Campbell, I think I should tell you that you're not to read that story or anything else Chamberlin writes again, or there'll be trouble on the line for you."

"Why should there be trouble on the line?" I asked.

"I'm just warning you," he said. "There's talk against it."

I couldn't think of any reason, other than jealousy, why the white students should object to the reading of the story. I did realize, however, that I was dealing with a very primitive mentality.

"I'm running this English class," I said, "and it's up to me to decide what I'm going to read."

"Telling you about this makes me a snitch, and I can get in a world of hurt," the student said. "I'm letting you know because I like you and don't want you to get into trouble."

Shortly after this, Chamberlin came to me and warned me not to read the story again or give him any encouragement in class. I told him I was not going to be intimidated by anyone.

"You know nothing about prison, and you're a fool," Chamberlin said excitedly.

"All right, I'm a fool, but I'm not going to back down," I replied. I was concerned because the situation was tense, but I continued to read the story in my classes; and a reprisal was taken against me, although of a completely different nature from anything I had expected.

One morning I was in the prison barber shop, having my hair cut. I was relaxed and garrulous, and very much a sitting target for what happened. When the barber had finished cutting my hair and I put my glasses back on to look in the mirror, I found I had been given a Black Muslim haircut. My head had been almost completely shaved, with only a tuft of hair in the center shading off to bare scalp at the temples.

"Well, I'll be damned," I said to the barber. "How much did you get paid to do this to me?"

"A carton of Pall Malls," he said foolishly.

"Why, you bastard," I said, smiling. I was relieved because I thought this a clever way to get back at me and, as hair does grow back, a relatively painless one.

When I returned to the educational area everyone, including Hugo Belson, immediately noticed what had happened to me. The students, black and white, laughed hysterically and were very curious about my reaction. I treated my new hairstyle with hilarity, and read Chamberlin's story for a third time in my class without incurring additional threats.

Hugo Belson urged me to turn in the inmate barber who had given me the haircut. I refused to do so, saying I had requested it, as it was going to be a hot summer and I wanted to give my scalp a chance to breathe.

The school officials and teachers put no additional pressure on me to report the barber, but one day as I was sitting in the snack bar, the Protestant minister nervously questioned me about what had happened. I told him I had requested the haircut. He ignored my reply and said, "You must understand when you don't report something like this, you threaten every free person in

189

the institution. It means inmates can ridicule free personnel without punishment."

I did not pursue the conversation with him.

A short time later Belson bum-beefed the barber, anyway, and sent him to the hole for ten days on a false charge. The barber had the opportunity to appeal his case but did not do so. Belson correctly guessed anyone stupid enough to shave someone's head for a carton of cigarettes is incapable of defending himself against rigged charges.

I talked to the barber after he got out of the hole. He laughed about the experience, not minding the bum beef since he thought he should be punished for what he had done to me. In any case, he had his carton of cigarettes.

Chamberlin continued his writing and produced an excellent series of vignettes about a mother and son on a southern farm. I encouraged him to expand these into a book. He became deeply involved in this project and went back to the class from which he had been transferred, as well as attending mine. He began writing love poetry in the other class. His female teacher became interested in his work and encouraged him. He told me he was no longer writing on racial subjects, that he wanted to do his time and be released in order to go to college. Chamberlin finished my class in June.

In early July we were already in the midst of a blazing summer. The temperature rose well over one hundred degrees. When the temperature in the classrooms reached ninety-eight, classes were cancelled and the men were released to the yard. The tension was increasing daily. It is difficult to describe a prison when a riot is in the offing. From my window I could see the trucks pulling up, unloading tear-gas cannisters, gas masks and other paraphernalia. It was as if they were delivering props for a spectacular play and all of us were going to have a part in it.

I had no fear for my safety. The trouble was brewing back in the cell blocks and on the yard. However, I realized a spark could ignite anywhere and it was possible the education wing would be the first to burst into violence. I had a plan if this happened. At the first sign of a ruckus I would shut and lock my door. (It was

190

left open during the summer to catch a breeze.) I would calm the students and instruct them that if the disturbance came our way we would jam the desks, chairs and whatever else we had against the doors—blacks, whites, Mexicans working together so nobody could get at us. We would wait until the bulls armed with tear-gas guns, mace and billy clubs fought their way into the education area, down the long corridor to my classroom and liberated us. It wouldn't take very long.

The students realized the classroom was the safest place to be and were reluctant to leave. Corridors, which during break times ordinarily swarmed with people, contained only a few stragglers nervously puffing on cigarettes. No one stirred until the bell rang for the next class and they had to move from one room to another.

About a week before the riot I walked into my first morning class and immediately sensed that something was terribly wrong. I could feel and almost see the waves of emotion coming from the students. Yet, to the naked eye, things were no different from any other morning. It was like a van Gogh landscape. Everything was in complete control, but you could sense the raging madness behind it. I gave the class a lengthy grammar assignment, which they eagerly accepted. They became completely involved in copying dull sentences, shutting themselves off from me and each other.

I left the room and walked the corridor. In every classroom the same scene was reenacted. No talking, no movement—only furious concentration over a meaningless book or piece of paper.

Near the end of the corridor I met Mr. Albertson, a free person in charge of janitorial services in the prison.

"I just called security," he said. "Come here, I want to show you something." He directed me to his mop closet. There on the floor, wrapped in wet brown paper towels, was the nastiest-looking instrument I had ever seen. It was all metal and at one time had perhaps been a piece of pipe. It had been shaved down, sharpened, and the thicker end bent into a handle. The powerful twist of a weight lifter's wrist could have driven it, to the curved hilt, into any human body.

"I discovered it taped to the ceiling of the closet. I never would have looked there in a million years. Someone rinsed it off in the shitter across the hall to clear it of fingerprints. Then he wrapped it in paper towels and stuck it to the ceiling with surgical tape from the infirmary. Lucky for us, he did. I was rummaging in the closet for supplies and felt a drop of water on my head. I thought a pipe had burst. When I glanced up, I found it."

By the time he finished his story, a whole group of security guards had arrived and were admiring it.

I returned to my classroom and observed the pain on the faces of my students. I now understood what was disturbing them. Through their grapevine they all knew a killing was supposed to take place in the education area this day.

No one said a word, but I knew what they were feeling. Someone's going to die here today. Someone's going to die—and it could be me. It's stupid and it's senseless. I'm petrified but I'm powerless to do anything about it.

"All right, men, I have good news," I said, slamming a book against my desk to get their attention. "Nobody's going to get hit. Mr. Albertson just found the shank in his closet."

There was great relief. Everyone wanted me to describe the shank. I refused to do it. Why trip them out on something as gruesome as that. By the same token, I knew it was useless to ask them the questions I had. Who was supposed to be stabbed? Why was he supposed to be stabbed? How did they all know it was supposed to happen? Why was the education area chosen for a hit?

A bull came into the classroom and politely informed us that all inmates were to be skin searched. Since my classroom was the last one down the hall, it would be some time before they got to us.

Here's how a skin search was conducted. The men lined up and came out of the room one at a time. They removed all clothing, including their shoes, and handed it to a guard. One guard inspected their clothing, another their bodies. After the clothes were inspected, the guard tossed them to the inmate and he was free to get dressed and return to his unit.

192

School was dismissed for the rest of the morning but would begin again right after lunch. I was expected to stay with my students until the guard took over. I didn't have to stick around to witness the searching procedure.

We were sitting around talking when suddenly a naked dude, smoking a fat cigar and carrying his clothes on top of his head, appeared in the doorway. He was completely bewildered, and after a blast from a police whistle and a shout from a guard he turned and fled. Apparently, after being searched he became disoriented and thought he was walking toward the stairwell, when in fact he was going in the opposite direction toward my classroom. Probably the guard found the cigar while searching his pockets and allowed him to smoke it while he was waiting. It was a trivial incident. But in that highly charged atmosphere it was uproariously funny for all of us.

The following day there was minor violence in my first afternoon class. We were doing *Romeo and Juliet* at the time, and although there is much violence in this play, I doubt that what happened was triggered by the antics of the Shakespearean characters. It is an unusual play to read with an all-male cast in one-hundred-degree weather in a prison that is about to explode.

Inmates love to read plays and have a flair for the dramatic. Most of them are avid television watchers, and all, of course, have been central figures in the courtroom scene where they were sentenced. They have all been expelled from school, where because of disruptive tendencies, they had not been asked to participate in group activities. As every play has several parts, many inmates can, for the first time, participate in something. There is much comedy in having huge men play female parts. I feel certain Shakespeare's shade would be more delighted by a prison reading of one of his plays than by a polished performance by professional actors.

Women's parts are difficult to cast, in this case, particularly that of Juliet. Only masculine men will play women's parts; men not sure of their masculinity will not. Homosexuals, surprisingly, are reluctant to play female roles. Perhaps they are worried the publicity will give them more business than they can handle. I volunteered to read some female parts but refused the lead, as I felt the starring role should be performed by a student.

Dipper played Ladies Montague and Capulet, as well a nurse. He was a strange, awkward man who worked hard in school but always managed to say the wrong thing. He was called a homosexual but I doubt he was. He had, in fact, been convicted of child molesting, but wouldn't admit to it because he stood a good chance of getting murdered if he did. Child molesting is the one crime prisoners detest.

Dipper had no previous record. At the age of eighteen he had been babysitting for a neighbor. The baby finished his bottle and was crying. Dipper had an erection while thinking about his girl friend and, acting on a wild impulse, he put his penis in the baby's mouth. At this moment the baby's mother returned unexpectedly and walked in on the scene.

As Dipper said, "The shit really hit the fan." The mother summoned her sister and both became hysterical. Dipper, in a daze, made no effort to leave and was picked up by the police. He got a five-year term and a molestation conviction permanently on his record.

As the mother was the only witness, I asked him why he had admitted to this crime. Dipper said, "Well, I done it." If he had denied it, he could perhaps have received psychiatric care and been released.

An inmate named Watkins played Mercutio. He was a tough kid who had some literary ability. In prison language he was what is called a gunsill, a loud-talking, aggressive individual, with a record that is not very bad, who tries to impress the other inmates with how dangerous he is and who preys upon weaker inmates.

Watkins made insinuating remarks about homosexuality to Dipper. I warned him about it. Later he again made a wisecrack and this time Dipper called him on it. Watkins swaggered over to Dipper, who jumped up and belted Watkins in his stomach and cheekbone, knocking him out.

It happened too fast for me to stop. Two inmates carried

194

Watkins to his chair and laid his head on the armrest, checking first to make sure he had not swallowed his tongue.

All such incidents and any letting of blood, no matter how slight, have to be reported. Watkins had a small trickle of blood on his cheek, but it was not serious. I didn't want to report the fight, for I felt Watkins deserved his punishment. I had to protect myself, however, so I asked the inmates, "You didn't see what happened, did you?"

"No, Watkins is a little sleepy and is taking a nap," they chorused.

All went well after that. As our 230-pound black Romeo declaimed, "What light through yonder window breaks ...," Watkins woke up and I sent him off to the washroom to clean himself up.

The following day at about 1:15 an inmate named Nickerson asked to be excused from class to go to the john. Nickerson was a quiet, slightly built white man who did his written work well but rarely contributed to discussion in class.

He returned in fifteen minutes, looking pale. He said he was not feeling well and requested permission to go to the infirmary. As it was extremely hot, I thought he was suffering from heat prostration. I instructed his friend Craig to go with him to the dispensary after checking in with the school office.

Craig returned ten minutes later and asked to speak to me in the corridor. "Nickerson was shanked," he said. "They got him in the gut twice. Then they whipped him with a sock packed with batteries and razor blades. He was chewed up something awful—he's all red meat on his belly and his back."

"When the hell did that happen?" I asked

"He left your room to go to the john. He was squatting over the shitter with his jacket off when four black dudes nabbed him and worked him over."

"Four black dudes? Does he know who they are?"

"He claims they aren't from Education and he never saw them before; even if he did see them, it all happened so fast he couldn't recognize them again. You know how it is, Mr. Campbell. He wants to live."

195

"Did you check in with Hugo Belson before you left for the infirmary?" I asked.

"Nickerson was in bad shape; we didn't stop for nothin'," Craig said.

"OK," I said. "Thanks for helping out. Go back to your seat and keep cool."

When we returned to the classroom I looked at the clock. It was only five minutes until the end of the period. My phone was in earshot of everyone. I was not going to walk to it, call Belson and inform him one of my students had been stabbed. I could have created a panic. I elected to go down at the break and inform him personally what had happened.

At the break I was at the stairs when I met Belson and the captain of the guards on their way up. Belson was angry because I had not notified him immediately. I explained I didn't know Nickerson had been stabbed when I sent him to the infirmary. I thought he was sick and he looked so bad I sent someone along to make certain he got there. The hospital had called security as soon as they admitted Nickerson. So as far as I could see, everything had been taken care of.

Captain Proctor, Belson and I inspected my room carefully. There was not one spot of blood anywhere. We reasoned that after he had been hit, he put on his jacket again and held it tightly about him, holding back the blood. Captain Proctor thanked me for helping him and agreed there was nothing more I could have done.

He didn't believe it was necessary to skin search the students because whoever had perpetrated the crime was long gone from the scene with the evidence. All his guards were needed back in the units, because when it became known in the cell blocks a white dude had been brutally stabbed and lacerated by four blacks, there would be trouble on the line.

I turned the last class of the day on to seat work. As yet they didn't know what had happened, but it wouldn't take long. I wondered about Nickerson's story. Why was he wearing that coarse denim jacket in the first place? The temperature was nearly a hundred degrees. He sure as hell didn't need it to keep

196

himself warm. There was the possibility he had been shanked in his unit and had put on his jacket and tried to tough it out. Maybe when he went to the bathroom he realized his wounds were extensive and he would have to have medical attention.

Or I could advance the theory that the shank planted in the closet in the early morning a week earlier was to be used on him in the afternoon. Maybe the shanking of Nickerson had nothing to do with riots or racial tension. Maybe he was hit by another white dude who insisted he tell the story it was done by blacks. The speculation was endless. What was interesting was that custody had no inclination to suppress the story that it was done by a group of blacks, whether it was true or not. They were not psychologists. Their response was to beef up their security so they could handle any disturbance. Everyone knew damned well there would be reprisals.

The next morning the California newspapers carried a story stating that a white inmate named Nickerson had been set upon in a high school prison classroom by four blacks. He suffered two stab wounds and twenty-seven severe lacerations upon his body, but he would survive.

That afternoon a black inmate was stabbed while in his unit. This was followed by two or three more stabbings. The next afternoon gunfire crackled from the yard. The guards claimed the inmates had begun to form into racial groups: white, black and Mexican. They signalled to the prisoners over loudspeakers to clear the yard. When it wasn't cleared fast enough, the guards in the towers fired bullets into the ground in front of the men to send them back to their units. (If the inmates refuse to return, the guards can fire directly into them.) The yard was then cleared.

The next day in class, my students protested that no racial group had tried to start a riot. They claimed that a crowd had gathered to stare at a homosexual in the protective custody unit who had stuck his bare ass out the window and was pointing to it and yoo-hooing. Although the two stories didn't jibe, there was no way to determine the truth.

The class finished *Romeo and Juliet*. The tension was so fierce I decided to assign a grammar lesson they could do quietly at their seats. One student said as I passed out the books, "Usually showing me a grammar book is like showing a cross to a vampire. Today I welcome it."

During the grammar work, a young Irishman named Flaherty came up to my desk and asked if he could address the class. Flaherty was an ex-marine who had been shot five times in an attempted holdup. He was strong and tough and not one to be messed around. He had served three years time and had read a good deal, something he had never done before he went to prison. He claimed he no longer had the desire for money that had led him to rob.

He stood in front of the class and pounded his fist into his hand as he talked.

"You all know what's happening here. Nickerson was stabbed, and the shit is about ready to come down. I think it's a mistake. You all know what happens when the riots start. You get gassed. We all get shot at. Those of us who survive get long time on account of it.

"Who gains from a riot? I'll tell you who gains: the guards. They get overtime. It's just like a Christmas bonus for them. All the time they're kicking the shit out of us, they get paid extra for it.

"If we want to stand up for our rights and accomplish things around here, we all have to work together, and that means blacks, whites, and Mexicans. These prison guards promote this racial shit because the truth is we run this prison, and if we'd stick together instead of separating into groups, we could bring the motherfucker down.

"As long as they set us fighting among ourselves, they can control us, and that's exactly what they aim to do. The jerks who say, 'Get the rugheads' only make things worse for all of us." He nodded to the black inmates and said, "Excuse me, I didn't mean any racial slur by this."

The black man who had played Romeo nodded back and said, "You're telling it like it is, man."

"We all know the shit's about ready to come down," Flaherty continued, "and the agitators ain't gonna be there when it

198

happens. You know who they are. It's the Hell's Angels standing around in the units, rapping shit and saying, 'Let's tear the motherfucker down,' and then when when the shit does come down, they ain't nowhere to be seen—they're locked up in their cells.

"You ever watched that the guys talk the toughest, when it comes down to the action, they're nowhere around. It's the quiet bastards that get out there and not get their heads knocked and bleed, and if we're all so God damned dumb we can't see it, we deserve what we get."

After this speech there was silence and then black Romeo said, "I agree with everything Flaherty said. I want to do my time and I ain't mad at no one. As far as I'm concerned, we should all mind our business and not get involved with this racial crap, but somehow it's not so easy. Sometimes a line is drawn—you have to choose; and you can't sit around and think about it or complain that's not the way it should be. You have to make a choice, and when you do, you choose your own people."

I asked the students why they thought prison guards promoted racial strife.

White Juliet replied, "If you're going to run any organization, you do it by keeping the people under you off-balance. Any large corporation does the same thing. You get people fighting for each other's jobs or more pay, and you have them off-balance and can control them."

I then asked the students how they thought riots could be prevented or stopped. The comment was made that the men in the high school classes were not among those promoting riots. Everyone agreed it was those with a lack of education who were the troublemakers. They were easily excited and were so restless and frustrated they simply wanted something to happen. No one took the position that if a riot came down it was a battle between the blacks and the whites, although there was certainly evidence that racial unrest did exist in the prison.

Although prison authorities pick leaders from the various racial groups and consult with them as to how to prevent riots, the students agreed that no individual leader could speak for a group, and doubted this practice helped. Once set in motion, riots seem to have a life of their own, independent of what is done to stop them.

I was in the snack bar after school, thinking about Flaherty's speech, when I smelled smoke. I went outside and noted there was a great deal of tear gas in the air. I could hear gas guns popping. A plume of smoke was coming from K unit. This is the isolation area, hole, or prison hotel. Here men are locked into individual cells, have thin mattresses, bad rations and are not allowed to smoke. They can only pace and think. It is considered the punishment area of a prison. A heavy iron grating separates this area from the rest of the prison. Inmates call this screen "the iron cunt." Several inmates had overpowered a guard, taken his keys and escaped from their cells. They ran amok, piled mattresses and chairs against the iron grating and set them on fire.

The inmates surrendered in less than an hour and were locked up again.

I later talked to a Mexican inmate who had been in K unit at the time. The guard who had been overpowered, an elderly man, had been in terror and had begged the inmates, on his knees, not to assault him sexually. This guard was hated for his many unnecessary cruelties. He had recently watered down an inmate's mattress, with the result that the inmate had to sleep on the floor for two nights. In spite of this kind of harassment, the guard had been so pitiful in his entreaties the inmates felt only disgust for him and ceased to threaten him.

That evening J unit blew. The inmates were watching a program in the TV room. At 8:00 P.M. a black inmate turned off the television set for an undetermined reason and racial groups formed immediately. Several inmates had socks filled with razor blades or batteries saved from transistor radios. Others carried homemade zip guns or knives carved from toothbrushes.

The TV room is in an enclosed area. The guards locked the doors, trapping sixty inmates inside, and shot tear gas into the room. This kind of situation is easy for the guards to handle. They have control of things and are in no physical danger.

Although tear gas doesn't suffocate, the inmates feel they are strangling, and this creates panic. The TV rooms have heavily leaded, inch-thick glass windows. The inmates battered at the windows with their fists, trying frantically to get air. It is impossible for the men to break these windows under ordinary circumstances; they have to be in a frenzy to do it. When they pulled their wrists back in through the panes, the broken glass shredded their wrists and hands. To the cleanup people, the place must have looked like a slaughterhouse, with blood smeared everywhere.

After an hour, the men were subdued and were let out of the TV room one at a time and locked up. The next day the inmates were allowed no yard time and had to go to chow in individual units.

School started on Monday as usual. Yard duty was allowed again, with the warning that the prison would be buttoned up for two weeks if more trouble occurred. The inmates in the education department were told that school might be discontinued, in which case no diplomas would be awarded.

During the day, rumors of blood and carnage started to circulate throughout the prison.

At 8:00 P.M. on Monday all units blew. I was in the bachelors' quarters, where I could hear screams and curses. The off-duty guards were called back. The guards ordered everyone out of the bachelor's quarters and instructed us to get tear-gas masks and help subdue the rioters. All the lights were blazing and there was pandemonium.

I wanted no part of subduing inmates and stayed in my room. At about 9:00 P.M. the tear gas became very strong, so I went to the snack bar, which was equipped with fans. The snack bar is run by trusties and no guards were present; they were all inside the prison, quelling the riot. I sat talking to some inmates who were glad not to be involved in the riot. They were, however, reluctant to discuss it with me.

At 9:00 P.M. the guards started coming into the snack bar, red-eyed from tear gas, but laughing. They were enjoying themselves and chattering like high school football players after the big game. I felt Flaherty had been accurate in his description of the guards' feelings toward riots.

The guards were discussing a shotgun blast that had been heard earlier. A Lieutenant Randolph had fired the blast from the catwalk, directly into a mass of confused, staggering inmates. A guard remarked, "Lieutenant Randolph really has balls." The inmates had, apparently, left the TV room more than one at a time, choking on tear gas and milling around in the corridors. It was then that Lieutenant Randolph had fired into them. The guards thought this a courageous action, as firing a shotgun incurs an investigation; they felt Randolph had put his job on the line. As it turned out, there was no investigation, so Lieutenant Randolph's courage was not challenged.

School was cancelled immediately. The institution closed down. When the prisoners went to chow, all free personnel had to stand in the corridor to keep watch on them as they went by. This was a slow process. The odor of tear gas still hung in the air the following morning and many prisoners were weeping. One inmate danced along singing, "Gas ain't shit, gas ain't shit." But most appeared exhausted and discouraged.

I nodded to my students as they passed. Flaherty looked at me and shook his head as if to say, "Well, I tried." Cunard, a brilliant student, became incensed at seeing me and said, "Look at that, Mr. Campbell is a cop, a fucking cop." Passing me on the way back from chow, he stopped and said quietly, "You were hired to be a teacher, not a cop. Why are you letting them do this to you? Why don't you show some balls?"

Cunard's comments hurt. I had had a good relationship with him. He had once brought me a poem by Edna St. Vincent Millay in which were the lines:

> Safe upon the solid rock
>   The ugly houses stand:
> Come and see my shining palace
>   Built upon the sand!

202

"That describes us, huh, Mr. Campbell," he had said.

I thought about "Romeo's" remark about choosing your own kind. In this case, my side had been the power group in the prison. To protest could have meant the loss of my job, and at the time I had thought it more important to continue working with the inmates than to show integrity. I understood better why inmates opposed to riots didn't take a more active part in preventing them.

After chow we had the unpleasant task of searching the cells for weapons. I was on a team with Mr. Farnsworth, a prosperous businessman who had retired and gone into teaching because he wanted to do something useful.

Before the search, the guard ordered the inmates out of their cells one at a time and made them strip. When the inmates' hatred showed on their faces, they were further humiliated by having to pull back their foreskins in a "search" for concealed razor blades.

The cells were pitiful. We were supposed to dump all personal belongings onto the bedclothes and then throw everything onto the floor. Farnsworth and I didn't do this and concentrated instead on looking for overdue library books.

Farnsworth and I went on to search another tier. The guard had all the inmates standing at attention, completely naked, waiting for their cells to be searched. I came across one of my copies of *Apology and Crito* in the cell of one of my former students. I picked it up and riffled through it. Parts of it were heavily underlined; comments were written in the margin. I couldn't bring myself to rip it away from him.

I went outside that tiny cell, where my former student was standing buck naked, milking back his foreskin under the watchful eye of a guard who was conducting a thorough search for concealed bits of razor blades, sometimes hidden, so the old timers say, in unlikely places.

"That book; it used to be mine. Please accept it as a gift from me," I said gently.

"Thank you, Mr. Campbell," he said proudly, cloaking himself with a dignity few of us with raiment will ever achieve. "All of us appreciate what you did for us."

Everyone in the prison had been weeping some that morning. Tear gas saturates clothing and lingers in pockets and the slightest breeze will fling it into your face and cause tearing many hours after it has been released.

I was glad of that, because what gripped me was not the residue of noxious fumes. It was a tightening in the belly which spread upward. I fought it by clenching my teeth and avoiding a womanish gasp. But it hit my eyes and splattered out. No one, not even the guard, suspected I was a sentimental son of a bitch.

At 2:30 we finished the inspection. No illegal instrument was found in the entire prison. Much contraband was found, including extra shirts and highly starched trousers called bonna rus, which the men, who are identically dressed, occasionally wore to stand out from the crowd. Over six hundred overdue library books were collected.

A teachers' meeting was called. Hugo Belson congratulated us on our cooperation. He stated the guards were usually jealous of teachers because of their higher pay. He said it had now been proved that teachers "could do a man's job." I did not feel we teachers had done a man's job, but rather that none of us had greatly honored our profession.

After the riot, I received an official written reprimand from Hugo Belson for not having reported the stabbing of Nickerson immediately. I was told I could have a hearing. I ignored the citation and no punitive action was taken against me.

Chamberlin, who had written the story about Vietnam, was accused by his female teacher of stabbing Nickerson. I asked Chamberlin about this, and he claimed the charge was ridiculous; he was not that sort of person. He said when he had written the love poems, which were to his wife, the teacher had thought they were meant for her and became incensed on hearing this was not the case.

In her original report she stated Nickerson had been out of her classroom during the stabbing. The other students testified this was not true. The teacher then tried to claim Nickerson had been stabbed at noon rather than at 1:15 when he had been excused to go to the bathroom.

Chamberlin was interrogated and brought to trial in the institution. He was acquitted but taken out of school. He needed only a few credits to graduate. Chamberlin was later sent to the adjustment center, a nonpunitive section where those who couldn't satisfactorily conform to prison were sent.

Chamberlin claimed he had been railroaded. A guard had come to his cell before his transfer, called him a racist and torn up all his writing. The guard said he was saving Chamberlin from trouble, because if the authorities had read his "racist" literature, his sentence would be extended. Chamberlin was helpless to do anything about this.

The destruction of Chamberlin's writing seemed to affect me more than it did him. He shrugged and said, "What I have is in my head; they can't take that from me."

Chamberlin needed only one English credit for graduation. I requested the opportunity to give him credit for work in my class. The request was denied. I then checked with Chamberlin's counsellor as to why he had been put in the adjustment center. His counsellor investigated and told me somebody goofed.

I asked him what could be done to get Chamberlin back on the main line and into classes so he could get his high school diploma.

The counsellor advised me to back away from the case. He stated any further investigation on my part would lead to trouble for me and for Chamberlin. He mentioned that Chamberlin was coming up for a parole hearing and any inquiries would eliminate Chamberlin's chances for release.

I talked things over with Chamberlin and told him I was convinced he had been railroaded and I was willing to put everything on the line to help him.

Chamberlin begged me not to interfere in any way. He said he clearly understood how the system worked and I could only damage him.

"What they want is a good nigger," he said.

He then wrote a letter to the head of the Department of

Corrections in which he freely admitted his crime and listed the many things that had been done to help him while he was in prison. He enclosed a picture of his wife holding their baby in her arms and wrote, "This is a picture of a child holding a child. They need me and I need them."

There was no bitterness or recrimination in this letter. It was a classic cop-out. Chamberlin received his parole and two weeks later returned to his family in San Diego, confident he knew how to beat the system.

CHAPTER 11

*Prison is a place where you forget who put you
there, where you have the vague idea you are being
punished, but you don't know what for.*

From a Student Theme

After the riots, the prison settled down. Before we knew it, it
was fall. The itinerant farm workers in the surrounding valley
moved on. They came with the early spring asparagus, harvested
the summer tomatoes and corn, picked the autumn fruits and the
English walnuts that appear in our Christmas stockings, and
vanished like the mist.

Many left their dogs behind. Almost every day, driving home
from work, I would see a gaunt animal trotting aimlessly along
the blacktop road. Most of them would die of starvation and rot
in the lemon-colored sunshine of a California autumn, unable to
survive in one of the richest valleys in the world.

In late autumn came the heavy fog, rising and rolling from the
nearby delta land. Sometimes, in the early morning, the prison
was completely obscured. When the fog started to lift or burn
away, I could see from my classroom a solitary guard, big bellied
from the shotgun lashed beneath his coat, walking resolutely,
round and round the fence.

When the fog waited until early afternoon to bury us, the

207

recall whistle blew three blasts, and our students returned to their chilly cells. When the prison was buttoned up, we teachers in our lonely classrooms were free to work at or ponder what we chose for the rest of the day.

Things were starting to change in the prison. A new superintendent, Mr. Feather, was appointed. Petoskey, our inmate superintendent, was paroled. At this time, two remarkable men, both inmates, came to my attention. They were highly intelligent, educated gentlemen and both commanded respect in our strange community.

Reverend Darling was in jail for embezzling $200,000 from the Baptist Church. The prison, by orders from Sacramento, embarked on a program of using inmates who were college graduates as teachers in the educational system. By doing this, they could get qualified teachers at no salary. Reverend Darling, because of his academic background, was picked to be a teacher in our school and was put in charge of a first-grade class.

His first day of teaching, I happened to be walking by his classroom on the first floor. As he stood before his students, an inmate said, "Hey, Pop, what're you in for?"

"Let us say, like you, I am a bad man," replied Reverend Darling.

Reverend Darling had been a highly respected member of his community. Not only was he a fully accredited Baptist minister, but he was also on the boards of two colleges near his parish. As chairman of a church building fund, he held monies accrued. When the building committee decided not to go ahead with plans to build the addition, he found himself with the money and no accounting system for its disposal. Reverend Darling realized he could keep the money for himself and no one would be the wiser.

At this point, apparently, he received some kind of message from God, informing him he was going to die within a year. He could take the funds and use his remaining time to provide lavishly for his family and do good works. At the end of the allotted year, since he carried an insurance policy of more than a quarter million dollars, he could replace all the money he had "borrowed." He accepted this message as the will of God.

208

There were other ways in which he could embezzle monies. The Baptist Church puts complete trust in its ministers, and there is no strict financial accountability as in other religious denominations. He spent the money on a trip to Europe with his family; he bought a Cadillac; he gave money to parishioners who were in need; and he lived his life as he chose.

At the end of the year, instead of dying, he found himself in excellent health. This mystified him and he found himself wishing he were dead. Finally, when the pressure became too intense and he realized he was not going to die, he went to the authorities and turned himself in. It would have been possible for him to abscond to another country with the money. But he would not do this because he genuinely believed his fantasy and was certain he was following God's plan.

I checked Reverend Darling's records in Central Files and was interested in how the board members of his church viewed him. Some of the members were furious with him and felt he had betrayed God, church and family. They could find no excuse for his actions because he, more than other men, should have been scrupulously honest. Other board members continued to maintain respect for Reverend Darling and felt he had done what he did because of religious conviction. I remember specifically, in a somewhat stilted form letter sent by the prison, the question was: "Why did inmate leave his last employment?"

One board member replied, "Because you people locked him up." He then responded that it wasn't what the prison could do for Reverend Darling, but what Reverend Darling could do for the prison that was important. He added that Reverend Darling's high Christian spirit would make itself evident, and he would be a force for good in the prison.

Reverend Darling told the story that after he had been sentenced and was in the reception center being processed, one of his young parishioners whom he had counselled saw him. His parishioner, also an inmate, came over to him and said, "That's all right, Reverend Darling, don't feel bad. I believe everything you tole me about doin' good was true, anyway."

Reverend Darling organized a religious group which met every

Friday in the prison chapel. It consisted of approximately twelve people, both inmates and free. I attended one of these meetings. We joined hands and prayed together. I remember a black man who was in for a serious crime, and how, as we held hands, he prayed for us. He prayed so hard, sweat streamed down his face. It was impossible not to be caught up in the sincerity of the moment and the power of his prayer.

Reverend Darling was highly respected by his first-grade students and functioned, as much as the rest of us, as a teacher. Of course, his contribution was without pay. According to the philosophy that was developing in his mind, this was exactly the way it should have been. He did request from Hugo Belson to be removed from the main line and put in an honor cell. This was in a separate wing, had its own small TV day room and was reserved for inmates who performed special duties within the institution. However, Belson denied this request and kept him on the main line.

His family and children continued to be loyal to him, and Reverend Darling felt that what had happened to him had not destroyed his career, but had enabled him to find himself.

The second man, Demian Flowers, escaped from prison at this time. I first had contact with him when I was putting out the prison newspaper. He had been recommended to me as someone highly qualified to be the editor. I talked to him about it and he very quickly explained to me that prison authorities didn't want a newspaper and it wasn't a job anyone in his right mind would take.

I didn't see him again until about a year later. We both attended a meeting where a woman doctor explained her experimentations with LSD as part of a medical program at Menlo Park. I was astounded at his knowledge of psychology and psychiatric terminology. I had some experience in these areas, and it was obvious after a very short time that his knowledge was far greater than mine. In the years he had spent in Leavenworth, he had worked with Dr. Karl Menninger of the Menninger clinic in Topeka, and was thoroughly familiar with psychoanalysis.

210

Demian's speech was that of a cultivated man. He had been in prison most of his adult life, where he had been assigned to libraries and had read everything in sight. He also had training as an artist and, at one time, had earned a living duplicating the old masters. In only a matter of hours, he could reproduce a painting so flawlessly only a trained art critic could detect it was a forgery. He had a number of spectacular prison escapes to his credit. During one of them he stole the warden's airplane. He was a skilled pilot and he flew the plane to Mexico.

He had the dubious record, set ten years previously, of being the first person to escape from the prison where I taught. He escaped the first time by building a false bottom in a large water tank in the welding shop. When the tank passed through the gates for inspection, the guard thrust in a dipstick to determine that it was filled with water. After the tank was inspected and passed through the gate, Demian broke through the sheet metal and hoisted himself out of the tank to freedom.

He was due for parole about a month before his escape. Since he was soon to be released, he was allowed to work outside the prison fence. However, prison custody discovered he had a "hold" in Alabama for another crime. This meant that after he completed his term in California, he would be remanded to Alabama. He did not want to serve time in an Alabama prison. He was removed from minimum security and again put on close security within the prison grounds. It was at this time he planned his escape.

He painted a self-portrait in a khaki uniform and had the prison art teacher hang the picture so it was the first thing you saw in the visitors' entrance as you passed through a metal-detection device in the control unit. A week before his escape, he had the picture removed. Then he stole a guard's uniform and simply walked out the gate during a busy period. Approximately three hundred guards moved in and out of that gate on a daily basis. It was impractical to ask each one of them to show identification. Because of the painting, the guard on duty subliminally identified his face as someone he knew and didn't question him as he strolled out of the prison.

It took a long time for prison authorities to figure out that he had escaped. For at least two weeks after he came up missing, the grounds were patrolled by bloodhounds and special searchlights flooded the area. The assumption was that he was still within the prison somewhere, hiding, and that he would wait until late at night and attempt to scale the fence. However, a few weeks later he was picked up in New Jersey, driving a stolen car and impersonating a lieutenant colonel in the U.S. Air Force.

It is difficult to analyze why a man as talented and brilliant as Flowers would waste his life in jails. On the other hand, even if he were fully accredited and operating as a professor in some university, I doubt that academic life would fulfill him. Flowers enjoyed the notoriety he had in any prison where he was held. He delighted in exercising the cleverness that was necessary to pull off his capers. I doubt very much that he would have enjoyed the jockeying and infighting that is a part of academic life. He was a man who relished assuming many different identities, and could not pick out one that satisfied him.

He was returned to California custody, but not to the prison from which he had escaped twice before. I never saw him again.

At this time Hugo Belson called us teachers together and announced the approval of a grant from the federal government's Title I Project to improve prison education. The initial grant was for $150,000, and if things went properly an additional $300,000 would be forthcoming.

In order to qualify for the grant, the school was required to spend some monies on innovations in education. Belson asked for help in fulfilling that stipulation. I'd taken an education course with a fellow teacher, Colonel Rupert, who satisfied his requirement for innovation in education by demonstrating to the class how to fire a .45 revolver. He got an A- in the course.

After the meeting I talked to Hugo Belson and laid before him my credentials, including my original proposal for which a textbook publisher had given me an advance of $10,000. I told him I had been working with discussion for a year with splendid results and invited him to attend some of my classes so I could

212

demonstrate to him how a properly led discussion of ideas was an important innovation in education.

Hugo Belson didn't visit my classes. I submitted written material about my program, which he returned with the comment that it was interesting. He solved the innovation requirement by giving each student six dollars per month for as long as he stayed in school. In modern educational jargon, this is called positive reinforcement in a program of behavior modification. In less sophisticated times it would have been called bribery.

The school spent $70,000 for hardware to be used in teaching reading in the elementary school. All this equipment was put in the closet and not used during my time there. Money was spent on two additional security guards to patrol the education area, particularly around the lavatory where the stabbing that touched off the riot had occurred. Colonel Rupert was taken off his teaching assignment and put in the office, at a salary of $20,000, to administer the program. Three secretaries were hired and the college-trained inmate clerks who had had these jobs were sent back to the yard.

I requested 150 paperback books for my classes. My request was denied. Out of the $150,000, not a penny was available for a single book for me. A few days later Hugo Belson called me into his office and informed me that, as part of the federal grant, the school was reactivating a teaching post in the adjustment center. He said the men in the adjustment center were the men removed from the main line because they were the most dangerous, unpredictable men in prison. He also mentioned that two years previously they had assigned a teacher there, but the students shit in their pants and threw the feces at the teacher, and the teacher resigned. Since that time, no attempt had been made to give academic instruction in the adjustment center.

He said he was assigning me there one hour a day and I could continue teaching three courses on the main line. He also mentioned I could refuse the assignment if I desired. Hugo Belson wasn't very bright, but he was shrewd, and he knew damned well I would accept the job, which I did.

I returned to my afternoon classes, gloomy because I wasn't going to get any of the books I had half promised to the inmates. I explained the situation to my students and with some anger mentioned that instead of books we were going to get wall-to-wall carpeting and some miserable wretch to supervise them while they squatted over their seatless toilet bowls.

The students claimed the establishment was sinister and didn't want people to get an education, because if people became educated they would get rid of everyone presently in power. I had heard these arguments before, and didn't agree with them. I didn't believe the establishment to be sinister; I considered it unutterably stupid.

Then Milton, a black kid from East Oakland, spoke up and said, "Mr. Campbell, I know you've got something here. You've turned me on to *Antigone,* and some of those other things. I tell you honestly, I'm a knucklehead, and when you can reach someone like me, I know you got something good. But your problem is you can't front. And, man, if you can't front in this society, you can't survive. You gotta be more like Sydney."

Sydney was a character Milton had known who wore sharkskin suits and engaged in real estate and stock swindles and always had plenty of money and never got caught. Milton wrote fanciful themes about Sydney, and some of the other students picked up the format, so that Sydney became, in that class, the generic symbol for any slick high binder or supercon.

"What you should do," Milton continued, "is go to New York to one of those places where they know what to do with your program. Don't go inside. Just stand around outside and watch the dudes going in and out. If they got a short-brimmed hat, you get a short-brimmed hat. If they got a little, stubby briefcase, you get a little, stubby briefcase. Then after you get suited up, you walk in there like you got a million dollars in the bank and you're gonna show them how to make another million. That's how to sell your program. That's how Sydney would do it."

"That's a brilliant analysis," I said. "I don't want to offend you, Mr. Milton. But I don't love Sydney. I mean, Sydney makes me laugh and I respect it that you love him. That's your thing.

But what you don't understand is that if there is anyone in this world I don't want to be like, it's swindler Sydney. That's my thing."

"Aw, I do understand," Milton said consolingly. "I tell you what, Mr. Campbell, when I'm on the bricks again and we meet in East Oakland, I'll get you a high yaller with titties this big." Milton made exaggerated cupping motions in front of his chest.

"You big mouth, Milton, can't you tell Mr. Campbell ain't that kind of man?" another student said.

This broke the tension of the day for me, and I snorted with laughter. Two weeks later, I started teaching in the adjustment center.

215

CHAPTER 12

Prison is a place where you're smarter than the parole board, because you know which guys will go straight, and which ones won't. You're wrong just as often as the board members are—but you never admit it, and neither do they.

From a Student Theme

To get to my classroom in the adjustment center, I had to go through seven locked doors. The first door led from the main corridor of the prison to the adjustment center. This door had to be unlocked by a guard in the main corridor. No one inside the A.C., including the guards, had a key. This was so that if trouble did start in the A.C., it could not spread to the main-line prison. It also meant those free personnel inside the A.C. would be trapped there with no chance to escape should trouble arise.

After gaining entrance to the A.C., I passed through a wide corridor containing a cement-block partition in the center, with ten cells on either side. The partition was there so that prisoners could not see into the cells across from them. It was set up much like a mental institution, with strip cells for the more violent inmates on the first floor and the less violent ones housed on the second floor, where they had a few more privileges. There was a barber chair at the end of the corridor, where inmates of the first

216

tier received haircuts and shaves. On the second tier, inmates were allowed to shave themselves under supervision.

Whenever I walked this corridor, a forest of hands reached through the barred windows in the solid metal doors and I would hear:

"Hi, Teach."

"Hello, Teacher."

"Please talk to me."

On the other side of the partition, where I could not be seen, voices would also cry out.

"Who is it?"

"It's the teacher."

"What color tie is he wearin'?"

"It's a red one with black stripes."

"That's the same one he wore last Tuesday."

"When are you going to walk on our side?"

"I will when I come back," I would say.

When you are locked in a cement-block cell twenty-four hours a day, except for a weekly haircut, daily shave and shower, and an hour of exercise, the slightest change becomes a carnival event. This is unquestionably a cruel punishment. Yet prison authorities point out that if a man will adjust to this environment, he can work his way to the top tier and back to the main line in only a matter of weeks.

Some men do exactly this, although there is the possibility that, in the process, their spirit may be hopelessly broken. Others deteriorate into insanity, although it is possible their defiant inability to conform was in itself a form of insanity.

In this strange environment it is difficult to judge exactly what is insane. Smearing yourself daily with your own excrement is considered unpleasant, but not insane behavior. Throwing excrement at the guards is considered unruly and will cause a transfer back to isolation, where conditions are more stringently maintained. It is not considered insane. Screaming tantrums and attempted murders are, of course, normal.

During the time I spent in the adjustment center, one young man was judged insane when he stole picture-frame wire from a

217

painting in the counselling room and managed to puncture both cheeks with it. Then he ran it over his tongue, pierced his forehead above the bridge of his nose, ran it down through his nose and attached a pocket watch to it. He claimed he was tired of people asking him what time it was.

A picture was taken of him with his dangling timepiece and submitted to a group of psychiatrists in Sacramento. Within a month, he was transferred to the mental facility at Vacaville.

A few men refuse to bend to authority, and live in adjustment centers for years. They develop enormous inner resources, and are capable of intellectual concentration far beyond the reach of those who must contend with the constant distractions of society.

The second door led into the shower area, where a single inmate soaps and showers under the watchful eyes of a security guard. The bathing schedule continues all day long, as it is considered dangerous to allow groups of inmates to congregate.

One day when I was walking through this area, the guard noticed the showering inmate had pierced his foreskin and had a small key chain dangling from his penis.

"What the hell have you done?" the guard cried.

"I punctured the son of a bitch," the inmate said, smiling broadly.

"What in the hell would make you do a stupid thing like that?" the guard asked.

"My prick ain't nothin' but a decoration in here, so I just thought I'd make it a little prettier," the inmate said.

"Give me the chain," the guard barked.

The inmate unsnapped the silver chain and politely handed it to the guard.

"When I get out, I'm gonna tie a feather in it and drive the women crazy," the inmate said.

"Keep your mouth shut," the guard said humorlessly. "The idea might catch on and then we'll have blood and mutilation all over the place."

There were five other doors that led through corridors and then up to the second floor, where I had my classroom. I was the first academic teacher to be assigned there in more than two years.

218

Monies had been appropriated for the position, but after several teachers had been run off by inmates in the space of a few weeks, the authorities didn't make further attempts to fill the position.

The adjustment center houses men who are removed from the main line for a variety of reasons. Some kill within the institution itself. Some are sent there because they incite others to riot and are considered provocateurs. Others because they have attempted suicide and must be protected from themselves. Some are housed there because they have gone berserk under a prison discipline and must regain a certain amount of composure before returning to the general inmate population. Others simply have refused to obey orders and are sent there as punishment. Some are escape artists, and the adjustment center is maximum security.

I enjoyed teaching in the A.C. so much I requested to be assigned there full time. This request was denied. My classroom was a box-shaped room, with a row of barred windows looking out on a bare, paved courtyard. It held a desk and chair for me, ten armchair desks for the students, an easel-blackboard, several old math textbooks, a set of Encyclopaedia Brittannica published in 1887, and a large metal globe. I later removed the globe, as it tempted some students who chose to mistake it for a bowling ball. There was also a travel poster advertising the beauties of Port-au-Prince.

My first class consisted on nine inmates. Hackenjoss was the only one of my students to remain with me for ten months. He was in the center because he tried to kill a black pusher who had given him some bad stuff (talcum powder substituted for dope). Hackenjoss and a friend had taken the pusher into the Santa Cruz mountains, tied him hand and foot, shot him five times and then covered his body with maggots. Their hope was the maggots would soon devour the body, leaving only an unidentifiable skeleton. They didn't know that maggots have a therapeutic effect and probably saved the wounded man's life. They cleansed the wounds by eating away the dead flesh, and five days later the victim had recovered sufficiently to crawl several miles to a cabin and was rushed to a hospital, where he later recovered to testify against his attackers.

219

Hackenjoss's mother taught at Berkeley and wrote several impassioned and highly articulate letters to the Department of Corrections, requesting her son be segregated because he might be killed by black prisoners if they discovered his crime.

Hackenjoss didn't have a conventional makeup and never evinced pity, compassion or remorse. He was willing to go to the main line and take his chances, but his mother feared for his life and fought like a tigress to keep him segregated. He mentioned she was active in liberal causes on the Berkeley campus and felt humiliated, not because her son was an addict, attempted murderer and prisoner, but because he had perpetrated a crime against a black man. Hackenjoss claimed the fact that the man was black was accidental. The pusher was in the business of using and selling dope. It was a tough game, and if he didn't play by the rules, he would be ripped off. Hackenjoss simplistically attributed his difficulties to his faulty comprehension of the function of maggots.

I never discussed his problems with him in the classroom because he didn't want the other students to know the nature of his crime. He was the only inmate who knew how to run the movie projector, and we would talk while he was setting up for the pictures I showed. I doubt the black population would have risen against him had he been allowed to go on the main line. I had students on the main line who had been involved in interracial killings and they were not threatened.

Hackenjoss was intelligent and wrote poetry containing vivid and startling imagery. He mailed the poetry to his mother, who in turn submitted it to the *Berkeley Barb*, where it was published with no mention of who or where the author was. I suspect he was doomed to years of solitary confinement because his mother couldn't come to terms with reality. What do you do at a fund-raising rally for the Black Panthers when it is discovered your only son shot a black man and covered him with maggots?

Buchanon was a Vietnam veteran, a marine who was also a homosexual. He was emotionally very sick. While in the service in San Diego, a civilian picked him up in a bar and took him home.

220

After having sexual relations with the man, a fight ensued and Buchanon struck him. Believing the man to be dead, Buchanon panicked and, in his hysteria, recalled a movie in which someone had accidentally killed a man and then set fire to the house so that the cause of death was attributed to the fire. Buchanon piled clothing around the body and set it afire. The man expired of burns while in the hospital, but was able to identify Buchanon before he died.

Buchanon claimed he had been spared the gas chamber by a marine general who had intervened in his behalf. He claimed he had worked in a top secret decoding section and had information about where in Vietnam the United States had constructed a nuclear reactor and stockpiled atomic bombs. He was continually drawing maps of Vietnam, pinpointing these areas and asking me to smuggle out this information and inform the world.

I asked him why the general hadn't wanted him sent to the gas chamber so that all evidence would be destroyed. He replied the death sentence publicity would provide the platform needed for his story to be told. In the adjustment center he was in the deep freeze and there was no way his story could be made public.

Buchanon lasted in my class for about six weeks. On his bad days, he would come up to me after class and tell me he had an uncontrollable urge to kill someone. He assured me he would not kill me or anyone else while they were in my classroom. I informed Buchanon's counsellor he was about ready to blow and he agreed he was sick and suggested I remove him from my roster. I refused to do this, as I still thought I might be able to help him.

Two days later he was not in my class and I found out from the other students he had conked another inmate over the head with a bottle of hot sauce. His victim was a bloody mess but not seriously injured.

Buchanon was back in my class the following day, feeling much better. He said he had nothing against the man he had hit, but felt he had to kill someone in order to attract attention to tell his story about atomic bombs in Vietnam.

I told him that many people in this country would be pleased to know we had atomic bombs stockpiled in Vietnam and it wasn't worth his life or anyone else's to bring it to their attention.

This rattled him and a few days later he managed to get another bottle of hot sauce. This time he shoved the bottle up his rectum and broke it. He was sent to the hospital to have the sharp pieces of glass surgically removed and, after recuperating, did not return to my class.

Although there is no reason to believe his story about atomic bombs in Vietnam was true, I think he believed it, and when I pointed out to him that no one really cared whether or not it was true, I destroyed his fantasy that he would be able to do one worthwhile deed in his hopelessly fucked up world.

Hughes was another Vietnam veteran. He was a tall, muscular young man with enormous biceps developed by pushing iron (weight lifting) in the prison gymnasium. He shambled into class like an overgrown puppy and I wondered if he hadn't, as a child, imitated a canine friend for whom he could feel affection. As a child, he had been beaten and chained to a post. He freely admitted that he neither trusted nor liked people, but he did like animals.

He delighted in telling stories about Vietnam and how he had been used to interrogate Vietcong prisoners. He told sickening tales of how he would chain a Vietcong prisoner to a stake and then, from a distance, fire his carbine at the man's feet, moving in closer until finally he would club the man with the butt of his gun. Once he mentioned he had knocked a prisoner's eyeball "clean out of his head."

He stopped when someone got the idea of "hitting them with the green hammer." This practice consisted of taking several manacled prisoners who wouldn't talk up in a helicopter, releasing them from their chains one at a time and throwing them out without a parachute to splatter against the bright jungle or "green hammer." Hughes claimed he and another G.I. usually had to toss out only the first prisoner to show they meant business, and never had to toss out more than two to cause the rest to "jabber away like crazy, spilling their guts out."

Hughes was in my class only a few weeks and then was paroled directly from the adjustment center back into society. I excused him from class early on his last day, and after he had gone another inmate said, "They ain't no way that man gonna make it on the outside."

It was rumored he was given an early release because of his good war record.

Mendares was a musician in prison on a drug charge. He was in the adjustment center because he refused to do K.P. There was just no way to get him into the kitchen. He had been beaten up, threatened with life imprisonment (which can happen to someone who disobeys direct orders), served ninety days naked in isolation, and finally tossed into the adjustment center when the authorities couldn't think what else to do with him. He was gentle, sensitive, kind, and completely without bitterness toward anyone. He fully comprehended the prison authorities had to do their "law and order thing." But he had to do his "thing," too, and it did not include kitchen work.

He wrote lyrics every day; I felt incapable of judging them because of my inadequate comprehension of current taste. They lacked the innocent power of William Blake's "Little Lamb, Who Made Thee," were superior to "I Wanna Hold Your Hand," and perhaps were on a par with "Blowin' in the Wind."

The remarkable thing about Mendares was he had found for himself an answer in the wind. He was always cheerful and completely ignorant of degradation. I am confident he would have chosen the "green hammer" to scouring out a pot or pan.

Mendares didn't stay very long in the A.C. He was transferred to the gardening detail, where I encountered him one afternoon puttering around with the begonias. He was the only man I knew in prison who won his battle with prison rules.

Toledo was the kind of inmate who presented enormous problems to prison authorities. You do not see this type on the streets because they never get out of prison. He was identified as an institutional killer. At San Quentin, one or two inmates are

223

killed every month. It is almost impossible to apprehend the murderers. The crimes are committed out of sight of custodial personnel, and other inmates will not testify because snitches are, in turn, killed.

Toledo had been closely linked with seven prison murders but had never been convicted of any of them. He was a model student. His counsellor considered him the toughest nut to crack he had ever encountered and felt it miraculous I was able to open him up at all. Toledo was only twenty-nine years old, had been in prison for twelve years and had been permanently expelled from San Quentin, Soledad, and Folsom. He was eligible for main-line assignment if any prison would accept him. None would.

He had been in the adjustment center for two years and during that time had never once uttered a word during a counselling session. Although I did open him up, I didn't feel I was successful with him.

Vittoria was clearly a success story for me. He was in prison on a drug charge and was in the adjustment center because a syringe, needle and a small amount of heroin had been found in his cell. He had not been convicted of any crime because he had not been caught in the act of using the drug, and he claimed it had been planted in his cell. He had a cell mate and there was no way to pinpoint the guilty one. Vittoria was moved into the adjustment center to stop the flow of dope into the prison.

Vittoria was fascinated by discussions of literature. His favorite was an existential story by Sartre, "The Wall." It concerns a man sentenced to death in a Spanish prison, who can save his life by snitching on the whereabouts of a revolutionary leader. It is about the man's change of values when he knows he is about to die for a cause he no longer cares about. Vittoria liked the way the man could hang tough even though his values had been destroyed.

Vittoria later returned to the main line and was determined to get into my classes there. I tried to get him assigned to me but was unsuccessful because my classes were full. He laughed when I told him this, and with the same resourcefulness that had enabled him to indulge his habit in prison, bribed a roster clerk in the office and showed up in my afternoon English class with a broad smile on his face.

It wasn't a particularly exciting class because I didn't have the same freedom I had in the adjustment center. I was teaching grammar to a very ungrammatical crew, but I could do no wrong with Vittoria, who pitched in and became my best student.

He would not tolerate criticism of me, and when some of the students grumbled about the dull assignments, he became furious. He explained my method of teaching them, told them what I had done for him. He also pointed out they had to learn to walk before they could fly.

Elgin was another student without any identifiable criminal tendencies. He was in prison on a drug charge, and in the adjustment center because he insisted on wearing the peace symbol as an arm band on his fatigue jacket. It was forcibly ripped off several times and he was finally sentenced to thirty days in isolation for disobeying a direct command. As soon as he was out of isolation, the peace symbol reappeared and he was sent to the adjustment center because the authorities didn't know what else to do with him.

He was friendly and cooperative at all times and had insightful comments to make about every story we read. Despite his peace symbol, he never discussed the Vietnamese war or his attitude toward it, although I gave him every opportunity to do so. Perhaps he felt he didn't want to defend his views in front of people who couldn't possibly comprehend. When I asked him why he insisted on wearing the arm band, he replied, "It was a foolish thing to do, I guess."

He made no attempt to wear or display the arm band in the adjustment center and claimed he would not do it again when he returned to the main line.

He went on a hunger strike for a number of days and I became concerned because of the way he looked when he came into my class. He never made clear to me why he wasn't eating and I never pressed him for an explanation. One day he announced to me that he was eating again. I asked him why he had been on the strike and he said, "I don't know. I guess I just wanted to see what it was like." He shrugged his shoulders and dismissed my question.

In every other way he appeared to be a very open and well adjusted person. He had previously been at Soledad prison, where he claimed he and some other inmates had planted marijuana seeds near the fence and grown their own weed right inside the prison. As he was in prison on a marijuana charge, it pointed up the hopelessness of trying to convince the young it is wrong to use this weed.

Armonk was a shy, sensitive, young black man and I don't know why he was in prison or why he had been assigned to the adjustment center. My guess is that he was pressured by someone for homosexual reasons and he had been sent to the adjustment center for protective purposes.

I did Kafka's "Metamorphosis" with the students and the story blew Armonk's mind. It concerns a man who wakes up in the morning and discovers he has turned into a giant cockroach. Armonk grasped the symbolism in this story and did a brilliant job of analyzing it.

In one section the father throws an apple at the cockroach, where it lodges in its back to fester and rot. Armonk said his father used to chew him out and he could feel those words just like the apple in the shoulder blades. He said he felt a painfully sore place in his back for weeks after we finished the story. I won't go into the brilliant analysis Armonk gave, but I don't know of any professor of literature who could have equalled it.

Armonk's I.Q. was below eighty, and one psychiatrist had listed him as hopelessly feebleminded and had recommended that he be institutionalized after he finished his prison term. I gave Armonk "Metamorphosis" and a dictionary and he could read and comprehend every word in it.

Patterson was another student whose crime, or reason for being in the adjustment center, I don't know. He read at approximately

226

a second-grade level and, unlike Armonk, didn't show any evidence of having a powerful mind. Sometimes I would have the class read a story aloud, passing the book around a circle. When Patterson's turn came we were in for it, because he would take an interminable time to complete reading a paragraph.

Once I suggested that if he wanted, he could skip the reading, but before he could answer Toledo said, "Leave him alone; the man is trying."

"I like to read aloud," Patterson said. "Whenever I tried to read in school, they laughed at me. No one laughs here." I continued to encourage Patterson to read aloud, although it nearly drove me bananas. I also arranged for him to work with Armonk on their own time.

Buchanon came up to me after class, complaining I had not picked him to help Patterson.

"I'm sorry, I didn't know you wanted to do it or I would have assigned you," I said.

"I was thinkin', I could help him with his reading and we could be alone in his cell and I might be able to give him a blow job," Buchanon said wistfully.

At first I was somewhat shaken by Buchanon's honesty, because I had spent much time reassuring the director that no hanky-panky would go on if I had Armonk and Patterson work together. After thinking about it for a while, I decided I didn't care what they did as long as they improved their reading skills. However, I didn't replace Armonk with Buchanon and I am certain Buchanon's instructional method would never gain wide acceptance from the National Council of Teachers of English as an effective teacher's aid.

I arrived early for the first day of class and arranged the chairs in a circle around my desk. I was required to hand out only pencil stubs, so that no one could use a pencil to stab anyone else. I accomplished this by breaking the regular pencils in two and sharpening them down.

A guard opened the classroom door and the men filed in one at a time. The guard then shut the door and locked it. Then we heard him turn the key and lock the grating, too. At the time I thought the guard was trying to harass me by locking me in with

227

these men. Later I found out he was new at his job and was scared. He wanted to make certain that if trouble did start, it would be contained. As I didn't have a key to the classroom door, there was no way any of us could have gotten out of that room.

The men were all pasty-faced and not in the good physical trim my students on the main line were in. There was great tension in the room, not a tension of fear but tension caused by men who have been cooped up with no one to talk to, some of them for years. The room exploded with everyone talking at once. I didn't try to stop it; I encouraged it. I tried to see how much noise we could make and screamed at the top of my lungs. Mendares and Buchanon were both quiet and I yelled at them, "Speak up, I can't hear what you have to say." When the noise started to abate, I fired questions around the room to keep the excitement alive. I expected the guard to unlock the grating and come racing to the door to quiet things down. But it didn't happen, and I realized that if things had been out of control, no one would have rescued us.

It was beautiful. Finally we were all laughing.

"How come the guard locked the door on us?" Vittoria asked.

"Maybe he wanted us to feel secure," I said.

"We hear you're the best teacher on the main line. How come they put you with the fuck-ups?" Vittoria asked.

"Maybe they thought only the best teacher could handle the job," I said.

"That's a lie," Vittoria growled.

"Exactly. You keep that up and you'll get along fine with me. I don't intend to tell lies, and I don't expect lies from you. I'm interested in the truth. I'm not certain why I was assigned here, but if you heard I'm a good teacher you also heard I'm not a snitch. I'm not going to snitch off the people who assigned me here any more than I'm going to snitch off any of you."

I then explained how I was going to conduct the class. I would read a story to them and then we would discuss it. My first assignment for them was the same one I gave to all my classes on the main line. I asked them to take pencil and paper and write an answer to the question "Who Are You?"

228

"Why the short pencils?" Hackenjoss asked.

"That's so nobody gets shanked," I said.

"Do you believe those stories?" asked Hackenjoss.

"I'll see that you all get long pencils tomorrow," I said.

"You don't know this place yet. You better stay with the short ones," said Hackenjoss.

I brought them long pencils and never had any trouble.

The next day I read them a story called "The Ledge." This is about a fisherman off the coast of Maine who takes his young son, nephew and retriever duck-hunting on Christmas morning. They are on a tidal outcropping and they will all perish. The nearest land is Brown Cow Island, a quarter of a mile away, but the fisherman knows there is no chance of making it by swimming in the numbingly cold water. The fisherman accepts his fate with taciturn courage, and when the tide comes in they are all drowned.

The line of questioning I wanted to take with him was how a man should react when he is hopelessly screwed. Thinking these students were caught by a very hard fate, I wondered if they wouldn't be impressed by the fact the fisherman didn't snivel. But they weren't.

"The man showed no guts at all," Toledo said.

"What could he have done?" I asked.

"He could have tried to swim for it," Toledo replied.

"The man was a fisherman who had lived his life by the sea. He knew no man could last for a hundred yards in those waters," I replied. "He was playing the million-to-one odds the tide wouldn't come over their heads.

"He could have done something."

"What?" I asked.

"He could have killed the dog," Hackenjoss said. "Isn't there a bladder in a dog with air in it that he could use as a float to get to Brown Cow Island?"

"Yeah, or he could skin the dog, take the wood from the shotgun stocks, cover it with his coat and make a raft," Armonk said.

"No, he shouldn't kill the dog," Hughes said.

229

"Why not?" asked Hackenjoss.

"The dog could have helped him. Maybe the fisherman could have held on to the dog and steered to that island."

"Does anyone believe the fisherman was hopelessly trapped?" I asked.

"The fisherman wasn't a misfit, and that's the reason he did what he did," Elgin said.

"What do you mean?" I asked.

"We're a bunch of misfits. We're not like the fisherman and we don't calculate the odds. You're a misfit, too; that's why we can get along with you."

"How so?" I asked.

"You want to improve education. There isn't any way in the world anyone is going to let you do that. And that's why you're in with us—the worst teaching assignment anyone could have. The teachers only want more pay, and the politicians want something to scream about. If we started to educate people, those politicians would be out of a job, and they know it. So you can head for Brown Cow Island but you ain't gonna make it."

We had a lot of fun in that class. We read Sartre and Kafka and Sophocles and the Book of Job, among other things. Sometimes we just talked. I remember once we were talking about poverty, and Elgin mentioned he and his little brother used to go to a butcher shop in Sacramento that donated its rancid meat to the zoo. They were allowed to pick through the meat to take home what they wanted to their family.

"You mean you took the rotten meat away from the lions and tigers and fuckin' baboons?" Vittoria asked.

"Baboons don't eat meat. There was always good meat around the joint bones," Elgin said.

"Man, I'd get a gun and steal before I'd do that," said Vittoria.

"What about you, Mendares? Did you ever go hungry?" I asked.

"I had a system when I was hungry," Mendares said. "I'd go into the supermarket and eat apples, oranges and grapes right inside the store. Once I got caught with a mouthful of crackers and cheese and all they did was paddle my ass and kick me out. It's when you carry the food out of the store that you get busted and sent to juvenile hall."

"Yeah, that's right—you don't get busted if you don't carry it out of the store," several chorused.

I was going around the circle, trying to get everyone involved. "What about you, Toledo?"

No comment.

"What about you, Patterson?"

"I was lucky. I lived near a potato chip factory and it was easy to steal a case of potato chips anytime I wanted. I never went hungry."

"What about you, Armonk?" I asked.

"I was lucky, too, I guess," he said. "After my father split, my mother became a whore and the pimp always brought food and presents for all of us kids."

"You mean you took presents from the guy who was pimping for your mother? My old man used to beat the shit out of me with a tire chain. But I wouldn't accept presents from my mother's pimp. Hell, I'd go out and pimp for her myself," Hughes said.

"No you wouldn't," Armonk said matter-of-factly. "You're thinking like a man and you've forgotten what it was like to be a kid—when you couldn't do a damn thing about anything. And it isn't very different right now, if you want to know the truth. There isn't a damned thing any of us can do right now, either."

"Would you say you're all here because of the way you were treated as children or because of poverty?" I asked.

Strangely enough, I drew a blank. I fired the question to everyone in the room and no one wanted to answer it. Finally Elgin, who was the most articulate of the group, said, "No, that's what you cop out to when you're before the judge or trying to con someone. Everybody knows right from wrong. We're no better than other people, but we're not a hell of a lot worse, either."

Because I was proud of my students, I borrowed a tape recorder from one of the counsellors to document what we were

231

doing. I went to great pains to smuggle out a recording. However, I found that half the voices were not picked up and I couldn't use it as proof of what these men could do.

I did play the tape for friends in San Francisco and they were fascinated by it, particularly the wry comments of the inmates. For instance, on tape Buchanon said, "That is in violation of the commandment, 'Thou shalt not covet thy neighbor's asshole.' "

"Wait a minute, you mean 'Thou shalt not covet thy neighbor's wife,' " Hackenjoss said.

"No, that commandment don't apply to me, so I made it fit. I'm queer," Buchanon said.

The tape was a valuable sociological document and extremely funny. I am sorry poor fidelity rendered it useless.

I found that men who had great difficulty talking about themselves could handle abstract ideas easily. Then, to illustrate their ideas, they would dip into their private lives, almost unaware of what they were doing.

For example, Toledo had been going to counselling sessions without opening his mouth. Grim-faced and pale, nothing could break him down. He shied away from anything personal. And yet in my class he opened up when we discussed Plato's *Apology*. He became fascinated by figuring out what the term "justice" really meant. He had pondered this for years, staring into space in his lonely cell, getting up in the middle of the night to smoke a silent cigarette, rearranging the pieces of his impoverished life to try to make some sense of it.

Socrates was punished for breaking a law he thought to be wrong. Yet Socrates thought he should accept the penalty of death because the laws should be more important than the individual.

"Yeah, the law should be more important than the individual," Toledo said. "But when the law is bad, the individual can only be worse.

"Do you know what they did to me at Folsom?" he continued. This was the first time he had talked about himself.

"They tried to kill me. They had this maniac they had welded

232

into a cell for five years because they found a shank on him. The dude was wild-eyed out of his mind. Two guards were walking me across the yard and two others were walking beside the maniac. Then the guards pushed the maniac into me and run out of the way. Right away he jumped me and the guards were laughing and warning us that if we didn't break they would order the tower guards to shoot. I shouted that I didn't want to fight and was trying to get away. Just as I did break away, the tower guards opened fire. The maniac was killed and I got two bullets in the left leg. When the guards picked me up, one of them said, 'Don't worry, Toledo, next time we'll finish you off, too.'

"I filed about six writs on this incident and they ignored every one of them and assigned me to this hole, where I been ever since."

"What about the injustices you've caused?" I asked. "Couldn't any of the people you injured claim the same thing?"

"No, like in the story, the state should be better than the individual."

"What if the state isn't better than the individual?"

"I don't believe in the laws of the state."

"Then that's jungle law and you were dealt with in kind by jungle law."

"Yeah, but that's different. They were the state."

"So what, you don't accept the state law, so why should you complain?"

"I can fight an individual, but I can't fight the state."

"Do you need the state?"

"No, I don't need the state; and the state don't need me. It wants to kill me."

"Do you deserve to be killed?"

"No, why should I be killed?"

"In jungle law, anyone deserves to be killed, doesn't he?"

"Only for food or to protect yourself."

"Maybe the state wants to protect itself by killing you."

I had him on the dialectical ropes and he knew it. What he didn't know was how to turn the argument against me. He should have pointed out that since I believed in the state, it was up to me to correct the injustices that had been done to him, because an injustice committed by the state also threatened and harmed me.

Almost every day I saw injustice around me and heard tales that cried out for correction. But I did nothing about it. If you are going to work in a prison, you have to toughen yourself to survive. People with high ethical standards do not last very long. I survived because I kept my mouth shut and tried not to disturb the power structure. Whenever I did assert myself, enormous pressure was put on me.

For instance, I did insist on showing movies to my class in a vacant room that had been outfitted to show movies but had never been used. We had curtains to cover the windows and darken the room. They didn't have access to television or movies and I wanted to do something to break their monotonous life. Under ordinary circumstances this would not be risky, but these men were deeply frustrated and some of them were death-haunted. The authorities were reluctant to let them get into groups because of the danger of violence.

Although I had permission to use the room from the director of the adjustment center, the guard assigned to my wing considered movies for these men "damned foolishness." At first he tried to reason with me, but since I had permission, this was to no avail. Then he tired to discourage me by locking me in the movie room with the men and leaving the area completely. There was no phone in the room and no way for me to call for help if something did erupt. At the end of the hour, the guard would return and release the men to their cells.

I didn't like this setup and thought that the guard should have at least left the door unlocked, since there was no place the men could go except into the long corridor, which was sealed on either end by huge metal gratings.

However, I didn't protest being locked in, because this would have opened the question of whether or not I should be showing movies at all.

In a sense, I put my life on the line, and yet I was fascinated by the challenge and perhaps enjoyed taking the risk. I wasn't sacrificing myself just so these inmates could get a little diversion. I was testing my knowledge of human nature in a laboratory. Many times, I carried films over from the main line and didn't show them because the feeling wasn't quite right in the classroom.

No trouble did start in that darkened projection room. The men were instructed to scatter about the room and not come within six inches of each other. There were hard wooden benches in the room and one chair. I put the chair on top of the table in the back of the room and sat there smoking a cigar and watching the men and the movie. When a shadowy shape would inch toward another shadowy figure, I would boom out, "Dinna do it, laddie, dinna do it," and the figure would slowly retreat. Of course, in these cases, the problem was not violence but the strong biological urge to touch and fondle another human being. A very few times the figures would coalesce and I would hop down from my perch and quietly touch them on the shoulders and whisper tenderly, "Dinna do it, laddies." They would separate.

I can clearly remember those shadow shows and the hopeless refinement of passion displayed by very unrefined men; and I can't recall anything about the movies we saw.

Once in my journey though the seven locked doors to my classroom, a guard stopped me and said, "Mr. Campbell, I think you should know this. I heard some of the inmates talking to each other from their cells last night and they claimed one of your students jacked off another student during the movie yesterday."

"I keep very close tabs on them, and I don't think that is possible," I said.

"What's that, someone got jacked off during the movie?" a second guard said.

I was astounded by the highly moral code that is formed in a place like this. I suppose if the rumor had been that something more had happened, it would have been reported and I would have been forced to stop showing movies.

Almost everyone in the adjustment center wanted to get into

235

my class. Since I could handle only ten at a time, I volunteered to sacrifice my lunch hour three days a week to teach another class. Although it was run in approximately the same fashion as my English class, it was labelled officially a counselling session and we had no written assignments. On Mondays, one inmate would be "it." He would tell the story of his life and the rest of us would ask questions and get him to defend himself.

On Wednesdays, we would discuss topics chosen by the inmates in advance. This could be anything from the worthlessness of indeterminate sentences, to the Vietnamese war, to job opportunities for ex-cons.

On Fridays, I would read a story to them and we would discuss it. This became a problem to me, because the demand for this class was great and students fought to get into it. It is understandable that the other counsellors were offended.

My program worked because it had variety. I wasn't just interested in opening them up and getting them to talk about themselves. I was interested in supplying information through literature and getting them to handle concepts beyond personal history. I became bored by all the horrible confessions I heard and referred to them as "dumping the garbage." Although I realize it is necessary to get people to release their guilt, I firmly believe the next important step is to get them concerned about new problems and ideas and to show them how literature can be a worthwhile tool which can expand their minds.

I was a success as a counsellor because I had a free-flowing, dynamic group. But I don't think anyone in authority there comprehended the educational value of what I was doing. I extended an invitation to the counsellors to drop in on my sessions at any time. One of them accepted. When he arrived, I was in the midst of reading a story by Isak Dineson, "Sorrow Acre." This concerns a mother in medieval Denmark who can save her son from prison if she can harvest an acre of grain all by herself in one day. She succeeds but dies of exhaustion at the end of her ordeal. I was prepared to get into the problem of self-sacrifice and whether or not anyone should willingly give his life for another. The boy was forced to watch his mother perform her

236

task; I wanted to get their reactions to this form of punishment for the son. I knew many of them had caused great suffering to their families and I wanted to get at the pain through their analysis of this story.

To my surprise, they were immediately attracted to the beautiful language in the story. They asked me to reread several passages and we carefully went over the delicate and expressive use of language.

I am certain that if a group of English teachers had heard that discussion, they would have been impressed by what a group of ignorant and insensitive men could do. But when I talked to the counsellor after the discussion, he said that while the discussion was very good, it did not relate to his job as a counsellor and he didn't have the background to do something similar.

I tried to explain to him that what had happened was a fluke and I was sorry I hadn't steered the conversation back to my original questions so that he could better understand my program.

He didn't come back again and I doubt the other counsellors felt threatened by my popularity any longer. I was reading stories to the inmates and they were not in the entertainment business.

I gave the biographies of the first ten men in my class because they were a typical cross section. Students stayed with me for a few weeks and then were transferred back to the main line or to other prisons or paroled. I didn't get close to these men the way I did with some of my students on the main line with whom I worked for extended periods of time.

The constant change made it impossible for me to determine if I was doing any good. I battled to prove that an educational system can work. And it did work better than I thought it could. It opened up channels of communication in severely blocked young men. It created a desire for learning in semiliterate men. And yet no one cared.

As I drove to work on the road to Sacramento, the highway was choked with army trucks rolling toward Berkeley. Their mission was to pick up gagged and trussed demonstrators at

People's Park and dump them in a newly activated prison about forty miles down the road. The prisoners would remain there for a few days until they could muster up bail. Many of them would return to respectable jobs. When I turned on the radio, I heard an on-the-scene account of low-flying American planes dropping tear gas on the Berkeley campus.

It seemed to me the entire state of California suffered from a severe communication problem. And, in this highly polarized situation, no one wanted to listen to a different point of view. I felt there was enormous need everywhere for the kind of program I had. Yet, like Buchanon, I had no way to tell my story. I, too, was beginning to get discouraged.

CHAPTER 13

What is prison like? It's not the same for everyone. The prison I know is different from the prison you know.

From a Student Theme.

The adjustment center is not like a main-line prison. People who can't make it on the outside go to prison, and people who can't make it in prison go to the adjustment center. It is the official bottom rung on the spiralling ladder of success all of us are told we must try to ascend. It is a place where activity stops and isolation becomes a brutal weapon. It is a place where you can scream all night without worrying about what the neighbors think. It is nowhere. Yet, strangely enough, it is a place most of us have been. Only, society didn't lock us up; we turned the key on ourselves.

I was assigned a badly screwed up Mexican, Zapata, who had been in solitary confinement for nine months. He threw his own excrement at the guards and screamed and hollered until they threw away the key on him.

There is a law that prohibits anyone from being in solitary longer than twenty-one days. There isn't any supervising agency to enforce this law and when an inmate is out of control he is kept in solitary indefinitely. There is no way you can release a screaming, out-of-his head maniac back to the main line, anyway. To be technical, the guard could walk him around the cell block every twenty-one days and recommit him on a new offense. I did hear tales about one inmate who spent seven years in solitary. Periodically, custody did release him to the main line, and when he went through the chow line, he invariably picked up his tray of food and smashed it into the face of the nearest guard.

Zapata finally quieted down enough to make it to the adjustment center, where he was assigned to my class. The first day I had him, he was a little wild. He started saying, "Mr. Campbell is a sissy. Mr. Campbell is a maricon." At first I ignored this; then I briefly explained to him that homosexuality was not my bag and I didn't see anything wrong with it if it was his. I didn't allow him to ruffle me.

Next he picked up a chair and started walking around with it, raising it over his head. My first reaction was to look at the other students. If he had caused trouble with them, I would have gotten him out of there, fast. But the other students were letting me handle it. They realized I was trying to help him and understood that he had been locked away for nine months and no one could expect an easy social adjustment.

I wasn't intimidated by him, because he was in poor physical condition. I figured there was no way that pale, friendless human being could bring that chair down over my head. If he tried, I could move out of danger, call the corridor guard and have him removed.

Calmly, I first ignored him and then started talking to him until I got him quieted down. I assigned the other students seat work, which they willingly accepted. Zapata put the chair down next to my desk, sat in it and began to talk.

He launched into a conventional tale of being beaten by his father when he was small, one that I had heard a hundred times before. What festered in his mind during those months of blind rage in isolation was an incident that occurred in the Los Angeles area. Zapata had been part of a riot, and the cops had arrived on the scene, pulled him out and handcuffed him to a nearby telephone pole. After the police broke up the riot, in the excitement of the moment, they pulled away in the police van

240

and forgot him. Zapata found himself in his own neighborhood, cuffed to a pole. Instead of helping him get free, his own people gathered around, taunted him and asked him to raise his leg and bark.

He wasn't a part of anything. Parents, neighbors, his own blood kin considered him no better than a dog. His ruined dignity compelled him to want to howl his life away.

Later the cop came back to retrieve his handcuffs. The policeman cut him loose, kicked him in the ass and didn't book him, because he didn't want to bring his own carelessness to anyone's attention.

Zapata came to class the next day and wanted to rap again. It reached the point where I felt I couldn't spend all my time with him. I wasn't assigned there as his therapeutic counsellor. Zapata would participate with the group for a day or two, then lapse into a restless tear again, demanding my complete attention.

One day Zapta didn't show up for my class. He was down in the exercise yard, playing basketball. Some of the other students started complaining. They said, "Where's Zapata? He should be here. He ain't no better than the rest of us."

I agreed it wasn't fair to excuse him because he had a problem. I notified the guard of his absence and he brought him to my classroom. Zapata was hostile as hell that he had been pulled away from his exercise time and started giving me trouble again. I got through the class, but it was a strain on me.

I didn't want to write him up, because if I did there was a chance I would bring everything down on him again and he would go back to isolation. I talked to his counsellor, who was a perceptive man, and sympathetic to the fantastic problems of adjustment center inmates. I told the counsellor I was having problems with Zapata and didn't want to kick him out because he was making progress.

"I think that Zapata is ready to go back to the main line and try it there again," I said. "He's already made one big step; if he can take another I think he can handle it. We're going to lose Zapata if he goes back to isolation, because his mind will be permanently destroyed by that place."

The counsellor agreed with me and dropped him from my

241

class, not for disciplinary reasons, but because he had scheduled him to return to the main line, where he eventually entered an elementary school class and made a successful adjustment.

It was shortly after this that the structure of my classes began to change. The prison started pulling out the black militants and assigning them to the adjustment center. They weren't charged with prison crimes, but had been removed because they were considered potential agitators in the cell blocks.

Without my class, these men had nothing but bare walls and a tray pushed under the door for companionship. If they wanted to explode, my class offered them an opportunity to do so. This was, by any standards, a nearly impossible teaching situation. How would you like to face a group of angry black militants who considered themselves political prisoners and who faced the stark cinder-block walls of their cells twenty-three hours a day because, in their view, all they wanted to do was speak the truth as they perceived it?

I thought about going to the director of the adjustment center and telling him of my concern. The racial mixture of my class didn't come about by administrative design. When the militants were in a majority, the white and brown students dropped out. Even Hackenjoss requested and received a temporary vacation from class. Eventually, I found I had only one white student willing to remain. Still, I didn't request that the racial balance of my class be changed, because I taught individuals not ethnic groups.

One of the students was Chamberlin, who had been my student on the main line. Chamberlin had been falsely accused of stabbing Nickerson in the john, and this was the incident that had led to the riot. Chamberlin was the brightest, strongest leader of this black group, and I doubt I could have taught the class without his support. It was a tense, most unusual teaching situation—and it fascinated me.

Badger, the one white student, looked like he had been scraped off the bottom of the genetic barrel. He had a large head and awkward body and had been classified feebleminded by the prison psychiatrist. The psychiatrist had made the recommendation that when Badger was released from prison, he not go into general society, but be placed in a home for the mentally retarded.

Badger couldn't read, but he could write grammatical, co-herent prose. Apparently, he was given standard reading tests and, since he couldn't respond to them, it was assumed he couldn't write. Not only was he not feebleminded, but he was the possessor of a probing intelligence. When I checked his records, I noticed a form they had asked him to fill out. When it requested him to list his favorite hobby, Badger replied: "Being pushed in a swing."

I once asked him what he would like to do when he got out and he answered that he wanted to repair cuckoo clocks. He wasn't kidding. He ran down the whole trip about the wooden gear, the weights and counterweight, and the little wooden bird and how it popped out and went "you know what."

I discussed this with Badger's counsellor and he agreed that Badger was sincere. He also said if clockmaking were open to him, he believed Badger would work blissfully at it every day and lead a rich and rewarding life. Unfortunately, the prison had no facilities for training, and the outside world had no jobs waiting for an expert cuckoo clock repairman.

Badger functioned like a lightning rod in that class. All the racial frustration turned toward him, not me. But he refused to be intimidated and insisted on countering their arguments. I remember a black student named Bullet recounting some terrible things that whites had done to blacks. Bullet was tall and lean, with a closely cropped Muslim haircut. He described how whites captured blacks, put them in irons, brought them to this country in stinking ships and sold them into slavery for huge profits.

Badger interrupted him, "Wait a minute," he said. "I'm not against blacks. I know the whites done terrible things. But the blacks did the same things themselves. Black chieftains captured their own people and sold them into slavery for trinkets.

"Not only that," he continued, "I remember when I was little and still could read, they had this picture of this dude in my geography book, with a bone in his nose. I mean those dudes

243

were cannibals. If they didn't sell their people into slavery, they put them into a pot, cooked them and ate them. Don't tell me they were any better than the whites."

Pandemonium! I put my hands to my head and groaned, "Oh, no, no, no. Badger, how could you be so stupid?" It didn't matter what I said, because nobody could hear me above the shouting, anyway.

"Get the stupid honkie."

"Take his head."

"Off the dude, now."

Badger started screaming, "Kill me, kill me!"

Then Cranker, a six foot four giant, with an arm on him like a mahogany tree trunk and a fist doubled up like a slab of rough concrete, got up and started stalking Badger like a jungle cat goes after its prey.

There wasn't time to do anything. Badger was standing upright, his big round head bobbing up and down, a perfect target for Cranker's unbelievable fist.

I couldn't look. I closed my eyes and turned my head away. Not only was I certain that Badger was going to be killed, but I believed the impact of the blow would sever his head from his body and it would roll across the classroom floor like a pumpkin.

I didn't hear the fist connect, and I turned back again.

"I'll fight ya! I'll fight ya!" shouted Badger, flopping around like a rag puppet and doing some kind of crazy dance.

Cranker's fists were down and he was staring at Badger's comical performance. He was still angry, but it was obvious that Badger's gyrations were cracking him up.

The crisis was over. I moved between the two and gently instructed them to return to their seats. Cranker was the first to comply. He went back muttering, "Man, that stupid honkie clown is somthin' else. I mean that little dude is somthin' else."

Badger was still dancing around me, and it took a little more time to get him back in place.

I gave the class a little speech about how the disturbance was my fault for letting things get out of hand, and how we had to have discussions without blowups or I would have to send them all back.

Nobody was listening to me. I wasn't listening to myself. I was filling in to give them time to come down from their high. Men who are isolated all day long find that when they are stirred up, their senses are heightened. In the language of the streets, it's a situation where a mouse pissing into cotton sounds like Niagara Falls.

After my boring speech, Badger continued. He didn't come on like someone whose life had just, miraculously, been spared.

"Don't you see," he said. "It's the whole human race that's all fucked up. It ain't the blacks or the whites. It's both of them. What's worse, a kick in the balls or a kick in the head? You dudes are all complainin' because you got ripped off the main line and put on ice over here. We all know there has been a bloodlettin' on the main line. They're coolin' the joint down. Soon as it's cooled out, you're all goin' back. And you're all gonna be heroes among your own people.

"But what about me?" he continued. "You know what I'm in here for? I was caught holdin' hands with another dude, and they busted me on a homosexual beef. I ain't no homosexual, and I never was, neither. In the joint there ain't nothin' a man can touch. There ain't a dog, a cat or a rabbit. What's wrong in reachin' out to a dude and holdin' his hand? I mean people shake hands every day and it don't give them the hots."

"It ain't right, Mr. Campbell," Badger said, addressing himself to me. "They ain't never gonna let me back on the main line. They ain't never gonna let me out of this place."

Badger's plight bothered me. That afternoon, after I had checked his records, I started talking about him in the teacher's lounge. "I have this student in my adjustment center class, Badger. He's there on a homosexual beef because he was holding hands in the TV room. Badger told me that he wasn't a homosexual. He was lonely and liked to hold hands. He didn't see anything wrong with it. I've been wondering. What *is* wrong in one man's holding another's hand?"

"I'd be careful about that kind of talk," a teacher said.

"Why?" I asked.

"I wouldn't let it get around the prison that Campbell is in favor of inmates holding hands."

245

"Balls," I said. "I just checked Badger's jacket in Central Files. There isn't a hint of any previous homosexuality there. He's just an oddball kid."

"You're very naive," the teacher said.

I was convinced Badger was telling the truth and his logic was sound. However, it was preposterous to believe that prison reform could be enhanced by allowing inmates to hold hands and openly stroll, arm and arm, around the prison yard. Anyone who suggested it would be a candidate for Badger's cuckoo clock repair shop.

Badger was a dangerous man. If you listened to him and were foolish enough to combat what he was saying with logic rather than with the cultural prejudices we all inherit, then the fabric of our crazy society started to unravel.

I managed to keep Badger in line enough so that no one attempted to kill him. The racial discussions continued of course. These young men were full of hatred and I let the anger pour out of them until it became crushingly boring. I wanted to shout out, "All right, all right, but for God's sake don't snivel."

Instead, I pointed out that oppression was as deeply a part of the human experience as eating, making love or going to the bathroom. I explained how, in modern times, a nation turned innocent people into lamp shades and soap; and how, in earlier days, a king of a civilized nation had his judicial system try, convict and chop the heads off his used-up wives so that he could marry again without having to get a divorce.

"The good people have always been tricked into doing what the vicious and the cruel people wanted done," I said. "Do you realize, at one time young boys were castrated so they could retain their high-pitched voices and sing beautiful religious music? How would you like to have your balls cut off so you could sing soprano in the church choir?

"We could talk for years and not repeat ourselves, recounting the horrible things mankind has done to its own kind. At this very moment, jellied fire is dropping on ignorant farming people in a far-off Asian country.

"Of course, bad things have been done to black people. But

246

don't let it fester in your mind or make you think you are a member of an exclusive club. The important thing is to learn from the past and figure out how to make things better."

"It's easy for you to talk that way because it's not your ass that's getting stomped," Cranker countered. "Why should I build a better world for the honkie? The honkies control, and I don't want to be no honkie slave."

"What do you want?" I asked. "Would you like to live on a plantation and have the honkie work the fields for you, while you poured cool drinks in the shade and fooled around with his women?"

"Damned right. That would be cool. That's what the honkie bastard deserves," Cranker replied.

"Now we're getting down with it," I exclaimed. "Analyze your statement. You're howling against injustice. But you're not opposed to injustice. You dig what the slave owners did. It's just that you want the other guy to be the slave.

"Let me ask you this question," I continued. "What the hell is a black man in America? What lesson should he learn from the past? Should he try to be exactly like the person he hated and is convinced in his heart was wrong? What should the Jewish person do, dream of the day he can pop all the blue-eyed Aryans in the gas oven? What should the women do, dream of the time they can chop their husbands' heads off? What should the children do, dream of the time they can get even with the society that castrated them? What should the Vietnamese do, dream of the time they can paddle to our shores and destroy the civilization?

"Don't think the feelings you have are unusual. They're typical of the human race that never seems to learn a damned thing." I was pacing restlessly about the room as I talked.

"Look," I said, getting myself worked up. "When I see your faces, I don't see black people. I see the honkie oppressor who is racist to the core. I see the old Yankee ship captain and the red-necked southern farmer, reborn in a black skin. And he is hostile as hell, and he is self-righteous as hell, and he thinks he has God and everybody on his side, and he's trying to enslave again.

247

"You men talk like the ruling class. But don't tell me you speak for black people, because I don't believe it. I believe the body is like a suit of clothes, and when we wear it out or rip it up, we get another one. What's inside that body isn't any particular race, sex or age, but is a collection of all the crazy things that make a human being. When you really understand what it is to be unfairly treated, you're going to hate injustice inflicted on any man, regardless of the color of his skin. I do understand that and maybe that makes me the only black man in this room."

There was complete silence; then Chamberlin spoke up, "I told you Mr. Campbell is crazy, but he's got something to say if you'll listen to him."

"No, he's not crazy. He's sly like a weasel," Bullet said. "He's putting words in our mouths and he's twisting everything around. I don't hate white people; and I don't want to get even with them. I'm a black militant because it pays. People are listening to me. I don't know if what the black militants are saying is right or wrong. But it gets action and it gets respect. I'm going to be a black militant if it means they take my head. When we stick together we have power. When we start to question and argue, that's when they put us in the trick bag."

"All right, that sounds like the truth to me," I said. "It cuts through all the hambone acting all of us have been doing."

"Who's acting? I ain't been doin' no acting," Badger said.

"He's right, that little son of a bitch hasn't been doin' no acting. He's just a natural-born clown. I mean he's Halloween," Cranker said.

"Peace," I said, puffing on my corncob pipe in a professorial way. We've all had our say, but we're still trapped in this sardine can for one hour a day, and I have to figure out a way to teach you."

"I can tell you how. But you're not gonna like it; and you're not gonna do it," Bullet said.

"Give it a shot," I said.

"Sergeant Rounder works in the library on the main line,"

248

Bullet said. "He's a black security guard and he's got some books there that tell the story the way it is. The dudes that order the books and censor them are too dumb to read them and know what they're about. Sergeant Rounder keeps them under his control, so the authorities won't discover them and rip them up. If you could borrow those books from him and bring them over here so we could read them, that would be the best thing you could do for us."

"That's fair enough," I said. "If the books are in the library, I don't see why we can't use them over here. I'll talk to Sergeant Rounder about it. The important thing is for everyone to keep his mouth shut. Nobody is checking up on what I am teaching, but I know from experience that if we got a snitch in the group, it can cause trouble."

All eyes riveted on Badger.

"Don't look at me. I'm no snitch. I don't talk to nobody. But that don't mean I think it's a good idea," Badger said.

"What do you think is wrong with it?" I asked.

"You know what these dudes are here for," Badger said. "And you've heard them speak their mind. They're racist agitators. What do you aim to do? Give them schoolin' on how to be better agitators and send them back to the main line?"

"No, that's not what I aim to do," I said angrily. "I don't believe in censorship. If these books have meaning for you, then you all have a right to read them."

"Badger, if you snitch us off, then you'll die," Cranker said. He spoke without emotion. It was chilling.

"Cranker, you don't scare me," Badger said. "If I'd a been scared, I'd a dropped this class long ago. If I was scared now, I'd quit. I'm not going to snitch on anybody. I know I need schoolin'. Even though this class ain't much, it's the only thing I got to get back the readin' I used to could do. I don't see what you're talking' about can help me in any way."

Once again, Badger got to me. He sounded like Hugo Belson. If he were on the outside, I could have recommended special instruction for him. If he had been in a different class, I could have worked with him individually. But, like everything else in his impossible life, it was impossible for me to help him in a room full of hostile black students.

"Don't worry about Badger, he's not going to snitch," I said confidently.

That afternoon, after my last class on the main line, I went to the library to locate Sergeant Rounder. I wasn't certain that he existed.

He did exist and cordially invited me into a side room for a chat. Sergeant Rounder was a middle-aged, scholarly-looking man, somewhat heavyset, wearing a pair of round steel spectacles on his black nose.

"You're Campbell, the teacher in the adjustment center, aren't you. I had word you were coming."

"Incredible," I said. "How could you possibly know that?"

"Those inmates in the adjustment center are amazing," he said, laughing warmly. "Some claim they tuck messages in bedding or kitchen items that pass in and out of there. Or that they signal from windows facing the main line. Nobody knows how they do it. But it works better than the telephone."

"You know, then, that they want some library books," I said.

"It's no big deal." Sergeant Rounder said. "Sure, I got some books that I keep on reserve. They're not dynamite. I'm not certain that they aren't setting up special classes in some of the other joints in California where they're using them. But the key around here is to lie low. I don't want them to fall into the wrong hands; they might get ripped up. If someone started making noise, they might ban them completely. Hell, some of the knuckleheads around here would ban Mother Goose if you brought it to their attention."

"I know where you're coming from," I said.

"I make certain they get into the hands of those black brothers who can handle them. No waves, no rockin' the boat, no trouble."

He went to the shelves, selected three books and laid them out on the table in front of me. "Two of these books deal with black history. The third one is different. It traces the oppression and

250

crimes against my people from earliest times to the present. What it says is true, but it's onesided. It doesn't point out the enormous strides that have been made. I'm not certain those adjustment center students can handle it."

"Do you know them?" I asked.

"I know some of them. They're ignorant," he said matter-of-factly.

"I'll take whatever you give me," I said. "I'm not going to betray their trust in either one of us. But I'm not going to teach a course in black history, because I'm not qualified."

"Lord no," he said. "I recommend you let them read the books and not get involved in any interpretation. No matter what you say, you still represent the honkie; any idea you have will make them suspicious."

"We understand each other," I said.

Sergeant Rounder went through the process of checking out the books in my name and, as he handed them to me, said, "I want you to tell those dudes that if any of them writes in any of these books, wrinkles or smudges any of the pages, I'm going to find out who done it and personally kick ass."

My students were delighted the next day when I brought the books to the adjustment center. In their eyes, I had risked a lot to help them. I tried to point out that I was entitled to use any book in the prison library and hadn't risked anything. But they craved danger and excitement and were skeptical of civil rights.

I told them they were free to use them any way they chose and I wasn't going to participate in the discussion. I also mentioned that Sergeant Rounder cautioned they not damage the books and mentioned what he would do to anyone who did not comply with his request.

Immediately, they drew up a set of rules governing the treatment of the books and refused to let anyone even look at them until he had washed his hands in the privacy of his individual cell. It was as if a secret society were forming with its own mystic rituals and these, at least to me, quite ordinary books were their sacred texts.

They signed up so they could read each book in turn. The

251

order in which they read the books was, in part, determined by where they were located in the cell block.

At three every afternoon, the center was closed down. If they wanted to trade cigarettes or pass objects from cell to cell, they did it by strings, made by unravelling their denims, towels or other bits of cloth, tying the string to the object to be transported, and then, somehow, working the string so that it could be secured and passed along by the person in the adjoining cell. It was a slow and intricate process. But the one commodity they had in abundance was time.

I could imagine these books, wrapped in protective coverings, moving back and forth on the concrete floor all night long, disappearing for a few hours under one metal door and then reappearing to go scuttling along the corridor to the next person on the list, who would soap and wash his hands up to the elbow before opening his precious package.

I kept my word and didn't attempt to comment or demythologize. Although the ritual for reading the books was marvelous, the discussions about them degenerated into diatribes against the hated honkie oppressors. They were without leadership and there were no dissenting opinions. Chamberlin was a very perceptive and capable leader, but he didn't want to do anything that would be inflammatory. His eye was, temporarily, not on changing systems but on understanding how the system operated and how he could manipulate it to gain his freedom. It worked for him, because in only a matter of weeks he was paroled directly from the adjustment center.

Badger was also out of it. Since he couldn't read, it was pointless to insist that he get a chance to examine the books. Badger spent his class time writing highly critical notes to me. He wrote them on white, lined paper in his notebook. He took me to task for allowing the militants' allegations against white people to go unchallenged. He also thought they showed no respect for me as a teacher, and that I should assert myself and demand it.

I accepted his papers, read them, folded them and put them in my pocket without comment. Like Chamberlin I, too, played it cool.

In the midst of this reading period, we received a new student named Melody. Melody was a righteous queen, a girl trapped in a young black man's body. He was pert and vivacious, with large eyes that rolled around in his head, and he was absolutely quivering with delight at the good fortune that had placed him in social intercourse with many handsome young men. There were no inmates like Melody on the main line because they were identified immediately in the reception center and sent directly to protective custody.

No one could mistake Melody. She was a girl and very proud of it. She wasn't particularly racist, either. I remember when I asked her name, she said, "I'm Melody, and what is your name, intriguing one?"

The second day she was in the class, I made the mistake of allowing her and Cranker out of the room at the same time to go to the bathroom.

By this time, I had my own key to the classroom door. If someone had to use the toilet, I would unlock the door and let him into the corridor. He would walk to a heavy iron grating that completely sealed the corridor. By tapping on the grating, he could signal a guard who would unlock and raise the grating and escort him to his cell.

Badger, of course, was the one who pointed out to me what I had done. I had unlocked the door for Cranker, neglected to lock it again, and Melody scooted out on me. I considered this situation harmless; but I opened the door and peered out in the corridor just to be safe—and in time to see the wooden door to a walk-in closet near the grating click shut.

I had the key to that door, too. The closet was used to store mops and buckets and was lighted by a naked bulb that hung from the ceiling. It was a deep room, and at the back were piles of dusty textbooks and an ancient mimeograph machine that was stored there for some long forgotten purpose.

The director of the adjustment center, when he gave me the key, had told me that I was welcome to use the closet and any of the materials it contained. In the wildest flights of my imagination, I did not consider that it would one day become the leafy

253

bower, the trysting place for two of my enterprising students. I was not about to intrude upon them myself, or call a guard and catch them *in flagrante*. Not only would this destroy the confidence I was slowly gaining, but it would also cause embarrassing questions for me to answer as to how and why I had allowed it to occur.

After an appropriate interlude, they returned. Cranker was the first to appear; he was a changed man. All the meanness had drained out of him, and he was positively civil. Following soon after, Melody floated in, enraptured by the opportunities afforded by our bright dungeon.

The early-afternoon sun, shining through the latticework of bars, created a giant tick-tack-toe shadow upon the polished floor. No hatred against the honkie was vented for the rest of the period, and I couldn't help thinking that Melody had done more than Milton or the proverbial malt in reconciling man to man. Nevertheless, when they were both back in the classroom, I locked the door, confident they would never be able to run that game on me again.

After the period, Badger stayed to talk to me. He was in deep distress.

"Mr. Campbell," he said, "I understand the problems you have in teaching a class like this, believe me, I do. I know you're smart, but you got the mind of a child, a baby. You don't see nothin'. I mean if you can't figure out where these inmates are coming from, then you should get out of this line of work. These dudes are so different from you that it's almost as if you ain't on the same planet."

"I'm sorry you feel that way, Mr. Badger," I said calmly. "I think a child's mind is a good mind to have. It's not cruel or ugly. I don't believe what you say is true, but I'm flattered you think so."

"Oh my God, my God," Badger said. He was a very tough little fellow and he was ready to cry.

I understood why Badger was so upset. He couldn't read and was without radio or television, locked in a cage of cinderblock and steel, without family or friends until perhaps eternity, for the crime of holding hands. Yet he saw the real thing, performed practically under his nose by his worst enemy, go unnoticed and unpunished. And by the code all prisoners must live by, he couldn't even mention it to another human being.

I could have told him the truth. But that, perhaps, would have been worse. He wasn't being punished on a homosexual charge. That would have taken only a few days. If he had just dropped the guy's hand and kept his mouth shut, he would never have been busted at all. He was punished for saying exactly what he thought, regardless of the consequences. This is what had exasperated me, and had nearly gotten him killed in my class. He had a knack for coming down on the unpopular side of any issue. Consequently, trouble followed him wherever he was and nobody wanted him around.

The very next day, Melody was transferred out of my class. I didn't question why. Inmates came and they went and I rarely got involved.

Shortly after this, Bullet deposited the books on my desk to be returned to Sergeant Rounder. He thanked me for allowing the class to read them, and stated they had talked it over and agreed they would cooperate with me in anything I wanted to teach them.

I was flabbergasted. For a few moments the crazy hope flared in me that I could take this impossible class and turn it into a group of truth-seekers. But I didn't have a single thing for them to read, I mean, *nothing*. I could bring in something and read it to them, but I wanted each one of them to have a book in front of him so he could dig in and examine from every side an idea that might possibly change his life.

Then I remembered the books at the back of the closet in the corridor. I quickly unlocked the door and returned with an armload of ancient literature textbooks. I hoped to find something that would contain ideas that I could use to pry open their minds. A good play would have been perfect. But the only play in the book was *Life With Father*. I knew it was about a wealthy, upper-class family of red-haired children in New York City at about the turn of the century.

255

I thought, how in hell can I do *Life With Father* with a group of black militants? How can they possibly relate to that? I tried to explain this to them, but it only sharpened their curiosity.

We ended up doing a wild performance of the play. Whenever they had difficulty with the highly stylized language, they translated it into their own vernacular, and the rest was dynamite. They despised the father because he was an oppressor. Hatred boiled out of them in the scene where the son wants a new suit of clothes and the father forces him to wear one of his old ones, cut down. "He's just like my old man. Someone should off the motherfucker," a student shouted.

The son was going to Yale, and Cranker pronounced it "Yalu." He asked me if that was right, and I said, "Yeah, that's the best pronunciation I ever heard." Chamberlin gave me a cross look and started to correct me. "Come on, Mr. Chamberlin, keep your mouth shut. It's Yalu. That's the perfect name for it. And all the people who go there are 'Yahoos,' " I said, laughing wildly.

Every one of the students had a dramatic flair, and the atmosphere was so charged that it made for explosively funny theatre. Badger wanted to get into the act, and they assigned him the part of Aunt Cora to read. The little fellow was trying so hard the perspiration was standing out on his face. He did manage to decipher a couple of words, and the entire room cheered him as if he were a conquering hero. Even Cranker congratulated him. For the moment, their racial dispute was buried; all the blacks found it easy to identify with a guy who was all screwed up and struggling mightily to comprehend a few simple sentences.

No sooner had we finished the play than the class composition completely changed. The black students were transferred back to the main line and Badger was dropped from my roster. I have no idea what happened to any of them. That's the way things were in the adjustment center.

By my own standards, I was pleased by what had happened. We had started out with murderous hatred and ended up with hilarious laughter. But what did it mean educationally? Nothing. Who had been improved by it? Nobody. Who cared about what had taken place there? No one. It was crazy, completely crazy.

I started to get acquainted with my new batch of students. A Chicano student ran down for the rest of us about what it was like to serve time in a Mexican jail. He described how the inmates' relatives would bring food in and cook right in the prison yard. And if the prisoner had no family, he damn near starved.

Another student started rapping about a psychedelic dream he'd had the previous night. He described how some multicolored beasts chased him up a pole, and one of the beasts started butting the pole until it knocked him down. Just as he felt one of the horns rake his back, he woke up. In the morning, when he examined himself, he found a strange scratch on his body. Everyone jeered at the story; so he took off his shirt and, sure enough, there was a red welt cutting diagonally across his back.

"You know there is nothing in our cells that I could use to scratch myself like that," he said. "So, I ask you, where the hell did it come from?"

This caught their interest, and I had to figure out how to take this strange group and weld it into an educational community. As soon as I got something going, they, too, would drop from my roster and I would have to start again. Cuckoo, cuckoo, cuckoo.

CHAPTER 14

Prison is where you wait for that promised visit,
when it doesn't come you worry about a car accident.
Then you find out the reason your visitors didn't
come, you're glad because it wasn't serious and
disappointed because such a little thing should keep
them from coming to see you.

From a Student Theme

One ridiculous incident perhaps marked the beginning of the unravelling of my prison teaching career. I was starting my first afternoon class when I got a call from Mr. Feather, the new superintendent, who in a funereal tone, said, "Mr. Campbell, something urgent has come up, I want you to dismiss your class and come down to the education office right away."

When I arrived in his office, Mr. Feather, Captain Proctor and an assistant warden named Warren Amber were there to greet me, all looking very solemn. I couldn't imagine what was up or what the hell I could have done to encourage this reception.

"We want to ask you some questions," Mr. Feather said.

"Fine," I replied nervously.

"A guard has found women's clothes in the closet of your room in the bachelors' quarters," Mr. Feather said, getting right to the heart of the matter. "There can be no doubt about the authen-

258

ticity of this charge. When Officer Waldoon discovered this, he immediately contacted the captain of the guards, who made an on-the-spot investigation and confirmed it. Captain Proctor then got in touch with Warden Amber, who investigated and also confirms this charge."

"Of course," I said, "the clothing belongs to my wife and two kids. We gave up the apartment in San Francisco when they spent a month visiting her family in New York. Right now, we're living in a motel, but in two weeks we're moving into a lovely house in a walnut grove, not far from here. We stored the furniture in the city, but I decided to put their clothing in that deep closet. I'm no longer living in that dump, anyway. The rent is paid until the end of the month, and I'm using it for storage space."

"Is that your explanation?" Mr. Feather asked.

"I guess it is," I said. The three of them were a pompous hanging jury. They had the evidence nailed down. Their difficulty was that the crime existed only in their own neurotic fantasy. When Mr. Feather summoned me, I had no idea what to expect. When he presented his evidence, I at first smiled and then burst into laughter.

"I want to impress upon you, this is a serious matter," Mr. Feather said, attempting to recover his ruined dignity.

"I'm sorry," I said, pulling myself together. "I'm not certain I comprehend the problem. Please start from the beginning again."

"Well I–er—do you have anything to add?" Mr. Feather asked, addressing himself to the captain of the guards.

"No comment," snapped Captain Proctor, who was in full dress uniform for the occasion.

"What about you, Warden Amber?" Mr. Feather asked.

Warden Amber made a sour face and, with a hand gesture, pushed the entire matter away.

"I believe I speak for all of us when I say we will accept your explanation and not pursue the matter any further," said Mr. Feather.

"Is it all right for me to return to my classroom?" I asked.

Mr. Feather nodded.

"OK," I said. "I'll move my gear out of that place tonight, turn my blankets and sheets in to the supply room, and hand over the key to the watchtower guard. Please accept the remaining two weeks' rent as my gift to the state of California."

Later I recounted the tale with great hilarity to my students and other members of the faculty. I never did find out why they were so startled by their discovery. My first thought was they believed I was living with a woman there. It was a gloomy place, without indoor toilet facilities and only a single cot for a bed. I didn't see how anyone could consider it a likely spot to set up light housekeeping.

The other slightly more plausible theory was they thought I was a transvestite. However, at the time, I weighed two hundred twenty, and my wife was less than one hundred twenty pounds. There was no way I could have fitted into any of that clothing.

Since a prison is a place where kinky behavior abounds and snitches love to practice their craft, it was perhaps unfair of me to poke fun at them. I don't believe any of the men involved in this incident were vicious or deliberately tried to damage me. However, a few months later when I was in difficulty, I doubt very much if any of them were particularly anxious to protect or defend my civil liberties, either.

A few months after this incident, our school was visited by a group of teachers from Soledad prison. The state of California allows each teacher to spend one day a year observing another school system in operation. These teachers taught under completely different guidelines from ours. For example, we were not allowed to have long hair or beards. All the Soledad teachers sported beards, because one of their instructors won a lawsuit in district court that entitled them to be as hairy as they chose.

After a phone call to Mr. Feather to obtain permission, I invited one of these teachers to observe my adjustment center class. Just arriving at that A.C. classroom was a dramatic event, with the grinding of the keys in the seven locked doors, the many arms reaching out as we walked the long corridors, the solitary, naked bather sudsing himself under the close scrutiny of the guard.

260

At first the students were suspicious of the bearded intruder. I explained who he was, where he was from, and how he happened to have a beard. This led into a discussion of how the law can be changed or reinterpreted to protect individual rights. I was reading Kafka's "Metamorphosis" to them, and we were soon into a lively discussion of degradation. The mood was relaxed and thoughtful. It was a graduate seminar, its participants some of the world's leading authorities on the subject.

The bearded teacher wanted to take part, but I discouraged him. Finally he could bear it no longer and he pleaded with us to allow him to join in. We relented. Before we knew it, the hour was over and we were retracing our journey through those gloomy corridors, mystified by the magic that had taken place.

When we returned to the main-line education area, the Soledad teacher started describing to Hugo Belson the fantastic experience he had just had. He embarrassed me with his praise.

To my amazement, Hugo Belson agreed with him and lauded me, my teaching program and my ability. In the two previous years, he had not said one complimentary word to me. I couldn't believe it. He was lavish in his praise, except for one qualifying phrase which he repeated several times, "Campbell is either a genius or a complete nut."

Shortly after this, a group of black students petitioned Hugo Belson to provide a Swahili course for students who requested it, and recommended me as their teacher. I loaned them a Swahili grammar book I had purchased in London. They were so enthusiastic about it, they raised the money to buy additional books for as many students as wanted to take the course. There was much kidding, and some of them claimed I, as a honkie, had a tongue too thick to properly pronounce Swahili words. I, of course, scoffed at this.

Funds were available, under the Title I Project, for other educational programs. If Belson had approved, I would have been paid for teaching the course. He turned it down as a paid project sponsored by the institution. But the students persisted and talked me into volunteering to teach them once a week as an extracurricular activity.

261

If students had a free person as a sponsor, they could have clubs which met during scheduled evening periods. I, at the time, was the sponsor of the Chess Club. There were more than fifty members in it and I earned enough points to qualify as the number three man on their chess team. We had regular tournaments with other chess clubs in the area. I say with some pride that we never lost a match.

Belson refused to allow me to teach Swahili on a voluntary basis. He did, however, agree to a meeting with me and the students who were promoting the project. We sat around in my classroom and discussed his reasons. Belson was courteous and tried to explain his point of view, which was that the students should bend their efforts toward learning the rudiments of the English language rather than getting involved in another language, which would not be useful to them.

I explained to him that the students had a high motivation to learn Swahili and I wanted to use this as a tool to get them involved in the learning process. I didn't care whether they learned Swahili or Old Icelandic, I was interested in working with an eager group of students. I explained to him that we had a competition going to see whether a white man could learn Swahili as well as a black man. Belson was not persuaded by our arguments.

The same students put together yet another program. They enjoyed reading plays in my classes, and many of them had considerable acting talent. They wanted to form a play-reading seminar which would meet once a week in the evening.

I thought this was an excellent suggestion, but Belson vetoed it. He called me to his office and told me he didn't want me agitating among the inmates. I told him that what the inmates had done came exclusively from them. I had refused to accept the sponsorship of their group a number of times until they finally wore me down. I pointed out that I was already teaching one night a week in the adult school in town and spending another night a week working with the Chess Club; a third night a week was more than I could handle. I agreed to do it because I was

262

trying to help them, not because I wanted to agitate. If he didn't want me to help them, I would be delighted to comply with his request.

"Do your job," Belson barked. "Get out of the prison at night and don't volunteer for anything. It isn't going to do any good. Nobody is going to appreciate it. In the end, it can get you into a lot of trouble."

Right after this, Hugo Belson filed his annual performance report on me. It consisted of rating me in a series of categories on a scale of one to five. One was excellent and five was failing. He rated me from four to five in every category, including academic qualifications for the job, rapport with students, ability to handle the classroom, everything. Then he recommended that I not be rehired when my contract expired in a few months.

I looked at the report in disbelief. I had seen other people bum-rapped, but it had not occurred to me that the same thing could happen to me. I decided to go to his office to talk to him about it. The performance report was an absurdity, because during the entire time I had taught at the prison, Belson had never been inside my classroom when it was in session. The best part of his leadership was that he didn't poke his nose into what I was doing.

I went through the report to pick out something I knew I could nail him on. I couldn't confront him on the academic qualifications, because he could claim that Harvard hadn't prepared me for the kind of situation I would find in a jail. Except for one minor skirmish at the beginning of my prison teaching, I hadn't had to discipline a student or call for help during the two years I had taught there. My record in this regard was better than any other teacher in the institution. However, I knew he could counter this by saying he had heard laughter and noise coming from my room from time to time.

He also had rated me low in health. On this count I had him. I could tear that scrawny little bastard apart with my two hands. When I went in to talk to him, I dropped the report on his desk and said, "For openers, Mr. Belson, what's this about rating me

263

down in physical health. I've been absent one day in the last two years. Also, I'm strong as a bull. How can you possibly rate me a four when I'm healthier than any other teacher in this department?"

Belson looked at me and shook his head, "Oh, I'm sorry, I thought that category included mental health. It's your mental health that's not good."

I was speechless. I stared at him for a long time. It was obvious he was not prepared to go through the report with me. He knew what he was doing and so did I.

"You probably think I hate you," Belson said. "But I don't. I'm doing you a favor. You're still young enough to get a good teaching job. I'm getting you out of this place before you get trapped. I've been trying to get out of this hellhole myself, but I can't do it. All my teaching has been in the joint and no other school will hire me. You've got three months before your contract ends, and this will give you plenty of time to find a new teaching job. Believe me, someday you'll thank me for it."

I saw no point in further discussion with him. I picked up the report and walked down the hall to the office of Mr. Feather. Although Feather had been superintendent for a number of months, the only contact I'd had with him was when he'd called me into question about the women's clothes in my room.

I knocked on his door and he beckoned for me to enter.

"Are you aware of this report?" I asked, and I tossed it on his desk.

"What report?" he asked.

"The one Belson wrote on me," I said.

"Yes, he sent me a copy," Feather said.

"The whole thing is a frame-up," I said.

"Don't blame me, I didn't write it," Feather said. "If it's untrue, you have a right to file a report on it and counter his charges. Obviously I can't testify for or against it because I've been here only a few months and I have no idea what you're doing. It's between the two of you."

"All right, I will file a report. I'll answer every one of these unbelievable things. But first I'd like someone to come into my classes and see what's going on. Belson has never observed my teaching. He has no idea what the hell is going on. I am proud of what I've accomplished. When I get hit by this ridiculous report, it throws me, because it has nothing to do with what's happening. Let me ask you, Mr. Feather, will you volunteer to visit one of my classes?"

"All right, just set the time," Feather said.

We agreed on a morning class the following Monday. I explained to my students we were going to have a visit by the new superintendent of education and I wanted to show him what they could do. I told them I had talked to him about the kinds of things we were doing in my classes and I wanted him to see how they could enjoy reading, analyzing, and discussing the great literature of the world.

They were excited by the idea. We decided to have a discussion of *Antigone*. We had talked about the play previously, but we decided for this occasion we could have a repeat performance. My best student, a Frenchman named Ouimet, agreed to give a short talk about the play and explain something about Greek mythology so that Feather could follow the arguments.

Everything went off beautifully. Ouimet started out by telling how Kronos swallowed his children. He traced this epic exaggeration from Mount Olympus, to the vampire legends of Transylvania, to the modern superman. He showed that man has always had a desire for supernatural, superpowerful beings who could command both the good and the bad forces in mankind. It was a short, clever, brilliant introduction. I won't go into the discussion itself, but I had everyone contributing, digging out information and responding to each other. I was profoundly pleased.

Later I discussed the class session with Mr. Feather. He was mystified. "Don't ask me to judge a thing like that," he said. "I have no opinion about it. It could be you're doing work that's very good. On the other hand, it isn't something I can understand. I'm unwilling to comment about it. I did notice you had

265

all the students interested and participating. But what good this is going to do them later in life, I have no idea."

I didn't know what to say. There was no way he could relate to what I was doing. At the same time, he did have enough honesty to admit that he didn't have the background to comprehend what he saw. Another educator might have been fascinated that students in prison could respond to great literature in a very personal, highly intelligent, civilized way. But the problem was that even though I had precisely demonstrated this, no one cared.

The conventional wisdom was that students in a prison weren't capable of intelligent thinking. Of course, the evidence was absolute and incontrovertible that they could. I could counteract Belson's antagonism and ignorance, but apathy defeated me. I became truly discouraged. I went back to my desk in my prison classroom and started answering Belson's charges against me.

I didn't have a bulletin board in my room. This was true. But what did this have to do with education? What did this have to do with anything that concerned me or my teaching? Belson's training was in elementary school, and a bulletin board was of some importance there. What bulletins did I have for these students?

I didn't have an American flag in my room. I hadn't noticed that most of the other rooms did have American flags in them. According to California law, every classroom in the state had to be equipped with an American flag. But as far as I was concerned, it was the school's responsibility to supply me with one.

I couldn't continue with Belson's report. It made me sick. I spoke to the man in charge of custodial duties and asked him to get me both a bulletin board and an American flag. He scouted around and, in about a week, produced them.

I talked to the supervisor in the adjustment center and told him Belson had recommended that my contract not be renewed when it expired in about three months.

"Belson is insane," he said. "You've done an absolutely remarkable job here with the toughest inmates in the institution.

"I tell you what," he said, stroking his chin reflectively. "There is a possibility I can get you hired through the adjustment center rather than the educational system on the main line. Funds have been allocated for a permanent adjustment center teaching post, independent of the main line, but it hasn't been possible to find anybody to accept it. I'm certain we can't find anyone with your qualifications to do the job. Let me see what I can do for you. I'll see if we can't get you assigned here as a full-time teacher. It will also mean a several-thousand-dollar raise in pay. Would you like teaching here on a full-time basis, without having to put up with Belson and all that bullshit on the main line?"

"Sure," I said eagerly. "I have enjoyed this adjustment center teaching more than any other teaching I have done."

In a few days he got back to me. "I'm sorry," he said. "I had a talk with Belson and can't do a thing for you. Officially, Belson doesn't have jurisdiction over the adjustment center. But he has a lot of juice, and he is dead set against your teaching here. I am occupying my post without all the qualifications necessary to be the head of the adjustment center. Belson knows this. Belson is a schemer, and I can't risk having him go after me. I already lost one good job in the prison system through politicking. I don't want another battle like that again. I hope you understand."

"I understand," I said.

I had another avenue of appeal open to me. The prison education department was under the supervision of the adult education department of the local high school. I had taught in the local high school system's night school for two years and knew the head of the adult education department, who was officially the head of the prison education system, too. I enjoyed an excellent reputation in the night school and never had to cancel a class due to lack of attendance.

The director agreed that I was excellent as an adult education teacher, but could not vouch for my ability to relate to inmates. Furthermore, the policy was to let the prison people handle their own problems, and his only jurisdiction was to see that the credits were handled properly and the teachers were credentialed properly. In short, he didn't want to interfere with the way the prison conducted its affairs.

267

I asked this man to come out with me and spend the day so that he could see what was going on. Reluctantly, he did agree to pay a visit to the prison. He didn't agree to spend the whole day, but he said he would sit in on one class.

He cancelled out on the appointment at the last minute. I made another appointment. He did not show up for this appointment, either. Finally, five minutes before the class was over, he did appear, apologizing profusely for not getting there on time. I pointed out that it wasn't possible for him to judge a class on that basis.

He mentioned Belson had claimed that I wasn't teaching grammar to the students. I had on my desk, at the time, a pile of grammar papers nearly a foot high. "That charge is untrue, also," I said and I pointed to the papers. "Look through them and you'll see that every one of them deals with grammar. Teaching grammar is an integral part of my work. I don't think it is the most important part, nor do I think it is the part I'm most successful with, but I do it; and here is the evidence. Belson has no evidence to the contrary, because he has never visited my class. Look through that stack of papers and see if they don't completely refute that charge."

He looked at me and grinned foolishly. "I'm sorry, but I can't get involved. You have other recourses. You can fight it out in the courts, if you choose."

I knew I could win my case if I took it to court. But I asked myself what I would gain if I won. Belson could make life miserable for me if he chose. He could rip away my English courses and assign me to teach anything he wanted. I had no appeal for this. If he bum-rapped me once, he could bum-rap me again. I had no confidence in his sense of fairness or in the ability of the prison system to protect my rights. Not only that, but because I lacked education courses, Belson could claim I was inadequately credentialed and get rid of me without a hassle, simply by finding a teacher who had all the qualifying education courses.

I felt I was in a no-win situation. I threw in the towel. I wrote out my letter of resignation and handed it to Mr. Feather. He accepted it immediately. He thanked me profusely and proceeded to write me a glowing recommendation, praising me as a sensitive and brilliant teacher.

Shit.

Even Belson was cordial and said he would be glad to help me if I were looking for another job not in the prison system.

I was a good soldier. I programmed. I didn't have any more contact with them, and my last few months were completely free of harassment.

A few weeks after I submitted my resignation, my class held a debate on capital punishment. It wasn't the same kind of debate as the previous one, as it didn't involve another class. I had a student in my early-afternoon class who stated flat out that he was for capital punishment.

"I'm a convict in on a serious crime. If I thought I could kill and get away with it, I would probably do it. How can you argue with that?"

Argue we did. I had another student in the class who had been under sentence of death for killing a Catholic priest. This was the only inmate-related crime that I remembered reading about before I started teaching in the prison. A gang of youths, high on drugs, had beaten up a priest, set his clothing afire and backed over him in an automobile.

My student confirmed this but added additional information. He had been part of a gang that preyed on homosexuals who frequented gay bars in the Bay area. My student was a handsome young man with a moonlike face and was the bait for the trap they set. He would go into the gay bar and pick up a wealthy mark. He would agree to go with the mark for a drive in his car. My student's friends would follow in their car. After they had parked in a secluded place, his friends would descend on them and strip the mark of wallet, rings, jewelry, everything he had. Because of the nature of the situation, none of the marks ever reported the robberies to the police.

When he and his friends, who were all Catholic and Spanish speaking, discovered their mark was a priest, they went berserk. They tortured him horribly before they killed him. As I recollect it, they left him under his car and presumed he was dead. The priest regained consciousness and was able to supply the police with a description of his assailants before he died.

"He was a very bad man, an evil man," my student said with great conviction.

"Certainly what you did to him was far more evil than what he wanted to do to you," I said.

"No, he was a priest, a man of God. He must be better than other men. I am nothing. I am dirt. It doesn't matter about me."

I pressed him, but I couldn't crack him on that argument. I had the impression he felt the killing of a homosexual priest was the only decent thing he had ever done. He was not capable of evaluating what punishment he should receive for his crime. If the state had put him to death, he would have found that satisfactory. If he had to stay in jail indefinitely for his crime, he could accept that sentence as just. What he couldn't accept was that a man could be both a Catholic priest and a practicing homosexual.

The varied backgrounds of my students made the debate on capital punishment an extremely rewarding one, and it continued at a fever pitch for a number of days.

I remember another incident that took place during those last few months. We were discussing something that had to do with money, when all of a sudden a student sat bolt upright and blurted out, "Money, Jesus I love it. I don't mean the spendin' of it or the savin' of it. That's nothing. I mean the money itself. All those distinguished dudes in them oval frames lookin' right through ya like you're naked. And think of the edges—those silver and gray edges. Didja ever go into a place and see a woman stack up the bills and riffle the edges with her thumb? Particularly the edges of the new bills. Oh, God, I can see it and feel it in my gut, it's driving me wild."

He then told a story about how he once knocked over a liquor store, brought the money back to his motel, piled it on his bed, undressed and made love to it.

After this outburst, he asked to be excused from the room, and

270

after he departed one of my students remarked, "Dig that crazy dude. Did you notice when he left he had an erection? I mean that dumb jamoke is really queer for money."

That incident made me laugh. It makes me laugh now when I'm writing about it. In all honesty, I can't go into a bank and see a stack of bills without realizing that I'm gazing at someone's "dearly beloved."

A few weeks before I was to finish my prison teaching career, I received a visit from Pamplona, a former student whom I hadn't seen for a number of months. Pamplona had been in the class with Barkham, who had won the "Crime Does Pay" debate. It was when I was lecturing on Graeco-Roman literature and the Renaissance and was probably at the peak of my prison teaching career.

Pamplona wasn't very handsome, but he had excellent critical ability. I could still remember the brilliant way he had analyzed Greek drama and literature.

He was in awful shape. He looked like he hadn't eaten or slept in days, and his face was ashen. My first thought was that he had leukemia or some other form of cancer.

"What's happened to you?" I asked.

"I'm due for parole in a week," he said.

"Congratulations," I said.

"It's killing me."

"Has your health gone bad?" I asked.

"No, I'm healthier than I should be, considering I haven't slept in eight days."

"I know you, Pamplona. You're a tough dude. Nothing is going to eat you up alive."

"My wife, Maria, she's going to have a baby," he blurted.

Since he had been in the joint for the last three years, I knew what that meant. I remembered his visit from his wife and son came once a week during my class time. When he returned from meeting them, he would describe to me how his boy would race across the room and bury himself in his dad's arms. Pamplona would be incandescent.

271

"OK, Pamplona, have a seat and tell me about it," I said.

"I found out about it during her last visit. She was scared to tell me. She knew I was getting out and it was something we both had to face.

"She doesn't care about the other dude. She wants to live with me, but she wants to keep his child. I can understand it that she went with him. She is a woman, hot-blooded, passionate. If she had been locked up, I would have done the same thing. But I can't take another man's child, support it, raise it and love it like my own son." His face was drawn and he was in intense pain.

"What about having her put the child up for adoption?" I asked.

"I love Maria," he said. "How can I tell her I love her and not let her keep the child? It's from her own body. If I did that I would be saying to her, 'I'm not man enough to allow you to keep the child.' I'm also saying, 'I don't love you.' "

"Go back with her and try to work it out then," I said.

"No," he said determinedly. "I can't. It would be easy to give it a try, but I know my own heart. I've thought about that unborn child. It's completely innocent. It's got as much right to love as my own boy. But I could never accept that child as my own in a million years. My own life would become an injustice and a lie.

"That's why I came to you. I'm going nuts. I don't want to get out of the joint. I can't handle it out there, it's too tough. In here is kid's stuff. I asked a stay of six months on my parole and they wouldn't allow it. I don't know what the hell to do," he said. He was getting the shakes.

"First of all," I said, "you don't need my advice. Your reasoning is perfect. It's beautiful. Do you realize how badly screwed up this world is because people can't think critically? Uncritical thinking not only leads to senseless wars and ridiculous demonstrations; it makes people kill, commit impossible fornications, the list is endless.

"But you got no excuse, Pamplona, because you can think. I can't tell you what to do, but I can tell you you're lucky as hell

272

because you got a shot at a life of deep love, trust and understanding.

"Most of the rest of us are not so lucky. We laugh, we cry, we thrust, we pull back from, we trust, we trick, we storm, we pacify, we hate, we love . . . We live together and yet we are alone. We're blind and we stumble—and we understand nothing about each other."

He was so locked into his own misery I wasn't reaching him.

"You know what I'd like to do to you, Pamplona," I said. "I'd like to take my fist and smash you in the face. With one blow I might be able to break either your nose or your jaw.

"I don't want to hurt you. I want to take away the pain. What you're feeling is entirely in your mind. It's not real. But it's light years more severe than a broken jaw."

"I'd be pleased to have you belt me, Mr. Campbell," he said.

I started stalking him until I finally got him to smile.

"You're a lousy God damned teacher," he said.

We looked at each other for a few moments with powerful affection. Then he turned round and headed back to his unit.

I didn't want speculation about my resignation, so I waited until the last day to announce my departure. When I told my students, one said, "I suppose you're going to write a book about us."

"No, I have no plans to do that," I said.

"I've read those stories written by schoolteachers. They're always about how the teacher took a bunch of bad guys and turned them into good guys. Mr. Campbell would never lie about us like that."

"Thanks," I said.

"I'm glad you're getting out," another student said. "I hope you get to teach in a school with a lot of young foxes, smellin' of perfume and sashaying up and down the aisles, swinging their hips from side to side."

"I liked teaching here. It was a hell of an experience," I said.

"They didn't bum-rap you, did they? Just give me the word

and we'll start a riot. You've got friends back on the main line you don't even know about."

"No, I resigned of my own accord," I lied. I never once doubted my decision to resign when I did. But I never bragged about it to anyone, either. It has to do, I guess, with the way I was raised.

After that class, I packed my papers in my briefcase, walked out of the classroom, down the stairs, through the long corridor, and out the gate. I didn't say good-bye to anyone and I didn't look back. That's the only way to leave a prison.